AMERICAN LITERATURE AND THE FREE MARKET, 1945–2000

The years after World War Two have seen a widespread fascination with the free market. Michael W. Clune considers this fascination in postwar literature. In the fictional worlds created by works ranging from Frank O'Hara's poetry to nineties gangster rap, the market is transformed, offering an alternative form of life, distinct from both the social visions of the left and the individualist ethos of the right. These ideas also provide an unsettling example of how art takes on social power by offering an escape from society. *American Literature and the Free Market* presents a new perspective on a number of wide-ranging works for readers of American postwar literature.

MICHAEL W. CLUNE is Assistant Professor in the Department of English at the University of South Florida.

CAMBRIDGE STUDIES IN AMERICAN
LITERATURE AND CULTURE

Editor
Ross Posnock, *Columbia University*

Founding Editor
Albert Gelpi, *Stanford University*

Advisory Board
Alfred Bendixen, *Texas A & M University*
Sacvan Bercovitch, *Harvard University*
Ronald Bush, *St. John's College, University of Oxford*
Wai Chee *Dimock, Yale University*
Albert Gelpi, *Stanford University*
Gordon Hutner, *University of Illinois, Urbana–Champaign*
Walter Benn Michaels, *University of Illinois, Chicago*
Kenneth Warren, *University of Chicago*

Recent books in this series

157. KERRY LARSON
Imagining Equality in Nineteenth-Century American Literature

156. LAWRENCE ROSENWALD
Multilingual America: Language and the Making of American Literature

155. ANITA PATTERSON
Race, American Literature, and Transnational Modernism

154. ELIZABETH RENKER
The Origins of American Literature Studies: An Institutional History

153. THEO DAVIS
Formalism, Experience, and the Making of American Literature in the
Nineteenth Century

152. JOAN RICHARDSON
A Natural History of Pragmatism: The Fact of Feeling from Jonathan
Edwards to Gertrude Stein

151. EZRA F. TAWIL
The Making of Racial Sentiment: Slavery and the Birth of the Frontier
Romance

150. ARTHUR RISS
Race, Slavery, and Liberalism in Nineteenth-Century American Literature

AMERICAN LITERATURE AND THE FREE MARKET, 1945–2000

MICHAEL W. CLUNE

CAMBRIDGE
UNIVERSITY PRESS

CAMBRIDGE UNIVERSITY PRESS
Cambridge, New York, Melbourne, Madrid, Cape Town, Singapore,
São Paulo, Delhi, Dubai, Tokyo

Cambridge University Press
The Edinburgh Building, Cambridge CB2 8RU, UK

Published in the United States of America by Cambridge University Press, New York

www.cambridge.org
Information on this title: www.cambridge.org/9780521513999

© Michael W. Clune 2010

First published 2010

Printed in the United Kingdom at the University Press, Cambridge

A catalogue record for this publication is available from the British Library

ISBN 978-0-521-51399-9 Hardback

Contents

Acknowledgments   *page* vi
List of abbreviations   vii

Introduction: The economic fiction   1

1   Freedom from you   27

2   Frank O'Hara and free choice   53

3   William Burroughs' virtual mind   77

4   Blood money: sovereignty and exchange in
    Kathy Acker   103

5   "You can't see me": rap, money, and the first person   127

Conclusion: The invisible world   147

Notes   165
Bibliography   197
Index   208

Acknowledgments

My thanks go first to Walter Benn Michaels for his generous and acute reading of my work, and for the example set by his own. Allen Grossman's personal guidance was crucial early in this project, and his essays have served as an inspiration since. Aaron Kunin's suggestions and criticisms have helped to shape the book at every stage. Sharon Cameron, Frances Ferguson, Michael Fried, Richard Halpern, Kerry Larson, and the anonymous readers for Cambridge University Press offered important advice on various drafts. Johns Hopkins University, the University of Michigan, the University of South Florida, and the Mellon Foundation provided support for research and writing. I thank Ray Ryan and Maartje Scheltens at Cambridge University Press. I would also like to thank Jonathan Freedman, Jason Gladstone, Jonathan Goldberg, Hunt Hawkins, Colleen Hull, Joe Loewenstein, Chelsey Moore, and Rebecca Traynor. This book is dedicated to my parents, Michael and Barbara.

An early version of chapter 2 appeared in *PMLA* 120:1 (January 2005); an early version of Chapter 4 appeared in *Contemporary Literature* 45:3 (Fall 2004). Frank O'Hara's "Personal Poem" is copyright 1964 by Frank O'Hara, and portions of it are reprinted in Chapter 2 by permission of City Lights Books.

Abbreviations

BJ   Sylvia Plath, *The Bell Jar* (1963; London: Harper & Row, 1971)

CG   Karl Marx, "Critique of the Gotha Program" (1875), in *The Marx-Engels Reader*, ed. Robert C. Tucker (New York: W. W. Norton, 1978)

CPO'H   Frank O'Hara, *The Collected Poems of Frank O'Hara*, ed. Donald Allen (Berkeley: University of California Press, 1995)

CPSP   Sylvia Plath, *The Collected Poems* (New York Harper Perennial, 1992)

DL   Jane Jacobs, *The Death and Life of Great American Cities* (1961; New York, Vintage, 1993)

ES   Kathy Acker, *Empire of the Senseless* (New York: Grove Press, 1988)

HC   Hannah Arendt, *The Human Condition* (1958; Chicago: University of Chicago Press, 1998)

IM   Kathy Acker, *In Memoriam to Identity* (New York: Grove Press, 1991)

JR   William Gaddis, *JR* (New York: Penguin, 1975)

M   Michel Henry, *Marx: A Philosophy of Human Reality* (Bloomington: University of Indiana Press, 1983)

OWA   Martin Heidegger, "The Origin of the Work of Art" (1935), in *Off the Beaten Path* (Cambridge: Cambridge University Press, 2002)

PE   R. D. Laing, *The Politics of Experience* (New York: Pantheon, 1967)

SM   William S. Burroughs, *The Soft Machine* (New York: Grove Press, 1961)

TTE	William S. Burroughs, *The Ticket That Exploded* (New York: Grove Press, 1962)
UK	F. A. Hayek, "The Use of Knowledge in Society" (1949), in *Individualism and Economic Order* (Chicago: University of Chicago Press, 1958)

The economic fiction

I.

Frederic Jameson, midway through his study of postwar literature and culture, raises what remains one of the field's most troubling questions. After patiently examining the fall of state socialism, tracing the rise of neoconservative free market ideology, and offering a Marxist analysis of these developments, he suddenly throws up his hands. "None of these things, however," he writes, "go very far towards explaining the most astonishing feature" of the period.[1] What remains unexplained is "how the dreariness of business and private property, the dustiness of entrepreneurship ... should in our time have proved to be so *sexy*."[2] Here Jameson confronts the fact that the prospect of a global free market has become an object of nearly universal fascination since the end of the Second World War. By the eighties and nineties, this fascination with the market was ubiquitous, expressed in phenomena as diverse as daytime talk shows, the Contract with America, news features on the New China, movies about the stock market, science-fiction novels, and music videos. Americans were captivated by the impulse to replace relations to governments, to traditions, to cultures, and to communities with a relation to market price. The specter of a purely economic world casts a shadow over the history of this period.

And what is so fascinating about markets, prices, buying and selling? Why has this fascination gripped so much of postwar literature and culture? How can we account for the sexiness of what William Gibson calls "biz," for Jane Jacobs' belief that commerce makes cities interesting, for Frank O'Hara's idea that he can't appreciate life if there aren't any stores around, for rap's picture of a world where "money rules everything around me"? Jameson thinks the market itself cannot possibly fascinate, and he argues, somewhat surprisingly, that in fact no one is fascinated by it. He speculates that people must have gotten the market confused with something else, the mass media, perhaps, with which the market maintains an "illicit metaphorical association."[3]

Jameson's response, though I believe it to be inadequate, is hardly unusual. It is echoed, in various forms, in the intense discussion about the free market that has ranged across a dozen disciplines and in the popular media. One of the surprising features of this discussion is how quickly the market is displaced by something else. For the left, for writers like Jameson or David Harvey, market relations are simply a mystified form of social relations.[4] What lies behind the market, what is real or valuable or important, is society, intersubjectivity, community. For the right, for neoclassical economists like Milton Friedman and conservative philosophers like Robert Nozick, the market simply and transparently reflects the personal values of sovereign individuals.[5] What lies behind the market, what is real or valuable or important, is the individual.

Thus the discussion about the market proceeds via a series of displacements. The left is against the market and the right is for the market. This means that the left is for the social and the right is for the individual. And this means that the left is for social justice and the right is for individual rights. In the academic versions of the discussion, ethical commitments often give way to ontological claims. The left thinks the sovereign individual is an illusion, and that market relations express, conceal, or mystify social relations. The right thinks society is an abstraction reducible to the individuals who compose it and who express their values and desires through the market.

So we can see why Jameson thinks that the fascination with the market must be a fascination with something else. In the terms of familiar academic and political positions, that fascination is simply inexplicable. Behind the economic, all parties agree, lies something else. The market, prices, buying and selling cannot be objects of desire in themselves. They function as a means of registering or expressing or concealing some other desire, some other fact, some other agent. How can you love the market for itself? What could the desire for a purely economic world possibly be? How can we understand the cultural appeal, the utopian glow, the "sexiness" of the market in this period, if not as a disguise for something else?

The thesis of this book is that to understand an important dimension of the postwar fascination with the market we need to understand the role of artworks in eliciting this fascination. In postwar America, the question of the distinctiveness of the economic becomes entangled with the question of the distinctiveness of the aesthetic. Existing criticism, reflecting the terms of the broader debate, has proceeded on the assumption that behind the literary image of the market lies an image of either society or the individual.[6] But a third option emerges in the transformation of market relations in postwar literature and culture. In forms from experimental fiction to popular film and rap, money becomes a means of shaping action distinct from both society and the sovereign individual. As Jameson recognized, postwar cultural and aesthetic forms have been irresistibly drawn to the market. Analyzing what happens to money when it combines with aesthetic form provides us with a critical opportunity to describe the aesthetic-economic entity that elicits this mysterious and "astonishing" desire.

Undoubtedly, much of the enthusiasm for the market can be explained by reference to the rhetoric of individualism. But the mode of fascination that puzzles Jameson, and that seems so strangely in excess of individualism, can be illuminated by exploring a kind of art that circulates increasingly widely as this period progresses. The works that concern us do something other than represent actual or imaginary economic relations and conditions. They give form to a special kind of experience. These works set market forces to work organizing experience. Money and the price system are not fictional. The market is an actual formal structure of our world. But in actually existing capitalism, the market is a conduit for actions, intentions, and desires formed by either social forces or private individuals. Market price can tell people how hard an object or service is to get, but it cannot give them a reason for wanting it or a way of using it. The right believes individual preferences determine what market agents want. A central tenet of economic theory is that an individual's preference for a thing is absolutely independent of that thing's price.[7] The left believes social relations, norms, and dynamics determine what market agents want. The left criticizes neoclassical price theory by arguing that both price and personal preference conceal the determining influence of social forces and relations.[8] Market relations either express or mystify desires and relations formed outside of the market. So the idea of a desire formed by price, of a purely economic experience, is astonishing.

But in the forms produced by the writers I study, market forces influence desire and shape experience. This shaping happens in a variety of ways across these works. A striking and central instance involves the transformation of market price in novels by writers such as William Gaddis and Kathy Acker. Outside these aesthetic spaces, an individual's formulation of intentions regarding the things in an environment – one's sense of what they are, what can be done with them, and whether one wants them – is distinct from the individual's awareness of the price of those things. But in the space opened by these works, the characters' awareness of a thing's price shapes other aspects of their relation to it. Price structures their experience of things from the outset. They do not form an interest in a thing, and then look at its price to see how hard it will be to get it. In these works, interest and desire play across an environment already organized by price. Instead of price imposing a limit on one's ability to procure what one already knows one wants, the limit imposed by price acts to shape one's perception of what one wants. At a certain price, a thing enters an individual's horizon, catches the interest, gets associated with this or that use. At another price, it disappears, gets associated with a different use, elicits a different desire or none at all. Just as up-down orientation defines one's spatial field, so price defines the perception of one's environment.

In the space opened by these works, the market is a self-organizing system that links every object of an individual's experience to every object of everyone's experience. One sees things through price. In these novels, the price system structures subjectivity. The structure transformed by the aesthetic varies with different works – in nineties rap it is money, in Frank O'Hara or Jane Jacobs it is an urban environment saturated with commerce – but in each work the capacities of the economic undergo the same fundamental change. The market structures choosing in Frank O'Hara, looking in nineties rap, touching in William Gibson. I don't claim that the market works this way outside of aesthetic space, nor do I argue it's possible that it might.[9] I do argue that the way the economic works in these aesthetic spaces has helped to make the idea of a purely economic world an object of cultural fascination. To observe the fictionalizing of the market in postwar America is to see the construction of a relation to the market that does not conceal either society or the private individual, but replaces them.

By "economic fiction" I refer not to some general relation of the aesthetic and economic in postwar America, but to a particular set of artworks defined by the special form the economic takes in them. The selection of works I discuss in the following chapters has been largely motivated by two related concerns. I chose works that are particularly vivid examples of what I take to be the central dynamics of the genre, and that foreground stages in its development. But there is a third aim. My claim for the influence of the economic fiction on a dimension of the postwar fascination with the market does not rest on empirical studies of the circulation and reception of these works. Rather, I pursue this claim by way of theoretical and interpretive arguments about the peculiar form of fascination observed by writers such as Jameson, the peculiar form market relations take in these works, and the peculiar relation of art to the society they intimate. That said, the works I discuss circulate among audiences of diverse composition and size, and have in part been chosen because of this diversity. The poems in Chapter 2 circulate first among small literary readerships, and later in college classrooms. The novels of Chapters 3 and 4 are important for various subcultures, from the sixties counterculture to post-punk Los Angeles. The film considered in Chapter 1 and the rap recordings and videos in Chapter 5 reach mass audiences. The economic fiction enters American culture at several different levels, and is disseminated broadly and deeply.

This introduction presents the aesthetic theory that underlies both my description of the economic fiction as a genre and of its relation to society. I then examine William Gaddis' *JR* as a mature example of the form. Chapter 1 presents a broad overview of the development of the economic fiction. I begin by arguing that the fascination of the economic is grounded in the desire for a nonsocial mode of relation. I take Sylvia Plath's *The Bell Jar* and *Ariel* as powerful articulations of this desire, locating her work within the context of the contemporary anti-psychiatry movement. I proceed to argue that in works as various as a poem by Amiri Baraka and a film by Paul Thomas Anderson, the alluring prospect of a relational alternative to intersubjectivity is understood in terms of a fusion of the aesthetic and the economic. I then provide a brief intellectual history of this fusion through the work of Karl Polanyi and Hannah Arendt.

Chapters 2 and 3 examine intermediate stages in the consolidation of the economic fiction. Chapter 2 explores the relation between the aesthetic, the individual, and the social in Frank O'Hara's effort to create a poetics of personal choice. In early postwar America, choice emerges as the fundamental interface between the individual and the collective. The nature of this interface becomes an aesthetic problem for O'Hara as he develops a poetics of choice that eludes what he identifies as the constraints of both the private and the social spheres. In the fictional space of O'Hara's "personal" poems, choosing is an immediate engagement with the environment. One looks around and picks out "whatever one happens to like," which is determined neither by the chooser's internal preferences, nor by social norms or values, but by the organization of an urban space that O'Hara and contemporaries like Jane Jacobs and David Riesman view in terms of the ubiquity of commerce.

If O'Hara's texts present an elusive agency that is neither social nor individual, the subject of my next chapter attempts to construct a detailed model of a "third" mode of experience. I read William Burroughs' practice of juxtaposition in his "cut-up" trilogy as an experimental system for coordinating embodied knowledge across a population without recourse to either intersubjective communication or social codes. I show how in developing this system, Burroughs discovers the same solution to the same problem as the most radical contemporary theory of the price system. With the "cut-up" works Burroughs thus constructs a powerful literary model that later writers will adapt to their economic fictions.

Chapter 4 takes up the late novels of Burroughs' disciple Kathy Acker, in which the fiction of a perfect language takes the form of a currency free of sovereignty. For Acker, 1989 emerges as the key year of the postwar period. This is not because of what changed with the downfall of "actually existing socialism," but because of what didn't. What Acker calls the "myth" of a purely economic world survives the celebrated "end of history." From the perspective established by her novels, the era is defined not by the conflict between capitalism and socialism, but by the conflict between actually existing capitalism and the fiction of a market without limit.

My final chapter considers a class of works that invent aesthetic supplements to actual economic forms. In it I explore the fictionalizing of money in the nineties rap lyric and related aesthetic practices as "diamonds that will bling-blind you." With money that blinds, the rap subject inverts conspicuous consumption, becoming transcendent by becoming invisible. "You can't see me": in rap the aesthetic supplement removes the economic from the intersubjective, sometimes in strikingly literal ways, such as placing tinted windows on expensive cars.

My focus in analyzing these works is on the dynamics of the aesthetic spaces they set up. While establishing the distinctive shape of these dynamics, I largely bracket the question of the ideological relation of these works to existing social and economic conditions. My conclusion takes up this question. I ask whether the economic fiction performs the ideological work of producing a fascination with the market by making actual economic inequality invisible, and find that it does, but in such a manner as to suspend any easy identification of an ideological function. I argue that to develop a critical understanding of the nature of the invisibility that emerges in these works requires a new description of the relation of the aesthetic to the social and of the relation of literary criticism to social science.

This book starts with poems moving among a small coterie of New Yorkers, and ends with lyrics, recordings, and videos circulating among hundreds of millions of people. The evidence of what Jameson calls the "most astonishing feature" of postwar life surrounds us. More economic forms become hybridized, aesthetic-economic interfaces circulate more widely, the economic fiction becomes a sociological phenomenon. What is disseminated in wider and wider circles is not a set of aesthetic representations of economic conditions, but a purely economic experience. Only in aesthetic form is the market independent of society and the individual. Only through economic form does the aesthetic become autonomous with respect to the social world. In postwar America, both attain their distinction by becoming lost in each other.

2.

In the following chapters, I will argue that certain aesthetic works open a space outside the social world. I do not claim that these works have no relation to society. In fact I will suggest that the fascination with the economic that they help to generate is a significant social phenomenon. But to see this particular relation of literature to society depends on being able to see literature as distinct. For two terms to be in relation, they must not be identical. Yet the possibility of thinking such a relation today encounters serious obstacles. Until about ten years ago, most literary criticism was dominated by the reaction to what became known as the "ideology" of the aesthetic. A broad range of critics during the late seventies to the mid-nineties, responding to an older critical sense of the intrinsic autonomy of the aesthetic, sought to demonstrate the continuity of literary texts with actual social relations. The New Historicist practice of homology, to take one influential example, operated on the principle that a Foucauldian social logic gave the same shape to both Renaissance property relations and Renaissance plays.[10]

A polemical commitment to the continuity of the literary and the social furnished these critics with a characteristic plot: literature tries to distinguish itself with respect to other social and cultural formations and fails. New Historicism characteristically showed the process by which literature's attempt to break free from a social system was contained and redeployed by that system. Marxism characteristically demonstrated actually existing capitalism's amazing powers of co-option.[11] Literary dynamics that seemed at odds with capitalist dynamics were redescribed as reflecting the "dialectical" tensions within actual conditions. The effect of this model was starkly demonstrated by Marxism's "utopian" strain, which evaluated writers on the way they dealt with the (nearly) impossible problem of producing something that wasn't just more capitalism.[12]

The appeal of these critical modes lay in their development of new ways of understanding the social and historical dimensions of literary form. Their weakness lay in their tendency to see literature as just another object generated by the processes defining a given social or historical context. By the early nineties, the story of the failure of literature to offer an ideological alternative to social power began to appear symptomatic of a critical failure. Available ways of describing the relation of the literary to the social offered limited resources for making principled distinctions between them. A desire to come up with an account of literature's *distinctive* relation to a social context was supported by a certain institutional pressure: If there is nothing special about literature, why should we study it?

Over the past fifteen years, a new sociology of literature has emerged in response to these intellectual and institutional pressures. While it contains a diverse assortment of approaches and methods, I believe it can be usefully discussed in terms of two general positions. The first argues that the production, exchange, and consumption of aesthetic works occupies a distinctive place in society. The second argues that aesthetic form enables a distinctive perspective on society. We can think of these two positions in terms of the different relations they propose between literary criticism and social science. For the first, aesthetic works are the objects of a special kind of social-scientific analysis. For the second, aesthetic works allow us to generate new social-scientific concepts and to criticize old concepts. Against both the "aesthetic ideology" and homology, these critics seek to establish a social basis for the distinctiveness of literature.

The possibility of giving a critical account of the postwar economic fiction arises within the context of this effort to describe what is special about literature without losing its social and historical dimensions. But to realize this possibility involves making a break with the theory and practice that has characterized much of the writing produced by this effort. I will argue that fictionalizing the market neither marks a distinctive place in the social world nor provides a distinctive perspective on it. It opens a hole in it. The new sociology of literature, which represents the best contemporary attempt to understand the difference writing makes in the world, is compelled to cover up this hole. By looking more closely at the two positions mentioned above, we can gain a clearer sense of the obstacles that confront any attempt to describe a form of art that exists outside the social.

The first position – the idea that the production, exchange, and consumption of aesthetic objects defines a distinctive social dynamic – is associated with the sociology of Pierre Bourdieu and with critics such as

John Guillory and Alan Liu who have developed its method and terms into a vital and influential approach to literature. One great advantage of this approach is that it enables us to see art not simply as representing, imitating, embodying, distorting, or reflecting social conditions, but as a social practice in its own right, complete with its own institutional context, and with material relations to other institutions and contexts. Another notable advantage of this approach is that it is able to distinguish economic and aesthetic value, to show their interrelations while preserving a sense of their differences.

Its great disadvantage is that it is able to analyze these practices, and make these distinctions, only by redescribing all economic, aesthetic, and social values as markers in intersubjective competitions. The economic and the aesthetic remain distinct while being submerged in the social, conceived as the sphere of relations between subjects. For Bourdieu, society is divided into various fields. Each one represents a kind of game in which individuals try to distinguish themselves relative to others. They distinguish themselves by accumulating social value, represented in the different fields by different markers. Each field has its own "capital" which enables individuals to participate in the accumulation of value. In the economic field, this is economic capital. In the aesthetic field, it is a set of learned dispositions which enables one to produce aesthetic value. This value can either take the form of judgments of taste (the "distinctions" that "distinguish"), or the production of artworks.[13]

These different fields, with their distinct value-markers, are complexly interrelated. These interrelations are possible because all the different forms of capital are ultimately convertible into a single kind of capital, which Bourdieu calls "symbolic capital." All values must be convertible to symbolic value, because symbolic value is value that is visible to others. Value must compel recognition of my status, because that's what makes value valuable. Value distinguishes me from you. It marks me as of higher, lower, or equal status in relation to you. Since value expresses a differential relation between subjects, the value I possess must be visible to you. Within this scheme, economic value and aesthetic value remain relatively distinct in that they are generated in different fields, take different forms, and are redeemable for different amounts of symbolic capital in different conditions.[14]

Aesthetic analysis, in the many studies that have taken this approach, thus consists in identifying what Guillory refers to as the "social value of aesthetic value."[15] The richness, nuance, and complexity of Bourdieu's analysis of Flaubert, or of Guillory's treatment of the canon wars, or of

Alan Liu's study of the aesthetics of knowledge work, or of Mark McGurl's study of literary value as "excellence," ultimately rests upon the simplicity of intersubjective recognition.[16] I see you drive a more expensive car than I do. Your stance before the Jackson Pollock painting shows you have taste, while I stand before it like a deer in headlights. "My web page is cooler than yours."[17] Money, excellence, canonicity, and cool are different colored markers in the same basic game. Despite being able to make the subtlest distinctions among literary works, this approach is no more able to describe a difference between the social and the literary than was the New Historicism.

In contrast, the second version of the new sociology of literature depends on such a difference. Where Bourdieu takes literature to be a distinctive object of the study of society, these critics think that the study of literature furnishes distinctive ways of studying society. Instead of being an object of social science, literature can make it better. Adherents of "the new economic criticism," for example, read literary texts as a means of demonstrating the paucity of such neoclassical economic concepts as "economic man" or "marginal utility" as descriptions of actual social dynamics.[18] Postcolonial critics show us how literature's ability to represent the nuances of intersubjectivity counters the abstraction of social-scientific descriptions in a way that suggests another cognitive dimension to the encounter of cultures. Posthumanist criticism shows us how artworks illuminate the dangerous flaws in the tendency of some economists and social psychologists to see society as a cybernetic order. If a Bourdieu-style approach to literature is a way of doing social science, a wide variety of writers practice literary criticism as a form of the criticism of social science.

Robert Kaufman's interpretation of Theodor Adorno's aesthetics, carried out in a series of essays over the last decade, represents a particularly elegant defense of this approach. Kaufman argues that Adorno was misread during the period of the critique of the "aesthetic ideology," when critics saw him advocating a rejection of formalism in favor of social and historical criticism. Trying to give a precise meaning to such enigmatic pronouncements of Adorno's as "the poem [is] a philosophical sundial telling the time of history," Kaufman suggests that attending to literary form is not an alternative to doing social criticism, but a better way of doing it.[19]

A traditional problem confronting the study of society is that the concepts of social science are themselves determined by the dynamics they propose to analyze. It is here, on Kaufman's account, that literature can help. Adorno's "key idea is that significant facets of society remain to be discovered and that such discovery is unlikely to occur through use of society's own extant concepts for understanding itself."[20] The critical encounter with literary form shows a way of generating new concepts that are not determined by society. "Criticism finally must work to enunciate ... the contributions *toward* conceptuality that art, that mimesis, has nondiscursively offered."[21]

Kaufman returns to Kant's aesthetics to show how this might happen. Kant attributes to aesthetic form a "quasi" or "as-if" conceptuality, and Kaufman suggests that these quasi-conceptual forms provide the structural basis for developing new concepts. They present the forms of possible concepts, but since they lack conceptual content, they are not bound by the necessity of fitting in with any current conceptual scheme. Thus when Adorno writes, "the aim of every artistic utopia today is to make things of which we do not know what they are," he refers to the way in which the encounter with an unfamiliar form can generate a new idea.[22] Studying a Shakespeare play might give us a new and unexpected idea of how Renaissance social relations work, one which we might test against nonaesthetic materials, but which we would never discover if we confined ourselves to those materials.

Kaufman's description of Adorno as a "Left Kantian" is a brilliant solution to the problem of showing the distinctive contribution literary criticism might make towards the study of the social world.[23] Literary form is an aspect of literature that everyone agrees is distinctive, and an object of study to which literary critics can justifiably claim a privileged access. But the critique of the "aesthetic ideology" made critics feel that they had to choose between practicing a formalist criticism, which they felt qualified to do, and a social criticism, which they wanted to do. By showing how formalist literary study can lead to the generation of progressive ways of understanding society, Kaufman suggests that critics can have their cake and eat it too. His work provides a coherent way of defending the project of using a Dickens novel to demonstrate the limitations of neoclassical economics, or a science-fiction film to show the limitations of cybernetics.

Thus literary criticism claims a critical relation to social science analogous to the relation philosophy once claimed to natural science. This claim comes with the risk that literature departments will become a home for social-scientific ideas not taken seriously by social scientists, and not verifiable by social-scientific methods. But its problem for us lies in how this criticism extracts "social value" from aesthetic works by focusing literary form on social-scientific problems. We have traded a criticism that sees literature as a special part of society for one that sees literature as a special way of thinking about society. But I am interested in the possibility that certain literary works might represent a material alternative to the social. To access this requires nothing like Kaufman's virtuoso defense of the cognitive capability of novels and poems. It requires only a rather simple negative capability, one that seems intuitively present when students begin the study of literature. We need merely to be capable of seeing that literature's value is not always a social value.

Why should this ability prove so elusive? The compulsion to collapse the study of literature into the study of society, visible from New Historicism through the new literary sociologies, seems to express an underlying conviction of literature's marginal status.[24] Critics are driven to account for literature's social dimension by interpreting it as either an object of social science or as an aid to social science. But both these approaches have a structural inability to see that literature might make a social difference by being different from the social. In this sense, what looks like a series of exciting new claims for literature represents successive stages of a melancholy new modesty. To escape this melancholy, we need to see art as something other than a marker of social value or a cognitive device for analyzing society. These positions, as my brief overview has shown, derive from one tradition of reaction against the aesthetic ideology. We need now to consider a different tradition.

In "The Origin of the Work of Art", Heidegger asks: "Does the work remain a work when it stands outside all relations? Does it not belong to the work to stand in relations?" (OWA 20). "Of course," he writes, at once distinguishing himself from the Kantian view of the artwork as the cleanly delimited object of disinterested judgment. But Heidegger now raises a further question: "It remains to be asked in *which* relations [the artwork] stands. Where does a work belong?" He answers, "As a work, it belongs uniquely within the region it itself opens up" (OWA 20).

Here the artwork is not, as it is for the Kantian tradition, cut off from all other relations. But the relations which are proper to it cannot be determined prior to an encounter with that particular work. The work is not set into an existing network of relations. Rather, Heidegger writes, the relations in which the work is embedded are "opened up" or "set up" by the work itself. What can this mean? Heidegger's elaborations seem to obscure rather than to clarify things. He glosses "to open" thus: "By the opening of a world, all things gain their lingering and hastening, their distance and proximity, their breadth and their limits" (OWA 23). And he glosses "to set up" as: "To open up the right in the sense of the measure which guides us along, in which form that which is essential gives its guidance" (OWA 22). And there are still other formulas: "In this work, if it is a work, truth sets itself to work" (OWA 17).

To understand these mysterious sentences, a little background on Heidegger's philosophy helps. Heidegger broke with Husserl by declining to identify that which organizes how we perceive things with the structure of consciousness. Rather, in *Being and Time* (1927), he calls the structure that determines how things show up for us a "world." Students entering a classroom don't compare the shapes of wood and metal to shapes in their heads and then identify them as desks. They immediately see them as desks, and approach them with a disposition to sit down, take notes, ask questions. The desk is involved in the dense network of relations, conventions, and actions that make up the world of the school. This network isn't explicitly perceived by the students; rather, the network is responsible for how the students perceive things. This world determines what shows up as notable; it limits the range of appropriate actions, focuses choices. Heidegger argues that the principles that organize our experience are in the world instead of in the pure immanence of consciousness. This means that how things show up for us can be shaped by structures that lie outside the mind.

An instance of such a structure for Heidegger is a work of art. So when he speaks of the opening of a space as "the measure which guides us along," he is referring to the artwork as a structure of experience, a particular way of organizing the experience of those who become absorbed in it. The work sets an *example*[25] before us. One first learns how to be a student at a new school by observing how others move and speak. Imagine a new student looking at the way the other students suddenly get up from their desks and stand in a line. In looking at this example, the new student does not wish to stand back from it, to perceive it disinterestedly in terms of shapes and colors. She wishes to inhabit the example, to perceive the world from its perspective. The way the students move is exemplary for a new student not because of any feature of the surface, not because of anything that can be seen. It is exemplary because of the way each movement is involved in an invisible network of relations with other elements of the world of the school. The new student can't directly see this network. But through the example of the other students, she gains access to it.

In taking the other students' movements as an example, the new student is moved along and stopped by a new ordering of bodily motion. Because of the example, the world of the new school opens up for her.

And for Heidegger, the artwork opens up a world for us in the same way. The artwork is an example of how it is to be in a certain world. One can gauge the scale of Heidegger's departure from traditional aesthetics by noting how for Heidegger the surface of the work of art disappears. For Heidegger, when one looks at Van Gogh's peasant shoes, one doesn't linger over the lines and colors of the painted surface. Rather, one gains access to the myriad relations of the world – of "uncomplaining" struggle, of closeness to the earth – which the painted shoes exemplify (OWA 14). Similarly, when one steps inside a Greek temple, one's eyes are lifted to the statue of the god; one views the sky from between the sculpted columns. The work organizes one's experience, creating patterns of reverence and perceptions of mystery (OWA 21).

But where does the "truth" that the artwork "sets to work" come from? Where does the "measure" that the artwork uses to shape experience originate? Of what is the example of the artwork exemplary? For Heidegger, the artwork opens the world of a "historical people" (OWA 21). Just as our hypothetical students' movements disclose the world of the American school, Van Gogh's shoes disclose the social and cultural world of the Dutch peasant; the temple opens the world of the Greek citizen (OWA 20). Hubert Dreyfus aptly calls the artwork a "cultural paradigm."[26] For Heidegger, the world opened by the artwork consists of the norms and conventions of a particular society.

So have we really gotten anywhere? In Heidegger's theory of art as opening a space, as in Bourdieu's and Kaufman's theories, the aesthetic is ultimately parasitic on the social. We can now see how, for the man walking down the street with an i-pod, or the woman reading a novel on the subway, artworks act as a mode of organizing experience. But where do the principles by which they organize experience come from? Society. An actual social world. By looking at a work from a different society we may gain a measure of access to different social norms, but the link between the aesthetic and the social seems as absolute in Heidegger as in Bourdieu.

In studying literature we identify the circulation of cultural capital. We study examples of the social construction of race. We describe plays that are homologous to Renaissance property relations, we describe plays that give us new ways to describe Renaissance property relations, we describe plays that show us the world of the Renaissance. What else is there? Can art be something other than a part of or a window on society? Heidegger's concept of the artwork as a way of organizing experience seemed promising.[27] But where might one find a way of organizing human experience that does not have its origin in the social world?

3.

Since 1945 the market has been increasingly thought of as a nonsocial way of ordering human action, perception, and desire. A variety of writers believe market relations – relations of buying and selling, relations oriented to market price – to be "disembedded" from society, to use Karl Polanyi's famous description. I will discuss Polanyi at length in Chapter 1, but for now I simply wish to note the status of this description in his work. When he describes economic relations as disembedded from the social, he refers not to an actual market, which he thinks of as thoroughly embedded in society. He refers rather to a fictional market, to the existence of the fiction that market price, buying and selling, are not social phenomena.

One might well consider such fictional, nonsocial economic relations to be pretty flimsy things, especially after our fruitless attempt to discover any nonsocial fictions. But our tour through Heidegger suggests a way of taking both nonsocial relations and nonsocial fictions seriously. Heidegger offered us a way of describing artworks as structures for organizing experience. What was then missing – but what a number of people writing after 1945 have found – is a nonsocial structuring principle. We can now define the genre that concerns us according to the following formula. The economic fiction consists of artworks that open a space in which market relations are set to work organizing experience. In opening this space, these works establish a fascinatingly new mode of experience, and a genuine, and disturbing, *relation* between art and society.[28]

But we have moved too quickly, and things are a little more complicated than that. In the first place, why should Polanyi or anyone else require recourse to the aesthetic to see that economic relations are not social relations? People from neoclassical economists to anticapitalist demonstrators have been able to see this quite clearly without the help of fictions, myths, or artworks of any kind. For them, the market has nothing to do with the social. It has everything to do with the sovereign individual. So to clear the way for a properly fictional view of the market's autonomy – a conception of the market that gives it a *unique* importance for literature – I must first untangle it from accounts of actual markets.

The argument that the market is not social goes like this: Society is the realm of interdependent and interwoven individuals. Social action is shaped by cultural norms; complicated by intersubjective dynamics; driven by class, status, political, religious, and racial conflicts. But in the market, things work differently. Here, I act as an individual. I decide what I want by myself. I know what I want, and I know how much I want it in relation to everything else I want. I find the thing I want. Now I see it has a price on it. This price gives me some information about the thing. It tells me how hard it will be for me to get it. I process this information. I calculate. I weigh how much I want this thing relative to the other things I want, and I examine the money at my disposal.

The information expressed by market price comes in to me from the outside; I process it, and send out my decision to buy or not to buy. There is no social relation here. No intersubjectivity, no culture, no politics. The market is perhaps the only place in the human world where this kind of purely individual action can occur. Through the price system, I act, I choose, I have individual freedom. The market won't guarantee that I won't starve, but it will guarantee that when I act, I will act as an individual.

So, for neoclassical economic theory, a private individual preference determines whether and how much I want something. And while individual preference determines price – in that market value reflects the preferences of all the individuals in the market – price never determines a single preference. The high price of diamonds reflects the fact that lots of people want diamonds and there aren't very many of them. The market doesn't determine whether or not I want a diamond. Price has nothing to do with my desire for diamonds. Price determines only whether or not I will realize my preexisting preference in an exchange. If the price shows me that the thing will cost me more than the benefit I expect from it, I won't buy it. I'll still want it; I'll just decide not to get it.

While demand theory works with personal preferences generated by individuals, others argue that social forces determine economic behavior. On this account there is nothing private about preferences, but these social desires are just as independent of price as the desires of sovereign individuals. I want a diamond because of the De Beers advertising campaign, or because I want to get married and a cultural convention associates diamonds with wedding engagements. Price has nothing to do with whether or why I want a diamond. Price reflects the fact that lots of other people want diamonds, which isn't surprising, since their intentions are formed by the same social dynamics as mine.

Here again, the market reflects the extra-economic determinants of desire and does not itself determine desire. The high price of diamonds reflects advertising campaigns or social conventions that position diamonds as engagement gifts or status markers. Price doesn't determine whether or not I want a diamond; these social factors do. Price just means that if I'm poor, I won't be able to realize my social desire in an economic exchange. Outside of the aesthetic, price never influences desire.

The example of the diamond ring, however, suggests a notorious special case where price does appear to affect whether or not I want a thing. This is the "Veblen effect," which describes the situation of the consumer for whom the high price of a luxury good makes it attractive.[29] Few people will believe, for example, that if I buy a Rolls Royce I do so because I prefer its smooth ride. Here, price is indeed a factor in shaping desire. It is not a cultural convention that associates Rolls Royces with high status; Rolls Royces just have incredibly high prices. And the desire for the Rolls is determined by price without ceasing to be thoroughly social: I want things with high prices because they enable me to project my social status.

But a complication arises as soon as one considers that it is not simply *any* high-priced thing that will attract me, but only things like cars, clothes, and jewelry. Price can shape desire in conspicuous consumption only when the aesthetic also plays a role. The high price of a thing can attract me only if something is added to it that enables it to project its high price to other people. As Veblen wrote, high price by itself is not enough, that price must be written "in characters which he who runs may read."[30] How do you turn an object into a projector of price? For designers, marketers, shop owners, and consumers, this is largely an aesthetic question. The silver angel on a Rolls Royce, Prada's distinctive colors: the iconic examples of conspicuous consumption tightly intertwine price and style. Chapter 5 examines in depth the tension between conspicuous consumption, where the aesthetic binds price to social relations, and the economic fiction, where the aesthetic cuts money free of the social. Here it is enough to note that the apparent exception of the Veblen effect proves the rule. To operate as a factor determining desire, market value requires an aesthetic supplement.

Without the aesthetic supplement, everything that determines my relation to things originates outside of the market and is then expressed or reflected in price. Market value reflects the extra-economic source of demand; it doesn't affect it. Ultimately, this is true even of the aesthetics of conspicuous consumption, since a thing's price can serve as a source of desire only because of an underlying desire for social status. Thus the common sense, expressed by Jameson, that the market cannot be anything other than a conduit through which social or individual energies pass. The desirability or utility of a thing is determined by the individual or society or both; it is then expressed by the market.

Here we have a basic reason why the market must remain dependent on either society or the individual. The market alone can't give you a reason for wanting a diamond or anything else. If you already have a reason to get something (a desire to give your fiancée a ring, a personal preference for a diamond's glitter), then it can tell you how hard or easy it will be for you to get it.

Thus the independence of the market is inconceivable; the fascination of an entirely economic world is truly astonishing. Market value represents information about forces, desires, and intentions formed without the influence of the market. Intention is extra-economic; there is no such thing as an economic intention. Even the desire for money itself is not economic. It is either a desire for the personally desirable things money can buy, if you are a strict individualist, or a desire for social power and status, if you are a strict social determinist, or some mixture of the two.[31] Money stays on the outside; the inner realm of the individual or the social, the place where intentions are formed and experience is shaped, is closed to it.

Alone behind the veil of individual subjectivity, or tangled in the realm of the social, I form a desire for a thing. Then I see what its price is, and I use this information to decide whether or not I will buy it. In actual markets, the moment I decide whether or not I am interested in an object or activity, and the moment I see what the price is, are two separate moments. But in the spaces opened by some postwar artworks, my experience and intentions are not distinct from my awareness of market value. This is the difference in the way the economic operates in these works. And this simple difference produces dramatic effects.

To make this difference in the way the market works requires a fiction. As Heidegger suggests, a fiction can make a certain perception, a certain action possible. For an astronaut fixing an antenna on a space station, there is no gravity. But she still may find the fiction of an "up" and a "down" useful in orienting her body to perform her task. When she opens a hatch on the station and enters it, she goes "down." When she reaches towards the fixture extending from the station's body, she reaches "up." This fiction is not a representation. It is not a picture of the space station, which she stands back to contemplate. It is a way of organizing her immediate experience of her environment. It's a way of entering the station, of getting her hand from one place on the antennae to another. Of course, to imagine a space organized by up-down orientation is hardly a challenge. But what does a space organized by the market look like?

4.

William Gaddis' 1974 novel *JR* provides a vivid example of an economic fiction. This work sets up a fictional mode of economic experience, agency, and perception distinct from both the social and the individual.

–Crawley here. What? No, I don't know what the hell's going on there nobody does ... What? no, it's not just two or three stocks, it's the whole market ... do what? Certainly not. If you want to quote me you can say the long overdue technical readjustments taking place in our present dynamic market situation offer no convincing ... now. These young ladies and gentlemen are here to buy some stock are they? (*JR* 83)

Gaddis' vast novel constitutes an extended meditation on the ubiquitous colloquial figure of the "crazy market." Like such writers as Sylvia Plath, R. D. Laing, and Amiri Baraka, who I will take up in my first chapter, Gaddis understands madness in terms of an alternative to social relations. Let's listen a little more to the sound this alternative makes:

"Must have been when Crawley was picking up the coins one second, I'm expecting a call from Washington, Senator Broos hello ...? No tell him I'll call him back now there, that one's not bad, not bad of Crawley but it looks like that pig is climbing in the window over his shoulder wait, here's my call now, hello? Senator? Moleenhoff? What does Mollenhoff want? ... No that was his memo to me not my memo to him ... what? Wait a minute ... who? No this isn't the maintenance department ..." (*JR* 215–16)

The speaker seems unable to get others to recognize his voice, and he is unable to recognize the speech of others. People in *JR* tend to speak on the telephone, a device Gaddis uses to represent communication without recognition.[32] And "communication without recognition" can serve as a useful shorthand for market relations in the novel. Here people are oriented towards market price, instead of towards each other. Price slices through interpersonal contacts. A typical exchange involves one character cutting another off by saying abruptly: "Don't worry about it just give me your figures" (*JR* 524). Here economic success is in direct relation to freedom from social recognition. When JR, the novel's eleven-year-old entrepreneur, is asked how he has managed to amass a vast business empire without anyone realizing his age, he says that he conducts his business "only in the mail and on the telephone because that's how they do it nobody has to see anybody" (*JR* 172). This absence of recognition persists even in face-to-face meetings. One character remarks of JR, "when you talk to him he doesn't look at you" (*JR* 246).

What kind of relation, what kind of consciousness exists in the absence of social relations? What does a nonsocial human world look like? Here, it looks like a five-hundred-page novel consisting entirely of unattributed dialogue. A new form of subjectivity emerges in this aesthetic space. In the character JR, Gaddis creates a figure who is exemplary in Heidegger's world-disclosing sense. JR, an eleven-year-old boy who makes millions of dollars trading picnic forks and scrap metal, could not be farther from the modern image of the entrepreneur. Successful market agents, in texts from Dreiser's *The Financier* to Schumpeter's influential theory of the entrepreneur, are the individuals who invent new manufacturing processes, who aren't afraid to buck conventional wisdom to pursue their dreams, who create new markets, who forge powerful organizations.[33] The heroic modernist entrepreneur imposes a powerful individual interpreta- tion on the world. JR's success as a market agent, on the other hand, is due to his awareness of opportunities. This awareness has a special structure. When JR looks around the world, he doesn't try to impose an individual interpretation on it. Rather, he looks to price to do that. The price system, interfacing with his individual body, transforms his awareness. Market price is threaded through his perception, through his agency.

Price shapes JR's awareness of the world. This awareness is collective without being social. "Just give me your figures" (*JR* 524). The displace- ment of speech by price is illustrated by the novel's favorite saying: "What's that got to do with the price of apples?" (*JR* 141) This reply is always apt, regardless of the question. We have prices, what is there to talk about? "At this price I don't think he'll mind the ahm, the smell you might say ... mind if I hang up?" (*JR* 452)

Clearly, price is doing something new and strange here. By imagining that price can replace social communication, Gaddis' novel transforms market value. Price can replace intersubjectivity because it introduces a collective dimension into JR's immediate first-person awareness of the world. In this aesthetic space, his awareness of price is a basic feature of his perception. And this represents a dramatic departure from the description of price given in the standard accounts of real-world economic behavior. As we have seen, in those accounts my intentions regarding the things in my environment develop without reference to my awareness of the price of those things. While economists disagree as to what determines my relation to things, all agree that I form a sense of a thing, a desire or lack of desire for it, independently of my awareness of price.

But in the fictional space of Gaddis' novel, JR's experience and inten- tions are not distinct from his awareness of price. Here, price organizes

JR's experience of things. As soon as he encounters a priced object, he experiences it as either easy or hard to get. Like shape or color or spatial position, the price is a feature of his experience of the thing. Price structures his perception by organizing the objects and activities in his immediate context in terms of how easy or hard it is for him to get them. Price does this by adding an element to his experience of a thing that positions it in relation to every other thing in the world. Because things show up for JR in this global context, he notices things that don't show up for people not attuned to price in this way.

JR's nervous, halting, fragmented speech is constantly interrupted by the words "see" and "look." Here are some examples of sentences spoken by JR. "No well look ... no well look ... no well look see ... Okay look." (*JR* 469); "Let's see hey what, holy look hey!" (*JR* 293); "No but see so ... No but see like ... No but wait hey." (*JR* 467). It is as if JR's seeing takes over his speaking; as if the special, collective structure of that seeing renders speech irrelevant. When JR looks out at the world through price, his first-person awareness has a global, collective dimension that renders intersubjective communication obsolete.

The special structure of JR's first-person awareness accounts for his insanely successful career. The modern image of the entrepreneur is of innovative individuals, like Dreiser's Frank Cowperwood, who have a heroic ability to outguess or "beat" the market. Their motto is "buy low, sell high." Such individuals rely for their success on knowledge, "instinct," or intelligence that places them in a privileged position above the market. Cowperwood, for example, does not believe in the information conveyed by price. In the dramatic scene where he regains his fortune after being released from prison, the market is falling precipitously, but he doesn't watch the prices.[34] Cowperwood relies on his own analysis of underlying social and economic conditions, an analysis at odds with the picture presented by falling prices. On the basis of this analysis, he guesses the prices will soon rise dramatically, and buys as much as he can. He turns out to be right, makes millions, and goes on to become *The Titan* of Dreiser's sequel.

But if the classic image of the entrepreneur involves out-thinking the market, JR's success depends on an incapacity to think, or even to perceive, outside the picture of the world presented by price. JR never outguesses the market. He is eleven years old, and manifestly lacks the finely-trained analytical skills of a Cowperwood. This very lack of a developed capacity to think outside the market constitutes his great advantage over all the adults he competes with. JR has an awareness completely tuned to price, and this enables him constantly to see opportunities beneath the notice of his elders. "Buy low sell high," for JR, simply means noticing that a price for picnic forks is low here, and high over there. The calculations of a Cowperwood are replaced by the careful attention of an eleven year old.

Gaddis' fiction turns the price system, the self-organizing system of a global economy of bodies, things, and actions, into a structure of attention, of experience. It links the watch or picnic fork in front of JR to everything and everyone else. It accomplishes this link by shaping JR's awareness of and relation to the thing. Shaped by price, JR's subjectivity is a collective subjectivity. The collective nature of his intention regarding the picnic fork rests on the determining influence of the single, nonsocial index of price. And in JR's fictional world, everything has a price.

Instead of a mechanism for mediating between the desires, expectations, and perceptions of separate individuals, the market looks like a mode of generating desire and perception. It looks like a subject. If a critical tradition from Simmel through Jameson has seen the market as a process of commodification or objectification, Gaddis' novel imagines market exchange as a process of subjectification.[35] Gaddis' critics, who see this novel, along with much of the rest of postwar literature, as a story about the death of subjectivity, miss this point. Most subscribe to some version of the reading articulated by John Johnson, who understands the "broken, fragmented" speech of the novel's characters in terms of the theory that "meaning does not originate in the individual's intentional act" but "is always produced out of its perpetual displacement in a preexistent and underlying system or structure."[36]

But this imagines a discrepancy between individual intention and underlying system. In Gaddis' market, there is no such discrepancy. It is not that JR's intentions fail or are displaced by a system. In fact, his intentional acts are wildly successful. It is just that JR's intention has a peculiar structure. His intention is not at odds with a system; the price system is partially constitutive of JR's intentional acts. In being shaped by the price system, JR's awareness of things is shaped by all the exchanges made everywhere in the world. This price system is an integral part of his awareness. It is not a system which he might use or not use, as one might use the number system to make a calculation. In this novel, the price system is an interface between an embodied awareness and a global collective. It ensures that JR's choices are coordinated with and shaped by all the choices being made throughout the world. JR, the boy who "doesn't look at you," embodies the subjectivity that arises from nonsocial relations. The child, who builds a vast commercial empire out of surplus navy boots, picnic forks, and various other odds and ends, replaces the industrial magnates and entrepreneurs of modernity as the classic post-war figure of the successful market agent.

With his acute awareness of the opportunities price reveals in his environment, JR exemplifies the kind of market agency described by F. A. Hayek in his 1949 article "The Use of Knowledge in Society." Hayek is the key postwar theorist of market price as a way of coordinating human perception and action, and I will engage with his thinking in several of the following chapters. Hayek's characterization of the price system as an autonomous process – and his tendency to locate this process in the fiction of a future when the various mechanisms that shackle the market to society have been destroyed – gives his economics a special relevance for my study.[37] Like Gaddis, Hayek is uninterested in the image of the market as driven by heroic, innovative entrepreneurs. He thinks it depends on a rather different kind of agent:

The shipper who earns his living from using otherwise empty or half-filled journeys of tramp-steamers, or the estate agent whose whole knowledge is almost exclusively one of temporary opportunities, or the *arbitrageur* who gains from local differences of commodity prices – are all performing eminently useful functions based on special knowledge of the circumstances of the fleeting moment not known to others. It is a curious fact that this sort of knowledge should today be generally regarded with a kind of contempt ... (UK 80–81)

JR makes millions with a simple awareness of the "fleeting moment" illuminated by price.[38] He notices advertisements for cheap shoes in the back of comic books, or unused picnic forks in a warehouse. An adult character like Edward Bast, a teacher and composer, who has marked individual dreams and projects, and a highly developed individual frame of reference, misses the things JR notices. Price is not integral to Bast's consciousness, and the piles of shoes or forks or scrap metal which occupy JR's attention simply don't show up for him.

Market price helps to constitute JR's intentional relation to the world. Who decides these mineral deposits are valuable? Who decides this failing media company has promise? Who decides this pile of scrap metal is interesting? With market price threaded through his perception, through his agency, JR embodies a collective market subjectivity, a collective market agency. He doesn't recognize any other subject, and others can't recognize him. They can't fix him in the space of intersubjectivity, in the gaze of recognition. JR's attention to things, his buying and selling, his phone calls and telegrams, exemplify communication without recognition, collective action without intersubjective contact.

Finally, it is this uncanny ability to elude recognition that most strikingly distinguishes JR from a titanic figure like Cowperwood. It's hard to see JR; it's hard to hear him. He ducks in and out of phone booths, speaks with a disguised voice over the phone, skips class to send out telegrams. Few characters in the novel see him, and nearly all of those who do don't realize who he is. Bast is one of the few who does, and he expends enormous and futile efforts to keep the social space between him and the boy open. The fragmentary conversations between Bast and JR, little glimpses of the clothes he wears or the color of his hair: all the information we have about JR emerges in a fragile intersubjective space which the form of the novel constantly undermines.

As the novel proceeds, as hundreds of pages of unattributed dialogue accumulate, JR gets harder and harder to see and to hear. Gradually, inexorably, the difference between JR's voice and the voices of everyone else, the difference between JR the character and *JR* the book, begins to fade. If the image of the eleven-year-old boy is not quite adequate to the collective agency that emerges in him, the book succeeds in producing a phantasmatic image of that agency. The form of the novel folds the voices of its named and anonymous characters into a single voice, which rushes along accumulating disparate bits of individuals and information, gaining direction, power, and grace by imitating what can only be described as the voice of the market itself.[39] Although readers may gain an abstract sense of the scale and integrity of this voice, they will remain unable to hear it. We have only the text; the voice remains virtual. The market has no relation to any other; in ventriloquizing it, Gaddis has created the fiction of a voice without an addressee.

The novel identifies the attempt to see, to recognize, this virtual-market subject as a mistake. Bast exemplifies one version of this mistake. Gaddis' critics exemplify another version when they attempt to recognize the relational space of the novel as a system, to bring it into focus as an analytic object. But if JR's subjectivity is not a private individual subjectivity lodged in a face and a body, neither is it displaced by a system. Unlike the concept of system that dominates the criticism, the coordination produced by price doesn't happen outside of or despite human consciousness. If JR can't understand the world without price, neither does price have a grip on the world without JR's minute awareness of the features of his environment. Picnic forks become interesting to JR, an ad in the back of a newspaper for scrap metal becomes noticeable to JR: this is how price works here. The agency exemplified by JR is located neither outside of the boy's body, nor inside it. The status of price system as *interface* erases this distinction, and frustrates every attempt to locate JR's intention, to recognize it in a delimited object. The choice seen by the criticism – either agency is located in an individual or in a system – is a false one. The agency manifest in JR's decisions is lodged neither within the boy's skin nor in some distinct, delimited system. In this novel, we witness a different kind of transformation. A recognizable object (the market) becomes an unrecognizable subject (JR).

Fictional economies of the kind exemplified by *JR* remove the tragic element from the economic. Ordinarily, the words "economic," "economy," "economize," are associated with the sacrifice that occurs when limitless human desires confront a limited world.[40] But in a fictional space where price shapes desire, this asymmetry vanishes. Here, the economic does not imply scarcity and sacrifice. Price limits experience in the sense that up-down orientation limits space, not in the sense that I want diamonds but can only afford zirconium. In these works, the economic loses its "dismal" or "dreary" aspect. The economic fiction is a comic genre.

The economic fiction is that genre of aesthetic works in which the market organizes experience. I understand "genre" here not in traditional formalist terms – as artworks that share a set of formal features – but, in the Heideggerian terms laid out above, as artworks that share a way of organizing experience.[41] The dynamics of this organization vary. In some works, price transforms perception as it does in *JR*. In other works – such as the fictional money that serves as a nonsocial mode of collective power and value in rap – the economic operates differently. By setting the market to work organizing experience in various ways, these works set up a purely economic relation to the world. Modernity means that most things in our world are entangled in the market. The postmodern fiction is that in the actual world the market lies semi-dormant, strangely inert, blocked and buried by social relations, fenced out by the shell of the individual subject. The fiction is that to free the market is to free it to organize the objects of human experience, to guide and shape human action. In the economic fiction, the collective rises in the moment-by-moment organizing of first person experience by market forces. These works turn market forces into the structuring principle of subjectivity.

To understand what Jameson calls the "most astonishing feature" of postwar culture, we need to examine how a purely economic form develops as a hybrid of the aesthetic and the economic. And to say that the market requires the aesthetic to become independent of the social, does not mean that it requires the social after all. Heidegger shows us how artworks can open a space in which experience is organized according to certain principles. In postwar America, the market appears to a number of writers as a nonsocial principle for organizing experience. The autonomy of the market from the social, and the autonomy of the aesthetic from the social, are indissolubly linked in this period. The aesthetic fuses with the economic to create works that offer an ambiguously fascinating alternative to social and individual life. To study the dynamics, the possibilities and limits, the circulation of this liberated market, to study the forms of its actual existence, is to study the evolution of an art form, as the following chapters undertake to show.

CHAPTER I

Freedom from you

In Gaddis' *JR* we encounter a mature example of the form I am calling the economic fiction. This chapter takes a step back in order to provide a fuller frame for its evolution as I will track it in the remainder of this book. My first aim is to explore the desire I believe to animate and to motivate this fiction. This is the desire for an alternative to social relations, and I approach it through three artistic images of madness. In the first part of this chapter, I set up Esther's insanity in Sylvia Plath's *The Bell Jar* (1963) as a rich site to investigate the belief that intersubjectivity is defined by intractable flaws and the corresponding longing for a different mode of relation. In the second part, my examples are the insane Plainview in Paul Thomas Anderson's 2007 film *There Will Be Blood* and the maniac in Amiri Baraka's 1972 poem "Das Kapital." I examine how these figures reproduce the key features of Esther's insanity, but now locate the alternative to intersubjectivity in the economic. To gain a perspective on this development, in the third part of this chapter I construct a brief intellectual history of the concept of an economic fiction, centering on Karl Polanyi and Hannah Arendt.

I.

For thinkers from Jacques Lacan to Martha Nussbaum, and from Charles Taylor to Gayatri Spivak, the social relation and individual consciousness have a single origin: the look of recognition. The gaze that loops between the self and the other, between the eye and the mirror, binds the human world together. The recognizing gaze ensures that the other side of every subject is an object. This gaze, whether housed in Levinas' other, in Lacan's mirror, or in Foucault's panopticon, ensures that subjectivity is associated with a face, a name, a position in the social field.

The ubiquity of the knot of recognition in postwar discourse has inspired a set of shadow questions. What happens when this knot is cut?

Is it possible to imagine human relations without recognition? I will follow these questions through a set of literary and theoretical works to trace
a route that has been invisible in the literary, cultural, and intellectual
maps of the period.

We'll begin with someone who has a particularly pressing problem
with recognition. One day Esther, the protagonist of Sylvia Plath's *The
Bell Jar,* discovers that she can no longer recognize herself in mirrors. At
a point early in the novel, she is startled by her reflection: "I noticed a
big, smudgy-eyed Chinese woman staring idiotically into my face. It was
only me, of course" (*BJ* 22). Later, the sense that the other in the mirror
is "only me" becomes more elusive: "The face in the mirror looked like a
sick Indian" (*BJ* 133).

Esther's inability to recognize her identity in her own reflection takes
the form of an intense and threatening sense of social difference. She
strikingly identifies the unrecognizable other in the mirror with unrecognizable social others. This decay exposes the radical otherness that
recognition conceals. Normal intersubjectivity and individuality is built
on this concealment, and when this secret otherness is brought into the
open, Esther recoils from seeing and being seen. She hides in her house
and creeps under the windows: "I didn't really see why people should look
at me" (*BJ* 134), and "I felt it was very important not to be recognized"
(*BJ* 135). The experience of looking at a crowd of other people reproduces
her experience of looking at herself in the mirror. She speaks of "faces in a
funhouse mirror," "dimly familiar but twisted all awry" (*BJ* 147).

Esther's problem with recognition is this: when she stops being able
to recognize, her relationships with others disintegrate, and her sense of
herself breaks down. Her whole life falls apart. And why shouldn't it?
Nothing is more familiar than the idea that when the knot of recognition is cut, a complete breakdown of social and individual life ensues.
Recognition, in Nancy Fraser's words, "designates an ideal reciprocal
relation between subjects, in which each sees the other both as its equal
and also as separate from it."[1] The idea that this relation is constitutive
of subjectivity itself is an old theme of western thought that received its
classic expression in Hegel's philosophy: "The self perceives itself at the
same time that it is perceived by others ... Self-consciousness exists ...
by the very fact that it exists for another self-consciousness; that is to say,
it is only by being recognized or acknowledged."[2] The conviction that I
become aware of myself as a subject by recognizing myself as the object of
another's gaze underlies Charles Taylor's influential argument that "recognition is not just a courtesy we owe people. It is a vital human need."[3] In

this view, recognition is not only the requirement for human relations, it is the basis of human consciousness. Thus Susan Stewart, to take another example, argues that "this imperative of recognition" is the "unending task" of the production and reception of artworks.[4]

Deprived of the ability to recognize and be recognized, Esther's life falls apart. This is not surprising. What is surprising is what happens next. Esther's crisis of recognition reaches a climax when she takes an overdose of pills, and hides herself in a hole underground where she passes out. She wakes in a hospital, in complete darkness. The nurse hands her a mirror. "At first I didn't see what the trouble was. It wasn't a mirror at all, but a picture. You couldn't tell whether the person in the picture was a man or a woman ... The most startling thing about the face was its supernatural conglomeration of bright colors. I smiled. The mouth in the mirror cracked into a grin" (*BJ* 208).

At first this passage reads, although in a curiously roundabout way, as if Esther has smiled at herself in the mirror, as if she has recognized herself. But suddenly a nurse runs in shouting and we realize that Esther has dropped the mirror and broken it. This information enables us to revise our understanding of the smile. Esther has not suddenly been cured of her mirror-phobia; the smile in the mirror is not a smile of recognition. The mouth that "cracks" into a grin is the mirror cracking. The line zigzagging down the center of the broken mirror is the jagged smile of a new kind of subject.

Esther's broken mirror holds the image of a new subject not defined by recognition. A desire for this new mode of being suffuses Plath's work. Consider Esther's soliloquy from the beginning of *The Bell Jar*.

"Doreen is dissolving, Lenny Sheperd is dissolving, Frankie is dissolving, New York is dissolving, they are all dissolving away and none of them matter anymore. I don't know them, I have never known them and I am very pure." (*BJ* 24)

Here Esther, lying in a bath she compares to "holy water," ritually invokes a consciousness immaculately free of recognition. It is a radical consciousness, radical in its freedom from the recognition which associates consciousness with an object, a body, a face, or a position. For Plath, this radical consciousness is the special achievement of artworks. One might compare the "very pure" subject summoned here with the speaking voice of the late poems, which Irving Howe described as expressing "a state of being in which the speaker ... has abandoned the sense of anyone but herself ... There is something utterly monolithic, fixated about the voice that emerges in these poems, a voice unmodulated and asocial."[5] Plath identifies the perfection of this "extreme," "asocial" subjectivity with the perfection of her art. Howe at times evinces a kind of horrified fascination with this state, but ultimately he finds it merely repellent, an entombment in the self, a self-defeating solipsism.

And yet Plath, in her poetry and prose, associates this new subjectivity with a vastly expanded and intensified access to language. The paradox of this writing is that the decay of recognition doesn't end the speaker's communications. Rather, the breaking of the mirror is associated with the removal of what had blocked the subject's ability to communicate. If this is solipsism, it is a strange solipsism that, instead of falling silent, begins to speak. Plath imagines that the freedom of her speakers from recognition endows them with unprecedented access to speech, to the community. This is not solipsism, but something stranger, a radical subjectivity where the failure of recognition produces an expanded access to communal value.

Plath sets up Esther's radical subjectivity by erasing the original mark of the intersubjective, a primal split she locates between her gaze and her image in the mirror. For Esther, the recognition by the other that constitutes the self is either performed by other subjects, as it is in Hegel, or, as in Lacan's revision of Hegel, by herself before the mirror. In recognition, as Plath writes in "The Other," "You insert yourself // Between myself and myself" (*CP* 201–02). With her visceral experience of her own nonidentity with her specular image, in suffering the gaze of the other as an alien force, Esther exposes the fissure that makes her subject to relationship. To enter intersubjectivity is to suffer the split between subjects within oneself, and Plath's writing makes this suffering vivid.[6]

If Plath had frozen Esther in this suffering, suspended before the mirror image she must identify with even as she recognizes its absolute otherness, her work could stand as an illustration of one of the most powerful recent critical paradigms. The past twenty years have yielded a large body of criticism that places a premium on the aesthetic exposure of the impossibility of recognition. Craig Owens' influential treatment of Barbara Kruger's work of the 1980s is perhaps the classic postmodern example of this trend. For Owens, oppressive stereotypes work by reflecting an image of the viewer which she then identifies with. Good art, like Kruger's, exposes "the contradictory construction of the viewing subject by the stereotype."[7] Drawing on Lacan's theory of the mirror stage, Owens argues that recognition is always misrecognition, that the space between oneself and the other in the advertisement or the mirror is never closed.

To stress the impassable character of that space, which swallows both the face and the address of the other, has become a preferred strategy of resistance to power. Judith Butler and Slavoi Zizek, among others, have celebrated this gap between self and (specular) other as entailing the necessary failure of oppressive interpellating recognitions.[8] To resist colonizing recognitions, Gayatri Spivak has adapted Levinas' argument that the attempt to cross the space from subject to other is the basic ethical wrong.[9]

But Plath, disconcertingly, does not stop with the failure of recognition. Esther, unlike the subject celebrated by these critics, does not remain rapt before the ineluctable difference between herself and the image offered by the mirror. She breaks the mirror, disposes of the divided self, and becomes "godlike."[10] What makes Esther's "internal divisions" so unbearable, what leads Plath to imbue them with an intense and visceral horror, is her passionate awareness of an alternative. Lying in the "holy water" of her bath she prays to the phantom of this alternative; by breaking the mirror at the hospital she escapes into it. The crisis of consciousness is precipitated by the revelation of a new kind of consciousness beyond crisis.

The critical equation of consciousness and recognition has made this dynamic difficult to see. Some later criticism, beginning with Jacqueline Rose's study *The Haunting of Sylvia Plath,* mistakes Plath's attack on intersubjectivity for an attack on subjectivity as such. For Rose, the poet's fractured subjectivity is the inevitable result of "the contradictory, divided, and incomplete nature of representation itself."[11] In a recent study, Christina Britzolakis writes that Plath "reinvents the lyric as the vehicle for a crisis of subjectivity."[12] Plath's writing shows how "the construction of the speaker must therefore increasingly appear as the effect of a prior splitting or doubling."[13]

In one important sense, Rose and Britzolakis are right. A major theme of Plath's poetry is the "crisis" of subjectivity, the revelation of its makeshift inauthenticity, its scars and gaps. However, as I will show, this crisis does not proceed from the inherent contradictions of subjectivity, as the critics believe, but from what Plath takes to be the inherent contradictions of recognition. For a critical tradition that identifies recognition or interpellation with consciousness, this difference doesn't make a difference. But it makes a difference for Plath because she doesn't think that recognition is the indispensable condition for consciousness. Plath's understanding of the separability of subjectivity from recognition underlies a dimension of her work that has remained invisible to the critics.

In some of Plath's most famous poems, such as "Lady Lazarus" and "Daddy," the speaker's subjectivity is indeed in crisis. This intensely fragmented consciousness, so interesting to recent critics, is not intended as the exposure of the truth about consciousness as such, but as the denunciation of the deformation of consciousness that constitutes the formal condition of intersubjectivity. The crisis of subjectivity is precipitated by the demand that the subject project a spectacular image of herself to connect with the other. Performance is not the only modality available to the subject, but it is the only modality available when dealing with the *other*, whether the other is in the mirror or on the street. Consider the following lines from "Lady Lazarus," a poem depicting the speaker's performance of her own death for a curious audience: "The peanut-crunching crowd / Shoves in to see // Them unwrap me hand and foot—/ The big strip tease" (*CPSP* 245). Death here is a "fake," and the moment of "resurrection" reveals its orientation to an audience: "It's the theatrical // Comeback in broad day/ To the same place, the same face, the same brute / Amused shout" (*CPSP* 245–6).[14]

"Lady Lazarus" exposes a subject entirely reduced to its relation to an audience, and completely bound to the object the audience sees. The self here is simply that which can be seen and recognized; there is nothing behind it. "Ash, ash – / You poke and stir. / Flesh, bone, there is nothing there—" (*CPSP* 246). As an object on a stage, the subject is fully present to the audience. Community and subjectivity are founded on this vivid visual presence of the self as object. In the theatrical space of recognition, intersubjectivity requires that the human body become an ever more spectacular and fascinating object. And nothing, Plath suggests, is so fascinating, so valuable to intersubjectivity as a brutalized body. The audience demands the display of "scars," and finally, in the poem's infamous concentration camp imagery, they want a more rigorously objectified body: "A cake of soap," a "Nazi lampshade" (*CPSP* 244). Here Plath scandalously imagines the Holocaust as the logical outcome of the regime of recognition. The gaze that binds the subject to an object ends by ensuring that the subject is nothing but object. Thus in "Edge," the "woman is perfected. Her dead // Body wears the smile of accomplishment" (*CPSP* 272).

For Plath, the dialectic of recognition is evil. I would suggest, for example, that her absolute hostility to the other in "Daddy" ("Daddy I have had to kill you"), has less to do with the specificity of the father than with what Plath perceives as the general condition of relations with others (*CPSP* 222). Anyone can (and in other poems, does) stand in for

"Daddy." Trauma is not inflicted by particular people, but is a general consequence of intersubjectivity as such.[15] The problem the speaker has with "Daddy," like the problem Esther has with the "Chinese woman" in her mirror, doesn't derive from the specific features of these different figures, but from their common status as other. As "Death & Co." puts it, "Two, of course there are two. / It seems perfectly natural now – (*CPSP* 254)." The roles and script vary, but "two" is the minimum requirement for the crisis of subjectivity.

The split, fractured, and tormented subject that fascinates Plath's critics is always the effect of a relation to another subject. For Plath this splitting is not, as the recent criticism would have it, simply the truth about the subject. The trauma of recognition is *un*necessary, and its superfluous character is precisely what makes intersubjectivity visible to Plath in the absolute, negative terms of her poetry. Intersubjectivity, with all its complexity, can simply be cast off. The late poems continually invoke a radical subjectivity as the alternative that funds this gesture: "The heart shuts, / The sea slides back, / The mirrors are sheeted" ("Contusion," *CPSP* 271).

The plot of *The Bell Jar* dramatizes the emergence of this new consciousness. It is invoked in the opening scene in the bath; towards the end of the novel it speaks in Esther's voice. "I was perfectly free," she comments, coming to the end of a list of people with whom she no longer has relations. Her attention is tuned to an absorbed, ecstatic inwardness: "I took a deep breath and listened to the old brag of my heart. I am, I am, I am" (*BJ* 289). This new subject, freed from intersubjectivity, echoes throughout the late poems: "And I have no face, I have wanted to efface myself ... how free it is, you have no idea how free" ("Tulips," *CPSP* 161). This new subject is godlike, godlike because invisible. "Now I resemble a sort of a god / Floating through the air in my soul-shift / Pure as a pane of ice" ("Love Letter," *CPSP* 147).

For Plath, the split subject is not the only possible mode of subjectivity; she sees this split subject not as a fact we must learn to live with, but as a symptom of the disease of recognition.[16] And in *The Bell Jar*, this disease has a cure. When Esther breaks the mirror the contradictions of the subject are resolved, its split is healed, the subject of recognition lies in fragments on the floor, and Esther is "freed." She becomes the avatar of a human consciousness that doesn't pass through recognition.

From the inside, this new subject feels like a god; from the outside, from the social world regulated by the regime of recognition, it is perceived as embodying a particularly threatening form of insanity. For breaking the mirror, for violating what the novel represents as the ultimate taboo,

Esther is evicted from the hospital. In the car on her way to the asylum, Esther's mother looks at her sorrowfully and says: "You shouldn't have broken that mirror" (*BJ* 210). The authorities in *The Bell Jar* declare Esther insane and shut her up in an asylum, where an alternately idiotic, sadistic, and tyrannical psychiatric staff attempts to cure her by forcing her back into the regime of recognition.

Esther's insanity negates the negativity of sane relations. The doctors locate her breakdown just where she locates her breakthrough: the breaking of the mirror. Here Plath illuminates a network in postwar thought that links madness, subjectivity, and the rejection of recognition. The thinking of the anti-psychiatry movement of the late fifties and sixties also moves along this network.[17] This movement represents a mode of thought and practice that has been obscured by the strict equation of recognition and subjectivity in the theory and criticism that succeeded it.

Anti-psychiatric writing, an international movement which includes early works by Felix Guatarri and Michel Foucault, is broadly characterized by a critique of the central premise of contemporary psychiatric practice: that insanity is an illness.[18] In an influential paper published in 1958, Gregory Bateson, an early American exponent of anti-psychiatry, defined schizophrenia as a subjective response to a formal problem with relations between subjects. He coined the term "double-bind" to describe this problem, which consists of the subject receiving contradictory demands from the other. For instance, if I tell you I don't mind seeing a certain film, but indicate by my facial expression that I do, I've placed you in a double-bind. Whatever response you give will be "wrong" in the sense of violating one of my directives. Insofar as the subject relies for her sense of self on the validation of others, the double-bind is "a dilemma of *self-preservation* in the most literal sense."[19]

The subject cannot escape through silence. Bateson claims that the space of intersubjective communication is defined by a command to respond. In some circumstances, the subject may transfer the contradiction to the interlocutor, perhaps precipitating a crisis of self-preservation on his part. If this proves impossible, for instance if the subject is a child receiving a contradictory demand from a parent, he may choose to "protect" his sense of self "by emitting messages that cannot be maltreated."[20] The subject introduces a "distortion" into her own speech that makes it impossible for the other to understand it either as failing or as succeeding to respond to the initial, contradictory demand. It is not that the subject abandons language, but by introducing "distortions" she signifies that her speech is not *for* the other. Through her distorted speech she affirms that the only relevant context for evaluating the success of her utterance is her own intention. She has effectively escaped the double bind and preserved the self. A subject who responds to the impossible demands of the other in such a way is schizophrenic.

While Bateson intends the "double-bind" to cover a wide variety of communicative scenarios, the logic of his claim applies to every scenario. Any situation when one person cannot be certain of understanding the other potentially constitutes a double-bind for one of the participants. The message itself doesn't have to be contradictory for there to be, or for one to perceive there to be, a disconnect between intention and interpretation. There is nothing to prevent a subject from finding a double-bind even in an apparently consistent message simply by reflecting that, after all, one never knows what the speaker really means. Since the intentions of different subjects are never entirely transparent to each other, and there is always the possibility that the speaker might say one thing while meaning another, the double-bind is formally applicable to *any* interaction between subjects.

The potential of any speech-act to constitute a double-bind is a result of the absence of any objective continuity between your intention and my interpretation: I can never really know what you mean. Of course, most of the time my response will assure you that I have understood your meaning, and your response will reassure me. But the possibility that you might mean something else is the condition of your subjectivity. My awareness of the potential discrepancy between your intention and your words and gestures – my awareness, in other words, of your subjectivity – constitutes, in Bateson's account, the sufficient conditions for the failure of our relationship.[21]

R. D. Laing, the most widely read anti-psychiatric writer of the period, follows the logic of Bateson's argument to its conclusion: "We have to ask if a personal relationship is possible" (*PE* 23). Laing clarifies the conditions for "personal relationships" so as to reveal the reasons for their inevitable failure: "Human beings relate to each other not simply externally, like two billiard balls, but by the relations of the two worlds of experience that come into play when two people meet" (*PE* 62–3). "Our concern is with two origins of experience in relation" (*PE* 54). The problem is not the contact of two bodies in physical space, but a different form of space, the space between subjects. This non-physical space between subjects is special in that it cannot be crossed. Thus we "experience every relationship as an absence" (*PE* 37).

For Laing, the attempt to "reach" the other, to close the gap between "two origins of experience," invariably takes the form of a "vicious circle of mismatched interpretations, expectations, experiences, attributions and counter-attributions."[22] "We act not only in terms of our own experience, but of what we think *they* experience, and *how* we think they think we experience, and so on in a logically vertiginous spiral to infinity" (*PE* 78–79). The crucial question for a subject in relation with another subject is: "what do I think you think I think?" Every attempt to cut through the vicious circle simply adds another layer to the spiral.[23]

In 1970, at the height of his popularity in the United States, Laing published a strange little book devoted to representing the "vertiginous spiral" he believes characterizes all intersubjective relations. *Knots* takes the form of a series of short poems, what Laing in his introduction calls "patterns" of "human bondage." He has abstracted these patterns from "the very specific experiences from which they derive" so as to define the "formal elegance" of these failed relations, or "knots."[24] A few examples of selected knots will suffice here. "Jill feels guilty / that Jack feels guilty / that Jill feels guilty / that Jack feels guilty."[25] "They are not having fun. / I can't have fun if they don't. / If I can get them to have fun, then I can have fun with them. / Getting them to have fun, is not fun."[26] "You pretend to be bored / because I am not interested / that you are frightened / that I am not frightened / that you are not interested in me."[27] As the second example suggests, and as he argues explicitly elsewhere, these "knots" are not limited to dyadic relations, but apply to any group composed of different subjects. Intersubjective group formation suffers the same null, knotted complexity that characterizes one-on-one relations.

Laing wants to cut through these knots, but not, as his critics often imagine, by establishing a healthy relation between subjects. The critics' mistake is easy to understand. Laing bases his influential attack on traditional psychoanalysis on the claim that it contains no registration of "the gap *between* persons" (*PE* 50), "no category of 'you,' … no way of expressing the meeting of an 'I' with an 'other'" (*PE* 49). His obsessive focus on registering this gap understandably led many to believe that he was interested in crossing it. But nothing could be further from his intention.

All Laing's efforts as a clinical practitioner were directed towards intensifying this gap, rendering it more vivid, more inescapable. "We hope to share the experience of relationship, but the only honest beginning, or even end, may be to share the experience of its absence" (*PE* 56). Or even *end*? The problem with traditional psychoanalysis is that, like Esther's doctors, it seeks to restore people to intersubjective functionality, and it does this by covering up the "gap," the impossibility, the "vicious circle" at its heart.

As with Lacan or Owens, Laing's version of the psychiatric encounter between doctor and patient amounts to a reverent acknowledgment of the impossibility of this encounter. But for Laing the payoff of this acknowledgment of the impenetrability of intersubjective space is the opening of what he will call "inner space." The psychiatric non-encounter that produces this opening is exclusively reserved for those society considers "well." The insane, having already rejected intersubjectivity, do not need Laing's treatment, quite the opposite. The schizophrenic is the avatar of a utopian new form of relation.

For Laing, as for Plath, to be mad is not to withdraw from the human community, but to withdraw from intersubjectivity while remaining within language, while maintaining an intimate contact with collective value. "Schizophrenia [is] a successful attempt not to adapt to pseudo-social realities" (*PE* 67). The schizophrenic refusal of "pseudo-social" relations opens the way to a radical form of genuine human relations. "Madness need not be all breakdown. It may also be breakthrough" (*PE* 133). This "breakthrough" has the same structure as Esther's breaking of the hospital mirror. Having totally forsaken intersubjectivity, schizophrenics "enter or are thrown into more or less total inner space" (*PE* 125). "Inner space" defines neither a pathology nor a personality; it is not the absence of relation but a new space of relation. Inner space is "a void which may be peopled by presences that we do not even dream of" (*PE* 133). Insanity figures the conversion of intersubjective relations into intrasubjective relations, the replacement of one kind of relation by another. Madness opens a space for relations without recognition. For Laing schizophrenia is a "social fact and the social fact a *political event*" (*PE* 121).

This event has been erased from the history of postwar thought. Laing's schizophrenic has been replaced by Frederic Jameson's, who shows us that *nothing* exists beyond the subject of recognition, of division, of alienation. Jameson places the schizophrenic at the heart of his periodizing study of postmodern literature in precisely these terms. Jameson associates "the postmodern vision of the ideal or heroic schizophrenic" with the evisceration of subjectivity.[28] By equating the refusal of recognition with the breakdown of subjectivity, Plath's recent critics have rewritten Esther's insanity according to this script. Laing has either been forgotten or dismissed as an exponent of what has come to be seen as an embarrassing sixties individualism.[29] But the conflict he stages between the schizophrenic and contemporary society, between "inner space" and the space between subjects, is not equivalent to the familiar opposition between individual and society. The real opposition is between two competing spaces of relation, between two different modes of the collective. In Plath and in Laing, the other side of the critique of recognition is the fiction of a mode of access to collective power that does not pass through recognition. The phantom of Esther's "perfected" subjectivity is the form this fiction takes in Plath's writing.

2.

What does this phantom signify? Where should we look for this alternative, non-intersubjective relational space? To approach this question, I now want to move across mediums and decades. Paul Thomas Anderson's film *There Will Be Blood* centers on a character who, like Esther, is acutely conscious of the flaws of intersubjective relations, and intensely aware of the fascination of an alternative mode of relation. In what follows I will be interested not simply in the themes that link the two works, but in the distance that lies between them. This distance in time and difference in mediums underwrites the film's ability to provide a perspective on *The Bell Jar*'s fiction of an alternative to intersubjectivity.

There Will Be Blood, a loose adaptation of Upton Sinclair's *Oil!* (1927), tracks the career of Daniel Plainview, a turn of the century oilman. In successive scenes, near the opening of the film, we see Plainview attempting to convince simple southwestern farmers and herders to enter into contracts with him to pump the oil below their land on terms that favor him. ("What will my share be?" one farmer finally asks. "One sixth," he replies.[30]) Plainview, as acted by Daniel Day Lewis, speaks in a loud, clear, and rather artificial voice, the voice of a salesman. "Ladies and gentlemen," his set speech begins, "I've traveled halfway across our state to be with you today." He speaks in a tone adapted to crowds of customers; it sounds odd in close, intimate spaces. In a striking feature of Lewis' performance, this salesman's tone is never dropped. Plainview talks in the same way both to a hall full of farmers and to his son.

In a key scene roughly halfway through the film, while talking by a bonfire with a man he presumes to be his long-lost brother, Plainview makes a confession that illuminates the desire that fuels the furious commercial activities that consume him. "I hate most people," he says. "I see the worst in people." "I look at people and see nothing worth liking." He expresses these sentiments in his perfect, artificial salesman's voice.

"I want to make enough money so I can get away from everyone," he says. These words reveal what the voice wants; they reveal the desire that animates Plainview's way of speaking. They show the deep compatibility of this clear, "friendly" salesman's tone with a desire for a total escape from personal relations. This marketing tone, this market voice is the way one who wishes to have nothing to do with people always speaks.

The film frames the pursuit of money as a way of not being with people. This is something we shall encounter again later in this book, and I want to linger for a moment over its strangeness. Plainview here is articulating the value of money itself. From the individual's perspective, as I discussed in my introduction, money is typically thought in terms of a power of procuring whatever one happens to want. Its value lies in its effectiveness in realizing a wide range of desires. When it is said that money can't buy happiness, that it can't buy love, it is understood that it can buy practically everything else.

Here however, money is understood not as the power of satisfying desire in general, but as the power to satisfy a very particular desire. Money is valuable, Plainview says, because it represents a way of not being with people. This is not to say that money allows you to be alone, to be solitary. You don't, after all, need money for that, as shown by the images of solitary, self-sufficient, and financially ignorant farmers in the film. Rather, what money does is to open a different kind of relation, a relation not between what the film calls "people." In *There Will Be Blood*, the category "people" is not identical with the category "human." The word "people" first occurs when Plainview articulates his belief that money will allow him to "get away" from people. As in *The Bell Jar*, an intense negativity towards people emerges alongside an alternative to dealing with them. Here, money allows the category of "people" to emerge by revealing certain kinds of relations that are not between people. "I look at people and see nothing worth liking," Plainview says. He glances across towards his brother and continues, "I can't keep doing this on my own with these …", there is a long pause in which he begins to smile. Then he finishes his sentence: "people." And laughs insanely.

At this moment, Plainview's relation to his brother is not a relation between "people," not an example of what he "can't keep doing." The relation between him and his brother is a blood relation. Blood, like money, allows Plainview to "get away" from people. The blood relation is guaranteed outside social space; it is secured in a different dimension. It doesn't require the kind of care that characterizes intersubjective relations; it is a relation beyond norms, beyond recognition, beyond the constraints and flaws that structure the hated world of what Plainview calls "people."

Kinship is one meaning of the "blood" of the title. Another is oil. For Plainview, the key feature of oil is its monetary value. If they can't find an inexpensive way to ship the oil, he tells his son, "then we aren't making money." And if the oil can't become money, then "it's just mud." But when Plainview can make money on it, when the enormous dark jet of oil spurts up blowing the roof off the derrick, the oil is blood. The fusion of these two kinds of blood – of family and money – creates the fascinating prospect of a way of not being with people, of a non-intersubjective space of relation.[31]

"I run a family enterprise," Plainview repeats, pointing to his small son whom he brings along to help make his sales pitch. There are different ways of thinking the relation between "family" and "enterprise." But for Plainview the allure of blood money is very specific. Like market relations, blood relations are nonsocial, free of the constraints felt to inhere in relations between "people." This way of fusing blood and money is not unique to this film, and in Chapter 4 I will pursue its sources and implications with reference to the novels of Kathy Acker. My present interest in *There Will Be Blood* lies in the perspective it provides on the desire for an alternative to intersubjectivity set up in *Bell Jar*.

This perspective is made possible by distance. The most obvious distance between the two works derives from the difference in mediums. *The Bell Jar* is a "lyric" novel, written in the first person, and Plath exploits the form to offer us the fiction of participating in Esther's subjective experience.[32] In key scenes, Esther achieves an alternative to intersubjectivity. As I have argued, when Esther drops the mirror she becomes a subject unmoored from any object; she possesses an experience not dependent on recognition. The fiction constitutive of the novel's form, the fiction that invites us to imagine we are "overhearing" her, also invites us to become partially absorbed in her experience. We are asked to participate in a phantasmatic, fictional subjective mode beyond recognition.

But in *There Will Be Blood*, we have no access to Plainview's experience. We encounter him only as an object, as an image on a screen. Thus where *The Bell Jar* can be understood as an attempt to exemplify a subjectivity free of recognition, the film cannot present its protagonist except as subject to recognition. We see through Esther's eyes, but we see Plainview as others see him. Seeing him thus, we are necessarily distanced from the fascination that grips him. This fascination appears most vividly in the scene when the great jet of oil catches on fire, and Plainview realizes he has discovered an "ocean of oil." In a long shot we see his oil-blackened face against the smoky night sky, staring fascinated at the oil fire, lips moving, ecstatic. The fireside scene discussed above provides the key to the particular fascination money has for him: "I want to make enough money so I can get away from everyone."

In addition to the distance imposed by the structure of the medium, we are distanced from Plainview's fascination in several other ways. In the first place, blood – both as money and as kinship – doesn't actually work in the film. Plainview's accumulated money leaves him aging, isolated, violent, and bitter. His "brother" turns out to be an imposter. His son is a foster child, who grows up to demand the kind of mutual recognition "people" want. This is not a blood relation after all, and Plainview cuts him off. In dramatizing the failure of blood, *There Will Be Blood* represses the participation in the fascination of an alternative to intersubjectivity that *The Bell Jar* solicits.³³ And in repressing the possibility that we might identify with this fascination, the film allows it to come into focus for us as an object. What does this perspective show us? It shows us an association of the desire for an escape from intersubjectivity with the market. When we step back from the person fascinated by the alternative to intersubjectivity and look again, we see someone fascinated by the market.

The distances opened by the medium and the plot of the film are entangled in a temporal difference. What difference does the four decades that separate *The Bell Jar* and *There Will Be Blood* make? To consider the difference between the two works as a difference between 1963 and 2007 is to suggest a progression reflected in the organization of this book. Throughout this period we find the progressive consolidation of an aesthetic form that approaches the desire for a new mode of human relations through an economic fiction. We see the elements of this form fusing as we move from Plath to O'Hara to Acker, Gibson, and rap.

But what can we say about how this film – which is contemporary with the composition of this study – distances itself from the lure of the economic? It is tempting to understand the tragic register in which the film renders Plainview's desire for money as symptomatic of the exhaustion of this particular fascination with the economic. It is tempting to suppose that, when looking back from the perspective opened by *There Will Be Blood*, we occupy a position outside the spell of the fascination I am here concerned to analyze. Tempting, but premature. After all, is it truly the case that the film – at least in its most intense moments – is unable to invite an absorbed participation in Plainview's fascination? I argue above that the film distances us from this participation, and if we distribute our attention across the narrative of Plainview's losses and disappointments, this argument seems right. But in scattered moments – like the moment when Plainview's wide, insane eyes are lit up by the spectacular flames of the blood money – that critical distance threatens to collapse.[34]

So we must suspend a decision as to what *There Will Be Blood* suggests about the future of the form we are studying, and concentrate on the perspective it offers us on the desire to "get away from people." In 1963, the insane Esther exemplifies the longing for an alternative to intersubjectivity; the 2007 image of the insane Plainview locates this alternative in the market. To investigate the logic of this link further I want to turn to a third example of madness in a poem by Amiri Baraka first published in 1972.

Das Kapital

> Most of us know there's a maniac loose. Our lives a jumble of
>   frustrations and unfilled
> capacities …
> Tomorrow you got to hit it sighs through us like the
>   wind, we got to
> hit it, like an old song at radio city, working for the yanqui
>   dollarrrr, when we were
> children, and then we used to think it was not the wind, but the
>   maniac scratching against
> our windows. Who is the maniac, and why everywhere at the same
>   time …[35]

At first glance, this poem's representation of an insane market looks straightforwardly Marxist. A closer analysis however, reveals connections between insanity, art, and intersubjectivity that situate this work in the context of concerns we've been exploring. In the first place, Baraka's poem reverses the logic of Marx's critique. *Capital*'s famous analysis of commodification as a relation between people that appears as a relation between things is built upon the exposure of a prior mystification: a relation between people that appears as a person. In his preface to the first edition, Marx writes: "I paint the capitalist and landlord in no sense *coleur de rose*. But here individuals are dealt with only in so far as they are the personifications of economic categories, embodiments of particular class-relations and class-interests."[36] What appears to the naive observer as the greedy, evil, or crazy intention of the capitalist, is in fact the effect of the capitalist system. Thus, "My standpoint … less than any other make[s] the individual responsible for relations whose creature he socially remains."[37]

Personification is a precritical mistake, and the work of critique is to move from the image of the person to the analysis of the system.[38] Marx draws a metaphor from biology to suggest that the personification of economic categories is related to another error: personifying the market itself. To an untrained eye, he writes, the market appears as a single body. This is because "the body, as an organic whole, is more easy of study than are the cells of that body."[39] Where the naked eye sees a body, the critic employs the "microscopes" of "abstraction" to expose the mechanical interaction of labor and capital, and to replace the initial, illusory image of a person with the abstract schema of a system.[40]

The poem "Das Kapital" moves in the opposite direction, personifying the system. Baraka accomplishes this personification by adopting the perspective of a child, mimicking the way we see "when we were children." And here, as in much post-Romantic poetry, the child's vision reveals a special kind of knowledge, knowledge repressed by the critical perspective represented by the poem's German title. Baraka sets up an aesthetic space where we can see the economy as a child might, as a "maniac" who is "everywhere at the same time." In this space, the systematic is translated into the intentional. And yet, this translation is not exactly equivalent to the substitution of human for system that Marx denounces. As the insistence that the maniac is "everywhere at the same time" suggests, personification here produces a kind of agent that cannot be contained by a body. The maniac is the result of a personification that heads in the direction of the person, and keeps going past it. The market system becomes an intentionality not locatable anywhere. As in Laing and Plath, madness here represents a radical subjectivity, a subjectivity not tied to a recognizable object, a face, or a body. The market is an awareness, an intention distributed throughout human space, "everywhere at the same time."

Baraka's personification conceals an even deeper difference with the analysis it reworks. In Marx's *Das Kapital*, the economy is a system of intersubjective relations that, to a naive observer, looks like it has an autonomous intention. In Baraka's "Das Kapital," the maniac's intention is not only nonreducible to a system, but violently antagonistic to actual social systems. This leads us to the second important feature of Baraka's poem. If the poem equates "Das Kapital" with the maniac, it distinguishes the maniac from America's hegemonic social structures. Consider the following examples of the poem's representation of the quotidian, characteristic figures and processes of American social life: "The baldhead man on the television set goes on in a wooden way"; "The people turn the channel looking for Good Times and get a negro with a pulldown hat";

"the commuters looking for their new yorkers"; "Tomorrow you got to hit it"; "After the church goers go on home." "The writing on them, the dates, and amounts we owe."[41]

The socius represented by these lines consists of "ashy fingered, harassed"[42] lives bound by endless loops of racist television programming, reams of extortive tax accounting, the daily repetition of the circuit between gray, barely differentiated scenes of domestic, professional, and religious discipline. The maniac appears "everywhere" against this social fabric not as its condensation, representative, symbol, but as its negation, its absolute other, its nemesis.

The maniac haunts the social world, disrupting its heterogeneous relations, interrupting the circuits, series, and chains of tranquilized bodies. There is a reference here to another classic formula of Marx's: the *Communist Manifesto*'s description of the market "pitilessly tearing asunder" every other social relation, replacing heterogeneous relations with "the single, unconscionable" relation of "Free Trade."[43] Marx, of course, felt that free trade itself was, ultimately, simply a particular kind of intersubjective relation between workers and owners. But Baraka radicalizes the sense in which free trade "pitilessly tears asunder" other relations. The maniac threatens the relations between subjects with total dissolution. Baraka, like Plath, Laing, and Anderson, figures insanity as the alternative to society. This asocial mania doesn't constitute solipsism, but draws its energies from an asocial mode of collectivity. "Das Kapital" pits relations between subjects against an asocial relation that constitutes a single collective subject.

In Plath and Baraka – as in Gaddis' *JR* – we encounter a new mode of subjectivity that cannot be reduced to or equated with any object. To succeed in identifying this subject with an object is to dispel it. Plainview's filmic objecthood, his imprisonment in how he looks to "people," constitutes his tragedy, and provides evidence of the failure of his desire. The tension animating *There Will Be Blood* is drawn between the effort to bring Plainview into focus as a delimited image, and the absorptive fascination of certain intense moments that let us into the orbit of his insane experience. During such moments in the film, and in a more sustained way in the novels and the poem, the fictive subject is neither identical with an individual face, name, or body, nor is it displaced by a system. Who wants what the maniac wants? Who chooses when JR chooses? This "who" cannot be identified with any object; it is unrecognizable. This "who" is "everywhere at the same time," as Baraka says; it is "godlike," as Plath writes: everywhere and nowhere.

In the regime of recognition, the image of the face or body, in the gaze of the other or in the mirror, inaugurates subjectivity. I become a subject by first becoming an object. But in these works, the image of the body has no special relation to the agency that emerges in it. As a medium, writing provides a privileged mode of access to this new, virtual subject. We can't quite see it. But we can hear it when Esther smashes the hospital mirror, when the maniac scratches against our windows. Perhaps its most perfect sound is the virtual voice that rises from *JR*'s collapsed dialogues. This inaudible voice complements Esther's invisible face as the form of the formless, the relation that is not between.

These aesthetic spaces open the fascinating possibility of a relation that is not between subjects. As the period progresses – and as my schematic juxtaposition of Plath with Baraka and Anderson attempts to show – this nonsocial relation becomes increasingly identified with the market. The aesthetic comes to shelter a purely economic relation. Before proceeding to trace this progression and to analyze the dynamics of these aesthetic-economic spaces, I want to conclude this chapter by recovering something of the intellectual history of this phenomenon. Against the background of Esther's achieved desire, Plainview's frustrated desire, and the ambiguous figure of Baraka's maniac, I want to pursue what has been thought and written on the three questions that now confront us: What kind of human relation is not social? In what sense is an economic relation not a social relation? And why should it be that this purely economic relation can exist only in aesthetic space?

3.

The linking of the distinctiveness of market relations with the category of the aesthetic emerges at the very outset of this period, with the publication of Karl Polanyi's *The Great Transformation* in 1944. His book presents a new history of capitalism. This history carefully distinguishes social relations from what he variously calls the "myth" or "utopia" of a purely economic relation.[44] Polanyi develops this distinction in terms of a conflict between "embedded" and "disembedded" relations. Whereas in actually existing capitalism, economic relations are "embedded in social relations," inseparable from the knotted complexities of intersubjectivity, the "utopia" of the free market projects a world "controlled, regulated, and directed by market prices."[45] For Polanyi, the aesthetic, the category of "myth" and "utopia," functions to "disembed" or to disentangle economic relations from social relations.

Polanyi argues that there is a "conflict between the market and the elementary requirements of an organized social life."[46] The desire to replace social relations with market relations is the desire "to annihilate all organic forms of existence and to replace them by a different type of organization."[47] This analysis of the conflict between economic and social relations represents a new kind of critique of capitalism. For Marx, Polanyi's important predecessor, economic relations are only apparently distinct from social relations. Marx famously argued that the relation between things expressed by price is simply a mystified form of relations between social groups.[48] For this quintessential modern critique, all conflicts are social conflicts, class conflicts. Polanyi's new critique of capitalism focuses on a different kind of conflict, a struggle between "mythic" economic relations and "organic" social relations.

Polanyi believes that the image of an economic relation disembedded from society exerts a growing influence on contemporary social life. This influence manifests in three related effects. In the first place, it gives a new emphasis to the conceptual distinction between market and social relations as two different modes of organizing collective life. In the second, it opens an aesthetic, "utopian" space in which a relation to price replaces social relations, creating the fascinating image of a purely economic world. In the third, this ambiguously fascinating image circulates through the social world, shaping new perspectives and new desires.

The possibility of seeing the economic and the social as conflicting alternatives begins with seeing them as conceptually distinct. For Polanyi, economic relations manifest a different logic than social relations. In our experience, the economic is so embedded in the social that this distinction can be hard to see, but analysis can bring it out. Price expresses the cost of a good or service. When I see the price of a car, for example, I see how hard the car is for me to get. Polanyi describes the price system as "self-regulating," a term that refers to the way the price of a good or service expresses the dynamic position of that good or service in the context of the economy as a whole. Price expresses the position of a thing in the economy – the market-wide demand for it, the market-wide supply of it – by making it harder or easier for me to get it. It links any good or service I might encounter with every good or service encountered by anyone, anywhere.

The self-organizing price system coordinates the various objects and activities of the human world. But the system itself depends on a different kind of organization. The organization of social relations is a complex, unstable process consisting of several interwoven dynamics. Cultural norms, to take one distinctive feature of the social, play a crucial role in shaping everything from car design to how close it is appropriate to stand next to a stranger in an auto showroom. Intersubjectivity, agreeing and disagreeing, taking the other into account, comparing one's status with the other's, is another distinct dimension of the social. Every economic exchange is embedded in an intersubjective relation. And finally, unlike the self-organizing price system, social organization relies on the display and deployment of power. "No society is possible in which power and compulsion are absent."[49] When I enter an auto-dealer's showroom, my relation to the cars' prices is embedded in my sense of how the different cars will project my status, in the norms that tell me how far to stand from the other customers, in the power relations that organize the institution I work for and the community I live in.

Market price coordinates the objects and activities before me with objects and activities across the world by telling me how hard each thing I see is to get. But why I want a given thing, how I will use it, in what institutions, with what associates, are determined by complex social relations and dynamics, not by price. The relation to price is not a social relation, it is an economic relation. In actually existing capitalism, this economic relation is always embedded in social relations. Ordinarily, the distinction between economic and social relations remains purely conceptual. But for Polanyi, an ominous new phenomenon gives the conceptual distinctiveness of price a new significance. This phenomenon is the mythic disembedding of the economic from the social, the utopian vision of a world in which economic relations *replace* social relations. In this image of an economic world, market price replaces culture, intersubjectivity, and politics. In the utopian image of a purely economic world, something happens to price. Instead of so obviously requiring the support of social relations in order to function, price begins to look capable of an independent function. The self-organizing price system, the single index of market price, begins to look capable of binding together a new world that can no longer be called social.

When Polanyi calls this vision of a purely economic world a myth or utopia, some take him to be dismissing it.[50] But in fact, *The Great Transformation* provides a powerful example of this myth at work. The book demonstrates that the image of a purely economic world now has the power to organize the writing of history. Polanyi divides all human relations between purely economic relations and social or "organic" relations. If by describing it as mythic we understand Polanyi to be saying that the disembedded economic relation is incoherent, we might puzzle over his impulse to make purely economic relations one of only two categories of human interaction. But when he says the free-market relation is a myth, he isn't saying that it is a mistake or hallucination. He is saying that when price enters aesthetic form it begins to look capable of independently organizing a world. And as the image of a disembedded market circulates through the social world, it elicits a powerful and troubling fascination.

It is important to be clear about the essential novelty of Polanyi's analysis. Before Polanyi, writers on capitalism traced its divisions to the social relations in which exchange is embedded. His analysis displaces the conflict of capitalist society from the struggle between owners and workers, to the struggle between "organic" relations and a "purely economic" relation. The conflict is not between various social groups but between *social relations as such* and a fundamentally different kind of relation. Many of Polanyi's readers, and especially proponents of the "new economic sociology" that has emerged in the past two decades, have missed this crucial point. For Michel Callon, for example, there is no embedded/disembedded dualism in Polanyi. He argues Polanyi thinks that apparently disembedded relations are just forms of embedded relations, which Callon proceeds to analyze in terms of his actor-network theory.[51]

But for Polanyi, the difference between embedded and disembedded price is real, stark, and powerful. This dualism helps to define our world. It drives a history. A relation determined only by market price is not embedded in noneconomic relations. This asocial relation takes an aesthetic form. And to describe this relation as aesthetic is not to say that it is embedded in the social after all, but to detect some new possibility of the aesthetic.

The appearance of this image of economic relations opens a new kind of division within capitalism. Polanyi traces a new fault line within capitalism, a schism every exchange reproduces. The appearance of this fault line, the awareness of this difference between social and purely economic relations, already contains in embryo the fiction that will multiply and spread through the subsequent decades. By 1944, the pure economic relation appears in America. It is embedded in social relations between individuals, but it is not identical with them. Through the aesthetic, it can be disembedded. In the form of myth, the shape of a purely economic relation is already clearly visible within the chrysalis of intersubjectivity. This visibility excites the dream of its release.

No writer of the early postwar period explores the implications of the fault line described by Polanyi more acutely than Hannah Arendt. She also analyzes the dynamic tension within capitalism in terms of a differ-ence between socially embedded exchanges and a kind of exchange freed from intersubjectivity. In the postwar world, something extra is added to the economic that causes it to appear independent of the social. In *The Human Condition*, first published in 1958, she calls this something extra "fiction." And like Polanyi, her discovery of this fiction leads her to write a new history of capitalism.

For Arendt, the economic fiction has its origin in the earliest modern attempts to describe exchange. The basic principle of this fiction is that a society organized purely by market price works like a single, collective subject. "It was not Karl Marx but the liberal economists themselves who had to introduce the 'communistic fiction,' that is, to assume that there is one interest of society as a whole which with 'an invisible hand' guides the behavior of men and produces the harmony of their conflicting inter-ests" (*HC* 43–44).

Like Polanyi's myth, Arendt's "fiction" projects an exchange relation that is not intersubjective. Through this "communistic fiction," market exchange appears as a relation that does not stretch between individual subjects, but circulates within a single, collective subject. The fiction that there is a "collective subject of economic activity" is "deeply rooted in economic terminology" (*HC* 33). The aesthetic supplement clings to the very terms we use to describe actual exchanges.

In the "communistic fiction" of exchange, the whole human and non-human world coordinates and organizes itself through each act of buy-ing and selling. The market does not merely mediate between the desires of various social or individual agents, the market itself shapes agency and determines desire. Arendt finds this communistic fiction so "deeply rooted," that if it were not for the fact that the state of affairs it depicts is quite impossible, we might well forget its fictional status. But the com-munistic fiction, as she writes, quoting Gunnar Myrdal, "amounts to the assertion that society must be conceived as a single subject. This, how-ever, is precisely what cannot be conceived. If we tried, we would be attempting to abstract from the essential fact that social activity is the result of the intentions of several individuals" (*HC* 44). The economic fiction projects an intention that does not originate in individuals, and a relation that is not between subjects. This is impossible. Arendt says all this clearly and repeatedly. It is thus tempting to read her description of this economic "fiction," as critics often read Polanyi's description of the economic "myth," as simply a dismissal of a purely economic relation as incoherent.

But her very insistence introduces a doubt. Arendt's readers have long been puzzled by her evident fear of something she herself calls "inconceivable" and "impossible": an "economic" collective subject not composed of social relations between subjects. What is she so afraid of? Hanna Pitkin, one of Arendt's best readers, argues that Arendt's fear of an economic collective subject mystifies the real issue, which is that people who "are interdependent and active ... behave individually in ways that preclude coordinated action, so that they cannot ... take charge of what they are doing in the world."[52] People enter into exchanges based on narrowly personal interests. But they live in a social world, and their exchanges have unpredictable and unintended social effects. So the results of their actions look as if they were completely severed from their intentions, and they become susceptible to the quasi-superstitious belief that society is controlled by some single, alien intention. What they should really do is be more aware of the intersubjective context in which they act. Then they could create better methods of intersubjective communication, so they can agree to coordinate their actions in ways that produce agreeable collective effects. This is what Arendt meant to say.

But Pitkin's neat attempt to rationalize Arendt's fear erases what that fear preserves. Pitkin never questions the fact that all human relations are intersubjective relations. But the source of Arendt's fear is that the communistic economic fiction alters this human condition. *The Human Condition* is convulsed by the fear that a fiction somehow threatens intersubjectivity. While Arendt calls the fiction of a collective subject "inconceivable," her almost compulsive generation of the figure of the collective subject of exchange shows she herself found it impossible to stop conceiving it.

For Arendt, as for Polanyi, to call the economic alternative to intersubjectivity a fiction is not to say it doesn't exist, but to say that its existence depends on the aesthetic. In the face of this threat, Arendt declares her belief that the endurance of the "between-space," the space of human intersubjectivity, must also depend on the aesthetic. The economic fiction, a perverse hybrid of the aesthetic and the economic, projects, in some as-yet "inconceivable" way, the collapse of the social space between people. Purely aesthetic works, in contrast, preserve, guarantee, and prop up this between-space.

Margaret Canovon writes of Arendt's "notion of the world as something that appears in the space between human beings."[53] Arendt writes, "To live together in the world means essentially that a world of things is between those who have it in common, as a table is located between those who sit around it; the world, like every in-between, relates and separates men at the same time" (*HC* 52). The things of the between-world both relate and separate; they relate people by separating them. Arendt believes that intersubjectivity is constructed with nonhuman objects.[54] Worldly objects sustain the borders of our individual subjectivities. You are over there, I am here, and the thing lies between us. "Everybody sees and hears from a different position. This is the meaning of public life" (*HC* 57). Our looking departs from separate points of origin, and converges in the same thing. We don't see it the same way, but we both see *it*. The thing's self-identity grounds our separate identities.

In a book convulsed by the fear of a collapse of intersubjectivity, this is hardly a neutral description of the world. The between-world is a human project; these worldly things are human artifacts. Any rock or tree can do the job of demonstrating that something seen from two different perspectives will look different. But something extra is required to turn this difference between individual bodies into a difference between subjects, to make the space between bodies intersubjective. Arendt calls this extra quality "permanence." The space of intersubjectivity arises because "everybody is always concerned with the same object" (*HC* 57–58). The things grounding the between-world endure. They are positioned in a central, public place, available for everyone to see. The gazes directed at these objects radiate from every point; these intersecting and intertwining gazes thicken into a between-world. The aura that surrounds these objects is not the aura Walter Benjamin spoke of; it is not the aura of the maker, but the aura of the millions of gazes directed at it. Separate subjects come together in this aura while remaining separate.

To attract and maintain this aura, these objects must be a matter of universal concern; they must elicit preservation, and they must endure. "Because of their outstanding permanence, works of art are the most intensely worldly of all tangible things" (*HC* 167). The work of the artist is the making of the between-world.[55] This is so because works of art elicit preservation, and make themselves public.

Society needs art. We need art to constitute a social world, to shore up this threatened between-world. Arendt's plea resonates. Subsequent decades will see many versions of her intersubjective aesthetics. Theorists from Emmanuel Levinas to Susan Stewart, from Gayatri Spivak to Charles Taylor, will elaborate the ways art preserves the between-space and facilitates the recognition of other bodies as *other*. The central conflict of Polanyi's new history, the struggle between social relations and economic relations, will be waged by Arendt and her heirs with purely aesthetic means.

Polanyi defines two kinds of relations: social relations, and purely economic relations. Arendt keys these two kinds of relations to two kinds of art: a pure art that preserves the social space between subjects, and a hybrid economic fiction that collapses it. Both writers perceive that something happens to money when it enters aesthetic space. In that space, economic relations appear independent of social relations. Purely economic relations look as if they could organize a world. For them, the troubling prospect of a purely economic world, of a purely economic relation, radiates from this hybrid of the aesthetic and the economic. In Anderson's Plainview and Baraka's maniac we see figures of this hybrid. In O'Hara, Burroughs, Acker, Gibson, and nineties rap we will explore successive stages in its consolidation as a form.

CHAPTER 2

Frank O'Hara and free choice

Personal Poem

Now when I walk around at lunchtime
I have only two charms in my pocket
an old Roman coin Mike Kanemitsu gave me
and a bolt-head that broke off a packing case
when I was in Madrid the others never
brought me too much luck though they did
help keep me in New York against coercion
but now I'm happy for a time and interested.
                              –Frank O'Hara (*CPO'H* 335)

How can a poem be personal? For O'Hara's early critics, the poetry's rigorous orientation towards the trivial, contingent, private details of a particular life presents a unique difficulty. Helen Vendler remarks of the personal poems, "The wish not to impute significance has rarely been stronger," and Charles Molesworth writes, "They make 'confessional' poetry seem alexandrine or allegorical by comparison."[1] These writers read the exact dates, particular streets and buildings, and proper names of friends in the poems as tombstones marking the inaccessibility of O'Hara's "particular consciousness," the "antipoetic weight" from which the "imaginative transformations" of his really poetic lines must be extracted.[2] The particularity of reference in the personal poems, what O'Hara calls their "dailiness," paradoxically disables the poetic persona by which the literal and particular are presumably controlled, the extraliterary processed as literature. "Mike Kanemitsu," "a bolt-head that broke off a packing case," "now when I walk around at lunchtime": these details stick in the critics' prose, they are both too personal and not personal enough to count as poetry. Clearly Marjorie Perloff is right in saying that a name like "Mike Kanemitsu," for example, is not imbued with the same kind of "inner reality" as Yeats' Lady Gregory;[3] and as Molesworth suggests, "Frank O'Hara" conspicuously fails to register in the way that the theatrical poetic personas of Robert Lowell and Plath do. Despite, or perhaps because of, the saturation of O'Hara's poetry with these personal details, the image of the person remains frustratingly elusive.

Recent criticism has tended to move beyond this problem, arguing that personal poetry represents the prototype of a progressive, "micropolitical" postmodern personhood. The personal detail, on this account, doesn't nullify the aura of the poetic persona as it does for the earlier critics, but preserves its resistant kernel.[4] But the first question remains the crucial route into O'Hara's mature work, one he took special pains to illuminate. How can a poem be personal?

In "Personism," the most famous of the prose pieces that supplement the project of his "I-do-this, I-do-that" poems, O'Hara puts this question slightly differently. How can the personal be abstract? He writes of his poetic stance that it is "so totally opposed to … abstract removal that it is verging on a true abstraction for the first time, really, in the history of poetry" (*CPO'H* 498). His personal poems do "not have to do with personality or intimacy, far from it," they are "true abstraction[s]" (*CPO'H* 498–99). Here O'Hara insists on exactly that feature of the poetry that troubles his early critics: the unsettling tendency of the personal detail to block rather than carry the poetic persona. But what does the careful, random particularity of personal poetry represent, if not a particular person? This question arises in relation to the personal detail. But the details noticed by the critics enter the poem only because they have been chosen. In a banal sense, this is true of all poetry, in that the author selects what to put in the poem and what to leave out. But O'Hara's work is characterized by its insistent and explicit thematizing of the process of choosing. The particular details here (an old Roman coin, a bolt-head) are the outcome of particular choices, particular interests, and specific acts of selection performed by the poem's speaker. The contingent personal detail should be read in relation to the basic unit of O'Hara's poetic discourse: the personal choice.

American political and economic discourse in the fifties depicted personal choice as the guiding principle of a liberal society where the institutions of collective life were directed by the command of the sovereign individual citizen. In his personal poetics, O'Hara reverses the liberal dynamic, opening the taboo and utopian prospect of a collective national subject. The poems dramatize the particularity of personal experience slipping through the grip of liberal subjectivity, and opening into a collective subjectivity. O'Hara marks a route from individuality to collectivity, from the personal to the abstract, through personal choices that aren't determined by particular persons. In postwar America, choice comes to be seen as the fundamental interface between the individual and the collective. In this chapter I will show how the form of O'Hara's choosing collapses the distinction between them.

I.

Consider how choices are staged in O'Hara's programmatic "Personal Poem," written in 1959 one week before "Personism": "I shake hands with LeRoi / and buy a strap for my wristwatch"; "we go eat some fish and some ale it's / cool but crowded we don't like Lionel Trilling / we decide, we like Don Allen we don't like / Henry James so much we like Herman Melville" ("Personal Poem," *CPO'H* 336). "Passing the House of Seagram with its wet / and its loungers and the construction to / the left that closed the sidewalk if / I ever get to be a construction worker / I'd like to have a silver hat please" (*CPO'H* 335). O'Hara shows himself moving through the city, making choices that are accompanied by an exhaustive specification of the scene of choosing. This specification of the *scene* of choice, O'Hara's tendency to give the coordinates of his position relative to space, time, and companions, replaces an account of the *reasons* for choices. Choice is determined by an instant response to options presented by the immediate environment, rather than by the speaker's fixed values, desires, or beliefs.

This reorientation of choice is most striking when O'Hara represents his serious literary commitments as if they were acquired in the same contingent way as the two "charms" he finds himself carrying when "Personal Poem" opens. A preference for Donald Allen, who gives O'Hara a prominent place in his pioneering anthology *New American Poetry*, over Lionel Trilling, the stock representative of the conservative literary establishment, seems an obvious and uninteresting corollary to O'Hara's personal and aesthetic positions. What is interesting is that his aesthetic should require representing this preference as if it were suddenly discovered in a conversation over fish and ale. "We decide"; the decision is insistently present tense, as if it did not express a considered position, as if "Don Allen," like the "old Roman coin Mike Kanemitsu gave me," and "a strap for my wristwatch," were simply things he happened to like at a particular moment. The emphasis on the details of where he was, at what time, with what companions, shifts the center of choice away from the interior of the choosing subject, and towards his local and contingent situation. "Now I'm happy for a time and interested": a state of being "interested," a disposition to prefer one thing to another, replaces definite interests and consistent preferences. The subject of "Personal Poem" doesn't arrive on the scene with a given interest or desire he then attempts to maximize or satisfy; he looks around and picks out what he likes, whatever strikes him. He's shopping without a list.

These examples of personal choice as whatever one happens to like are perversely out of key with the massive public discourse that accumulates around the concept of choice in the fifties. Postwar American intellectuals increasingly came to think of individual choice, the choice of what to buy, where to live, who to vote for, as the crucial link between the individual and society. The idea that national life should be directed by the private interests of the sovereign individual received its highest theoretical elaboration in the aggressive, colonizing discipline of postwar neoclassical economics and the "rational choice" political science derived from it. Individual choice is the sole determinant of value for neoclassical thought. "Modern subjectivist economics [has] converted the theory of market prices into a general theory of human choice."[5] Choices, in the neoclassical model, are rigorously determined by the rational individual's preferences. The system is always moving towards an equilibrium that is predetermined by the preferences of the individuals making it up, who trade with each other to get what they want. When all their preferences are relatively satisfied so that no one can benefit from further trades, the market reaches equilibrium. The order of the free market and, with the ascendance of economic models of voting, of the free state, is based on the determination of collective action by the personal choices of rational, utility-maximizing individuals. An array of demand curves, marginal-utility curves, ordinal-utility curves, and indifference curves can be constructed based on the mechanical regularities of choice. Agents are left to define the specific content of their preferences behind the curtains of liberal subjectivity. To count as a rational agent, you can want anything, as long as (1) you know exactly what you want, (2) what you want doesn't change, (3) you know how much you want it relative to the other things you want, and (4) all your choices are continuously directed towards getting it.

O'Hara's choices violate all these conditions. "In the GOLDEN GRIFFIN I get a little Verlaine / for Patsy with drawings by Bonnard although I do / think of Hesiod ... but I don't, I stick with Verlaine / after practically going to sleep with quandariness" ("The Death of Lady Day," *CPO'H* 325). "I just stroll into the PARK LANE / Liquor Store and ask for a bottle of Strega" (*CPO'H* 325). "It is 1959 and I go get a shoeshine" (*CPO'H* 325). In O'Hara, there is no causal account linking choice to the interiority of the subject. The speaker of the poem, the agent of these choices, is the ultimate "true abstraction" here. These trivial choices do not represent or reveal a subject; they order and constitute a world. This absence of an "inner reality," beliefs, taste, interests, or "personality" pre-defining or circumscribing choice, and its replacement by a desire that surfaces in a spontaneous engagement with a given array of options, a given environment, is the central feature of personal poetry. The self-centered world of O'Hara's "I-do-this, I-do-that" poems requires a self without a center.

For O'Hara, choice is determined neither by the stable preferences of the subject nor by the social value of the chosen object. The objects he selects conform to the model established at the opening of "Personal Poem": "Now when I walk around at lunchtime / I have only two charms in my pocket," an "old Roman coin" and "a bolt-head that broke off a packing case." He doesn't imply that these objects might be recognized as "charms" by other people. The absence of private individual standards governing choice is not compensated by the presence of social standards. The value of chosen goods is like the value of a "charm," something without a recognized social value, but also without a determinate personal value. It is not as if O'Hara conceals a preference that might be satisfied by an old Roman coin, or secretly believes in its value to others. Nor does the reason for his choice lie in a concealed personal history. Unlike an object with sentimental value, for example, a good-luck charm derives its worth not from a definite relation to a personal past, but from an open relation to a personal future. A charm is an object I value without having a good reason. Or, O'Hara suggests, even a bad reason: his good luck charms appear to lack good luck ("the others never / brought me too much luck"). Something strange happens to value in the space of these poems. The source of value here is neither internal preference nor social norms and standards. Choice is idiosyncratic, but its idiosyncrasies don't reflect the personality, values, history, or interests of the chooser. Something leaps to the speaker's eye, and he likes it. The source of value lies in the chooser's openness to his immediate environment. The personal charm functions as a store of this kind of value.

The model of the personal charm, something O'Hara happens upon and happens to like, is now transferred to other kinds of objects, a "silver hat," "Herman Melville," a "strap for my wristwatch." O'Hara submits these heterogeneous objects, drawn from different spheres of life, to an identical principle: does he like it when he sees it? "A lady asks us for a nickel for a terrible / disease but we don't give her one we / don't like terrible diseases" (*CPO'H* 335). The humor here is didactic: no demonstration, persuasion, or advertisement of an object's social value will get O'Hara to pay for something he doesn't happen to like. This is free, or abstract, choice.

In these poems, personal choice is not determined by the personality, the interiority of the chooser. But if individuals aren't behind their choices, who is? Are these choices simply random? How can whatever one happens to like count as a principle of order? The final movement of "Personal Poem" shows us. The end of the poem marks a change of tone from the "I-do-this, I-do-that" accelerated, unrhymed, quotidian patter, to a reflective closing movement, underscored by a final rhymed couplet. O'Hara's most perceptive critics have noted the oscillation in the mature poems between a documentary mode of representation verging on an automatic transcription of place, time, companion, and a symbolic, writerly mode. Most, following Perloff's influential study, have figured this oscillation as an opposition between the intractable material of O'Hara's personal circumstances and their "imaginative transformation" through the poetic faculty.[6] But if O'Hara's vision of the personal as "abstract" is, as he suggests in "Personism," already an "imaginative transformation," then we must find another function for the stylistic departures in the poems. The first part of the poem shows a certain kind of choosing in action. The latter part steps back and takes a look. What does all this choosing do? What kind of relation to the world does it make possible? The lyrical ending of "Personal Poem" locates O'Hara's choosing in terms of a new relation to collectivity.

> I wonder if one person out of the 8,000,000 is
> thinking of me as I shake hands with LeRoi
> and buy a strap for my wristwatch and go
> back to work happy at the thought possibly so.
> (*CPO'H* 336)

After a long catalog of choices, after carefully tracking the movement of his body through the city, the poem suddenly shifts perspective, and stages an encounter between the speaker and the city in its abstract, statistical totality. This encounter is resolved in terms of a personal relationship; the relation between the speaker and the city is transposed into a relation between the speaker and "one person." Interestingly, this "one person" is absent and unnamed. The relation to it occurs at a different level than the farewell handshake with LeRoi (the person who *is* present), and the purchase of the wristwatch strap, actions that happen "as" O'Hara thinks of the "one person" thinking of him. This reflective moment, suspended in possibility, "possibly so," this closing intimation of a depth to the personal behind or beneath the flow of actions and choices, is slightly jarring. The "one person," whoever it is, seems to have the "inner reality" "LeRoi" and "Mike Kanemitsu" lack. It also appears to supply the missing interiority of the speaker: this is what he thought about while making these choices, this is what he wondered, this is who he really wanted. Or, keeping in mind O'Hara's admonition against finding "personality or intimacy" here, we might read this moment as supplying the missing content of the way of choosing the poem represents. "One person out of the 8,000,000": this is what *choosing* wants. Free choice, abstract desire makes a relation to "one person" out of a relation to "8,000,000." "True abstraction" figures a relation to "8,000,000" as a personal relationship. It is a "happy" thought for O'Hara. Can it be possible? The whole city is "thinking of me," and nothing stands between us, not even myself.

Choosing whatever he happens to like raises the utopian possibility of a new kind of relation between the speaker and the city. The poem's ending suggests that something about the way of choosing the poem shows us somehow accomplishes this relation. Is this simply an unfounded assertion, a wish? If not, what in the dynamics of the choosing the poem shows us grounds this assertion? How exactly does this choosing marry the speaker to the city? How can the value discovered in whatever happens to strike one's eye possibly count as collective value?

We might illuminate the curious properties of this choosing via a contemporary writer whose work exhibits the same tensions and paradoxes. O'Hara's presentation of the city street as a fictional space where value is transformed, and where free choice becomes a pure experience of collectivity, finds an echo in a work that profoundly changed the way people thought about cities. Jane Jacobs' *The Death and Life of Great American Cities,* published two years after "Personal Poem," argues that free, "abstract" choice exposes new possibilities for urban life. Jacobs mounts a wholesale attack on the theory and practice of city planning. She argues that if all social and government planning were to cease, a spontaneous urban order would arise, and she devotes her book to detailing the workings of this "healthy" city. As in O'Hara's poems, the free choices of individuals constitute the mechanism driving the unplanned order of Jacobs' city streets. She borrows her characteristic rhetorical move from free market discourse, asking city dwellers whether they would prefer to make their own choices, or to have their choices made for them by planners

(*DL* 14–15). On the surface, the difference between planning and free choice thus looks like the difference between social and individual determination of action. But a closer look at the dynamics of choosing reveals that free choice for Jacobs, as for O'Hara, represents a form of agency that is neither social nor individual.

Jacobs' term for value, like O'Hara's, is "interest," a word that is ubiquitous in her work. People must be "interested," streets must be "interesting," a healthy neighborhood is full of "interest"; planned developments are "uninteresting," the people that move through them are "uninterested," a "great blight of dullness" follows in the planners' tracks (*DL* 43). And like O'Hara, whose poems continually show him buying wristwatches, books, sodas, tickets, and hats, the closest meaning of interest for Jacobs is economic. Her "healthy" streets are saturated with commerce (*DL* 216, 229); the fundamental building block of a healthy city for her is the presence of shops, bars, and restaurants on every corner and in every block.[7] What sparks individuals' interest are the goods for sale that surround their bodies on the narrow, congested streets of Jacobs' city. If one does away with zoning laws, she predicts our actual "dull" residential and industrial districts will light up with "interesting" commerce.[8] For her, as for O'Hara, what is important is not simply the equation of interest with the economic, but a new perception of how economic interest works.

Interest for Jacobs means responsiveness to one's immediate environment. One's environment is interesting, and one becomes interested. In Jacobs' book, an individual's interior is a blank. Individuals have no internal preferences; their choices are entirely determined by the "opportunities" presented by their environment. As an example, she uses that stereotypical city figure, "the stranger." This stranger enters a city street, and is captured by it. If the street is "dull gray," with few shops, few restaurants, bars, or salons, the stranger might take the opportunity to snatch your purse or slit your throat (*DL* 42). If the street is "interesting," the same stranger might pick out a wristwatch he likes, have a soda, and look around (*DL* 35). There are no context-independent desires for Jacobs; the individual chooser is entirely motivated by a disposition to be interested in what surrounds her.

Free choice, for Jacobs, consists in this sensitivity to the opportunities presented by an interesting street. The interesting street is a context containing various opportunities – to look, to eat, to drink, to wear – arranged around one's body. And like O'Hara's poems, which contain no distances, no long views, Jacobs' fictional streets are designed in such a way that they do not permit one's vision to extend beyond the reach of one's body. Practically the only planned intervention she advocates in her fictional city is that long streets allowing one to see far into the distance be broken up with corners, walls, and café awnings, in order to concentrate the individual's attention on the immediate context of embodiment (*DL* 372–92). Free choice requires an intense and minute awareness of this immediate context. The shape of Jacobs' streets, and of O'Hara's narrowly focused poems, protect this awareness from any temptation to reflect, to look inside, or to look away.

Jacobs' text thus elicits the same question as O'Hara's poems. When my choice is circumscribed and defined by my environment, when I never ask myself what I want, and instead simply wait to see what catches my eye, who is choosing? But perhaps we should ask a different question first. Can this choosing happen just anywhere, or does it require a particular kind of space? Choice in Jacobs and O'Hara consists in responsiveness to the environment. Perhaps a clue to the dynamics of this choosing lies in the peculiar features of this environment. The relevant space is a city street. And for both writers, the distinctive feature of urban space, compared with rural or suburban space, is the density of commerce. As O'Hara writes, "I can't even enjoy a blade of grass unless I know there's a subway handy, or a record store" ("Meditations in an Emergency," *CPO'H* 197). The enjoyment, interest, and attention displayed in the poems depend on the proximity of commerce.

For Jacobs, if there are no stores, restaurants, or markets on a street, choice won't work on that street. Only in this commercial urban environment can free choice, choosing whatever strikes one's interest, be more than random. Choice is determined by context, and for Jacobs, the commercial urban context has special properties. When individuals choose freely among the shops, restaurants, and galleries, their choosing gets woven into a self-organizing collective system, an "organism" composed of 8,000,000 human bodies, which she describes not with the terms of social science, but in terms drawn from biology.[9] As with the end of "Personal Poem," a choosing oriented only to whatever strikes the eye opens directly out into a collective subjectivity.

We can now isolate four features of the choosing that happens on O'Hara's and Jacobs' fictional streets. (1) Choice is determined by the arrangement of things in the immediate context of embodiment. (2) This urban context is defined by the density of commerce. (3) A collective process operating in this commercial urban space shapes the context. (4) Individual choice has a collective subject.

We will want to distinguish the fictional element in this choosing. Let's begin with the first feature. That the makeup of a chooser's immediate context plays some role in actual choices seems fairly intuitive. It is striking only in that it took so long for economics to accept it. In 1974, two experimental psychologists published a study challenging the foundational premises of the modern theory of choice. Daniel Kahneman and Amos Tversky's argument, given the stamp of orthodoxy nearly thirty years later with the award of the 2002 Nobel Prize in economics, is that the neoclassical assumption of "stable, context-free preferences," is a myth.[10] The rationality of "economic man," his status as a strategic, self-interested agent, is dependent on consistent internal preferences. Instead, the authors argue, "stable preferences do not exist prior to or independent of the menu of choices available to a decision maker."[11] "Preferences are constructed in the process of making a choice."[12] While the people studied will sometimes delay their decisions in order to get more information, perversely, this information will not affect the decision itself, but rather the *reasons* they often feel compelled to give for their choice.[13]

A choosing that is not determined by internal preferences, but that chooses from the given menu of options presented by an environment, is not fictional. It is, after all, the principle that determines the "impulse buy" arrangements by the checkout in grocery stores. Context-dependent choice is not a fiction, but seems to many economists and psychologists today accurately to describe actual choices. One way of approaching O'Hara and Jacobs would be to say that by foregrounding the extent to which real-world choice is context-dependent, they reveal the problem with the descriptions produced by neoclassical economics.[14]

But this would be to distort a central feature of these texts. O'Hara and Jacobs don't represent actual choices. They fictionalize choosing. That choice is context-dependent is not fictional. What is fictional in these texts is the particular way that the urban environment determines what catches my interest. In Kahneman and Tversky, context-dependent choices are examples of mistaken or compromised individual agency. In O'Hara and Jacobs, context-dependent choices are examples of collective agency. Special features of O'Hara's and Jacobs' fictional spaces hold the key to this difference.

Most economists assume that the function of the market is to record and transmit the private values of individuals. One decides how much one wants a thing, and then looks at how much it costs to see whether one can afford it. But in O'Hara and Jacobs, the ubiquity of commerce means that the city street is a context for something other than the calculation of internal preferences and external costs. In this space, value is not the projection of individual preference onto the world. Rather, the perception of value is figured as a connection between the individual and the collective.

How does this value-as-connection show up for agents? As we saw when looking at O'Hara's charms, value is experienced as a force that renders things more or less interesting, more or less noticeable. My perception of an object's value consists of my perception of its place in my environment, in the way it "leaps out" at me. A valuable object is one that catches my eye. This value is not a private individual value, nor does it consist of social norms or standards. This context-shaping force is the fictional form economic value takes in the commercial spaces of O'Hara's city streets.

Here, the agent's perception of a space is organized in terms of this value; value brings things within one's "range," or it moves them away. Ordinarily, to say that preference is context-dependent either means that choice is determined by contingent features of the context, or that it is determined by the social forces that shape the context. But if commerce as a collective process determines the context of choice, then context-dependent choice is neither determined by society, nor by purely contingent features of the individual's environment. If preference depends on context, and context is shaped by commerce, then choice has a collective dimension. An omnipresent commerce knits everyone and everything into the fictional city's vast nervous system. Who chooses? Everyone.

O'Hara insists his poems cannot be set in a place without "a subway handy, or a record store." If his poems were set in a commercial desert, choosing what strikes his eye would be choosing at random. It would not marry him to the collective. In his fictional streets, choosing whatever happens to strike one's eye is not random. If the economic is imagined as arranging the things in one's environment, bringing them closer or moving them farther away, making them more or less interesting, then choosing whatever strikes one's eye has a kind of rationality. It is rational choice, but rationality works rather differently here. Rationality is "in the air," woven by commerce into the changing environment, not contained within the individual chooser.[15] To be rational is to be interested, to be alert to the circulation of collective value that defines one's environment. Choice is determined by the arrangement of things in one's immediate context, and the economic works to determine the arrangement of things in that context. The careful specification of the *scene* of choice in O'Hara's programmatic personal poems registers this collective determination of personal choice. This specification of context replaces an expression of internal preferences as an account of the intentionality of choice.

The submission required by the collective takes the form of keeping your attention firmly on the interesting things around you. In "Personal Poem," O'Hara renders this submission as love. As various critics have noted, this poem is ultimately a love poem, but attempts to identify the beloved with a particular *individual* in O'Hara's private life miss the point.[16] The object of his desire is not a person but a collective. In choosing, O'Hara enters into a direct relation with the *whole city*. The apparently random, trivial choices of the speaker (buying a strap for his watch, picking out a charm) conceal a powerful and utopian claim.

O'Hara's poetry constantly reproduces this sense that the preference of the moment activates the communal dimension of personal experience. Consider the following lines, drawn from the personal poetry of the late fifties. "Did you see me walking by the Buick Repairs? / I was thinking of you / having a Coke in the heat" ("Song," *CPO'H* 367). "My ton of books and John's ton of clothes bought / in a wild fit of enthusiasm in Madrid; all jumbled / together like life is a Jumble Shop" ("A Little Travel Diary," *CPO'H* 357). "To try to make something appear between divided selves / clear and abstract" ("Those Who Are Dreaming, A Play About St. Paul," *CPO'H* 374). "I … buy a strap for my wristwatch." "The meaning / of abstraction, a color of general significance and beauty … belonging only to you" ("Those Who Are Dreaming," *CPO'H* 374). "57th Street / street of joy / I am a microcosm in your macrocosm / and then a macrocosm in your microcosm" ("A Warm Day for December," *CPO'H* 375–76). "One person out of the 8,000,000 is / thinking of me." Free choice is the route to a total relation to America. In choosing freely and abstractly, "I" move closer to "you," to the "one person," to the whole. This is a political desire: I want to become you, and you to become me. Instead of a nation of individuals, O'Hara's America is a nation of individual choices. Collective action is determined not by general consensus, nor by an equilibrium point between everyone's preferences, but by a single, collective subject. O'Hara creates a striking image of this new subject in another major poem of the late fifties, "Ode to Joy."

> We shall have everything we want and there'll be no more dying …
> Buildings will go up into the dizzy air as love itself goes in
>   and up the reeling life that it has chosen for once or all …
>   pouring hunger through the heart to feed desire in intravenous
>   ways …
> great cities where all life is possible to maintain as long as time

which wants us to remain for cocktails in a bar and after dinner
lets us live with it.

No more dying. (CPO'H 281)

The opening line establishes the poem's utopian tenor. "We shall have everything we want." In contrast to the "I-do-this, I-do-that" everyday-ness of the personal poems, "Ode to Joy" self-consciously appropriates the gestures of high art. The title, for example, evokes Beethoven, Keats, and Schiller. A collective "we" replaces the ubiquitous "I" of the personal poems. The sublime declaration of absolute freedom from necessity in the "No more dying" that frames the stanzas, the evocation of "legends" and "great cities," and the development of elaborate metaphors, situate the "Ode" in an elevated discursive mode compared with the poems considered above. However, the apparently random and trivial personal details characterizing "Personal Poem" also appear here, incongruously embedded in the utopian proclamations. This juxtaposition of the profound and the trivial is reproduced throughout the poem. Its lines are littered with "racing forms," "photographs of … movie stars," "cocktails in a bar." This ideal world, where there is "no more dying," overflows with the same kinds of "charms" chosen by the drifting, everyday speaker of "Personal Poem." In these juxtapositions O'Hara illuminates his vision of personal choice opening out into the life of the collective. "The reeling life that it has chosen for once or all." The collective choice of a way of life, chosen "for once or all," is brought into relation with the contingent, spontaneous choices of priced objects, of "racing forms" and "cocktails." The "we" emerges with these trivial, immediate choices; the desire of the collective blows through the priced objects of everyday life, infusing them with its aura.

"No more dying:" the phrase frames the poem, declaring this to be a space free of the scarcity and sacrifice that have always constituted the tragic dimension of the economic. In the conventional understanding of the market, desire forms in a private space, only to be confronted with the tragic gap between unlimited human desire and the limits of the world. The economic does not shape desire, but places cruel limits on the private desires of individuals. Neoclassical subjects might want Rolls Royces and mansions, but often find, to their dismay, they must settle for "racing forms" and "cocktails." But in the aesthetic space opened by this poem, there is no possibility of such a gap between what I want and what I can have. Desire forms out among the things themselves, not in an interior vacuum. I choose whatever strikes my eye in an environment organized by commerce. Shaped by the economic, desire is wedded to the world. In this aesthetic space, the world we encounter will always be enough. "We shall have everything we want."

Whose desire is satisfied here? This densely textured, delirious desire winds among "supper clubs," "buildings," "gold," and "limbs." It circulates within a composite, collective body composed of organic and inorganic materials. "To feed desire in intravenous ways." This circulation does not occur between individual subjects, but within a collective subject, "intravenously" not intersubjectively. O'Hara's unusual depiction of sexuality extends this representation of the collective as a kind of body. "Buildings will go up into the dizzy air as love itself goes in / and up." This strange image eludes the queer readings that make up much of the most interesting criticism on O'Hara in recent years.[17] Terrell Herring's claim, for example, that "The personal poem … is a cruising ground on which gay men come together," suggests exactly the kind of relations *between* individuals that do not characterize this poem.[18] Rather, the city itself is sexualized in "Ode to Joy." The phallic "buildings" that rise into the air "as love itself goes in and up" do not represent an erotic relation between individuals; they show the collective as a desiring and desirable body.

O'Hara's poetry sexualizes the collective. The "we," the composite body of the city itself, becomes the *subject* of desire in "Ode to Joy." Queer readings of O'Hara offer productive ways of understanding the hostility of this desire to the norms of liberal subjectivity. Leo Bersani's analysis of gay cruising as "eroticism uncontaminated by a psychology of desire,"[19] for example, represents a version of homosexuality particularly relevant to my account of choice in O'Hara as whatever happens to catch the eye. But in O'Hara, the point of choices undetermined by the interiority of the chooser is to open choice to the city, which becomes a kind of nervous system knitting bodies and objects into a new, collective subjectivity.[20] If readings informed by queer theory have advanced our understanding of the emancipatory character of desire in O'Hara, the subject of this liberation has gone unrecognized. The aim of his radically free desire is not to form new kinds of relations between individuals, but to free this "we," this virtual collective, from the liberal individual.

2.

In a set of early poems that constitutes the prehistory of his mature program, O'Hara develops two opposing images of America, which represent, respectively, the America he wants to escape and the America he

wants to become. Writing in a decade obsessed with the fear of conformity, he identifies the organizing principle of American public life in the
fifties as a command to conform. In an essay on *Dr. Zhivago*, O'Hara
reads Pasternak's novel not as an indictment of Soviet political oppression
but, perversely, as a penetrating insight into the problem with American
democracy. Quoting Pasternak, he describes the American public sphere
as the space of artificial homogeneity and constraint, the hateful "duty,
imposed by armed force, to live unanimously as a people, as a whole
nation" (*CPO'H* 508).

For O'Hara, the archetypical space of our public life is a memorial that
organizes people as an undifferentiated mass centered on reverence for the
dead. The figure of George Washington, in his semi-mythical, blandly
virtuous image as the "father of the country," is imagined as the center of
stifling and oppressive public spaces. In "To Canada (For Washington's
Birthday)," O'Hara flees from the spectacle of the nation's birthday: "I
am so tired of the limitations of immobility / all of America pretending
to be a statue" (*CPO'H* 396). Here the unity of the nation, the "e pluri-
bus unum" of democracy, looks like a demand for everyone to imitate
George Washington's statue. The subjects of democracy are frozen, compelled, mechanical. The poet is sickened by "the pretensions of their wor-
ried faces"; they are not "interested" or "interesting." Elsewhere the figure
of Washington is associated with militarism, "The arch bestrides me …
The soldiers filing / at my feet" ("Washington Square," *CPO'H* 83), and
with the violent clearing of natural space to create the "perfect aridity" of
political space ("The State of Washington," *CPO'H* 220).

Throughout these poems participation in American public and political life is neither free nor natural, the organizational principle is malevolent and coercive, and the poet represents himself as continually "fleeing
a hunter, / which is our democracy" ("In Memory of My Feelings,"
CPO'H 256). "Military Cemetery" develops a surreally literal image of
democracy as a hunter, and the nation as a grave. The poem begins with
a political crisis: "We've got to get our war memorials corrected" (*CPO'H*
262). It has been discovered that the names were "spelled wrong" on the
graves, "that is, there was but one man in every grave," an abstract, ideal-
ized "unknown" soldier instead of the real bodies that should be there.
Correcting the memorial involves getting him "out of all the graves but
his own / and then kill the others, they've been romping too long / and
pop them into the graves" (*CPO'H* 262). "To be public spirited, alas! / is
to seem mysterious to the very people / you are trying to fill the graves
with. They get away" (*CPO'H* 263). Finally, the right live people are

killed and buried, and there is an absurd ceremony to certify that there is "a different person in each grave"; the integrity of the public space is restored, and "the wind will again whisper through the poplars" (*CPO'H* 263). Liberal democracy here as in the Washington poems is a categorizing scheme. The integrity of individual bodies is subordinated to the claims of a method of organizing persons into one people, and the perfect metaphor for a functioning nation is a cemetery where the names match the bodies in the graves.

O'Hara situates his earliest articulation of an alternative vision of America in a redundantly aesthetic space in a poem about a painting: Larry Rivers' *Washington Crossing the Delaware*. Rivers' aim, as he says in an interview with O'Hara, is to reimagine the scene of the familiar nineteenth-century image of the same title, in which Washington strikes a "heroic, slightly tragic pose," in order to capture the physical immediacy of "someone getting into a chilly river around Christmas time."[21] As might be expected considering O'Hara's view of what Washington represents, he at first strongly resisted this work, finding its subject "hopelessly corny."[22] On seeing the finished painting, however, O'Hara had something of an epiphany, and the poem he wrote in 1956 to record this moment figures his discovery of a personal relation to Washington as the discovery of a personal relation to America.

"On Seeing Rivers' *Washington Crossing the Delaware* at the MOMA" begins in an impersonal, public, and alienated space. The poem depicts O'Hara approaching Rivers' painting as it hangs in the museum as if George Washington were approaching him, struggling to free himself from the clichés and "false abstractions" that cling to him. "Now ... our hero has come back to us," having extricated himself from "the jealous spiritualities of the abstract" (*CPO'H* 233–34). Suddenly the exciting, chaotic, "immediate" presence of Rivers' image of Washington comes into focus, and the false abstractions "have burned up / See how free we are! as a nation of persons" (*CPO'H* 234). The emergence of Washington from "the national cliché" is accompanied by a kind of declaration of independence "as a nation of persons." The "dear father" of the nation O'Hara suddenly embraces is imagined, in the poem's final movement, in a direct and immediate relation to the poet: "Here are your bones crossed / on my breast like a rusty flintlock / a pirate's flag, bravely specific" (*CPO'H* 234). This Washington is not the imposing, moral figure who "cannot tell a lie"; the founding father is not entombed in a memorial or a statue, but lends his authority to the impulses of O'Hara's random heart. A "pirate's flag," symbol of unrestrained and anarchic desire, replaces the American flag. In a striking anticipation of the formation of "one person" out of "8,000,000" at the close of "Personal Poem," the "nation of persons" here is refounded as a person. O'Hara and the symbol of America no longer stand opposed, as in the earlier Washington poems. They have become indistinguishable.

O'Hara develops his aesthetic as a way of moving Washington from the outside, the public sphere where the image of the nation oppresses and stifles, to the inside, the personal space where collective energies are focused in a new, amplified subjectivity. Historians of the fifties often associate the critique of the conformity and oppression of contemporary America with the political left. But this critique is equally pronounced in the writing associated with the postwar resurgence of free market discourse. The terms of this discourse often resemble O'Hara's fantasy of a personal relation to America as a whole. But just as Jacobs' appropriation of individualistic free market rhetoric conceals a commitment to the collective, O'Hara's appeal to free choice conceals a radical fictionalizing of the market. Reading O'Hara alongside contemporary free-market discourse allows us to mark the fissure between actual and fictional economics.

Free market thinkers of the fifties and early sixties sought alternatives to what were seen as the intractable flaws of the political institutions of liberal democracy. These institutions, by interposing an abstract majority, or "general will," between the individual and society, were seen to produce conformity, mediocrity, and unfreedom. The oppressiveness of American democracy, according to this discourse, differs only in degree, not in kind, from the crushing political regime of the communist enemy. The alternative to representative democracy, with its dismal mediating apparatus of majority, tradition, representation, and a phantom "civil society," is a direct relation between the individual and society, a relation afforded by the market.

Milton Friedman was a particularly visible spokesman for this position. In 1962, he criticized John F. Kennedy's inaugural speech in terms strikingly similar to O'Hara's rejection of "public-spiritedness" as the "duty to live unanimously as a people, as a nation." Friedman attacks the "paternalism" of the famous line, "Ask not what your country can do for you," and suggests that Kennedy had it backwards. The effect of the demand "to ask what you can do for your country" is "to force people to act against their own immediate interests in order to promote a supposedly general interest."[23] Such a general interest is a "false abstraction" in O'Hara's sense; it belongs to no one, and is properly predicated only of "people pretending to be statues," neither "interested" nor "interesting." The tendency of American public life to generate this abstract "general interest" and require submission to it, is seen by Friedman as an unavoidable effect of political structures as such, no matter how superficially "democratic." "The characteristic feature of action through explicitly political channels is that it tends to require or to enforce substantial conformity."[24] Political action, whether totalitarian or liberal, imposes conformity to the "general interest" through essentially coercive means. "The fundamental threat to freedom is the power to coerce, be it in the hands of a monarch, a dictator, or a momentary majority."[25]

Friedman sees the market as the alternative to a society organized by political means. "The great advantage of the market, on the other hand, is that it permits wide diversity. It is, in political terms, a system of proportional representation. Each man can vote, as it were, for the color of the tie he wants and get it; he does not have to see what color the majority wants and then, if he is in the minority, submit."[26] Instead of filtering the individual's choice through everyone else's choices, the market offers an individual direct access to the capacities of the entire society. She speaks, it listens; she demands, it supplies. Clearly, representing the market as a direct and personal relation between the individual and the society "has implications that go far beyond the narrowly economic," in that the distinction between economic and noneconomic spheres of life disappears.[27] The market is not, as per the classic laissez-faire arguments, the "private" complement to a public life centered on the minimal state, but is imagined as *replacing* the state itself. It fulfills the same role; it is *like* a system of proportional representation, only much better. Here Friedman advocates a form of social organization in which the basic problem with other forms, the friction between the public and the private, the individual and the general, evaporates. In the free market, the individual obtains a personal relationship with the whole society: he tells it what he wants, and then he gets it.

But how does he know what he wants? Friedman's representation of true freedom as a choice between different colors of tie betrays the vulnerability of his position. The free market discourse, in reducing political and economic issues to the question of the best means of registering the individual's private desire, depends on the strong, and to many contemporaries, implausible, neoclassical account of individual self-identity and self-determination. If individuals do manifest such mechanical preferences, it is only because they have been artificially placed there. As J. K. Galbraith writes in *The Affluent Society*: "A determining factor in production ... is, in fact, not consumer choice but, in substantial measure, producer manipulation of consumer response."[28] "Production only fills the void it has itself created."[29] This manipulation can be direct (everyone has to wear ties to work) or indirect (advertising creates a desire for red ties). Either way, the result is crushing conformity, obtained without any formal violation of free choice on the market.

Adorno and Horkheimer's famous 1947 attack on American consumer society in *The Dialectic of Enlightenment* is also predicated on the sense that market choice is determined not by the free individual, but by manipulation. The individual's needs are "predetermined" by advertising; a manipulation facilitated by the fact that individuality itself is neither free nor natural, but is manufactured by the system, along with the matching ties.[30] The American individual is "the eternal consumer," the "product" of the culture industry.[31] Individual consumers make the choices, but the capitalist producer makes the individuals and their desires. The neoclassical subject is the product of differential power relations that are invisible to her. The free choices of unfree individuals on the market replicate systematic conformity and oppression. Galbraith suggests that the advocates of a new market revolution look elsewhere for utopia. "Among the many models of the good society, no one has urged the squirrel wheel."[32]

O'Hara's personal poems attempt to rescue free choice, and a free nation, from the rigid, mechanical model of the individual that accompanies it in liberal free-market discourse. If for Friedman the market allows one to satisfy one's stable individual preferences, choice for O'Hara dissolves the individual in the flows and processes of the collective. If Friedman sees the individual's desire as intensely private, O'Hara sees it as thoroughly collective. In the personal poems, as we have seen, individual choice becomes collective choice. O'Hara's "personal" method is abstract; it demonstrates the uniqueness not of particular subjects, but of particular choices. Once the stable world of stratified subject-positions dissolves into the floating world of atomic choices, the relations of production, which determine the market for writers from Adorno to Galbraith, assume a different aspect. "If / I ever get to be a construction worker / I'd like to have a silver hat please." "We just want to be rich / and walk on girders in our silver hats" (*CPO'H* 335–36). The ultramasculine, (re)productive character of the construction worker is replaced by a prancing, loafing figure whose perverse and trivial desire substitutes for hard labor. It is not that production is displaced by consumption; it is that both production and consumption are understood to be matters of free choice. The imbrication of work and desire, production and consumption in these lines reflects the dynamics of a poetics where making poems is a matter of liking things.

O'Hara develops his aesthetic of choice in the context of the New York art world during the fifties and early sixties, a world he personally inhabited as friend and lover of the artists, and professionally as a critic and curator of the MOMA. Abstract expressionism is the dominant school of the period, and the account of abstraction given by its preeminent champion and theorist, Clement Greenberg, provides the background for O'Hara's innovations. For Greenberg, like Kant, the aesthetic establishes the "subjective universality" of judgment by allowing a kind of experience devoid of personal interest. Abstraction is the paradigmatic example of an art freed from the taint of interest. In "The Case for Abstract Art" Greenberg writes that abstraction "has emerged as the epitome of almost everything that disinterested contemplation requires, as both a challenge and a reproof to a society that exaggerates, not the necessity, but the intrinsic value of purposeful and interested activity."[33] Greenberg attributes abstraction's value, at least in part, to the abstract subjectivity it cultivates in the audience. An impersonal attention, a "disinterested contemplation" is called forth by the picture "like a stimulus that elicits an automatic response."[34] Abstract paintings are a kind of Skinner box that "train[s] us to relegate [our self-interests] to their proper place," freeing the universal subjectivity of pure, or abstract, "attention."[35] Greenberg thinks abstraction, to extend his Skinnerian metaphor, is highly reinforcing; the impersonal, disinterested contemplation developed before the Jackson Pollock canvas can now be trained on other objects in different contexts. Abstraction "refine[s] our eyes for the appreciation of non-abstract art," and in so far as "necessity" permits, for the objects and scenes of everyday life.[36]

At first glance, O'Hara's aesthetic, given in his characteristically talky, "personal" criticism, seems the antithesis of Greenberg's version of abstraction. In "Larry Rivers: A Memoir," published in 1965, the year before his death, O'Hara clarifies his sense of the aesthetic appeal of this artist. Rivers' work is "very much a diary of his experience," O'Hara writes, in terms that clearly apply to his own mature work, "where much of the art of our time has been involved with direct conceptual or ethical considerations, Rivers has chosen to mirror his … enthusiasms in an unprogrammatic way" (*CPO'H* 514). "Rivers veers sharply, as if totally dependent on life impulses, until one observes an obsessively willful insistence on precisely what he is interested in" (*CPO'H* 514). Again, as in "Personism," O'Hara suggests that this personal art is not the opposite of a "program" or a "concept," but represents a different program, a new concept. Rivers' work only appears to be "totally dependent on life impulses," but the "obsessively, willful insistence on precisely what interests him" imposes a disciplined structure on the material. Rivers paints only what interests him, and his painting is interesting to O'Hara. Good art doesn't cultivate disinterest, but interest. "What his work has always had to say to me, I guess, is to be more keenly interested while I'm still alive. And perhaps this is the most important thing art can say" (*CPO'H* 515).

O'Hara's aesthetic of personal, contingent interest thus seems to anticipate the postmodern critique of Greenberg's praise of abstraction as inspiring "pure" and "disinterested" contemplation. Barbara Herrnstein Smith, in *Contingencies of Value*, provides the paradigmatic instance of this critique, claiming that the tendency "to isolate or protect certain aspects of life or culture," such as artworks, "from consideration in economic terms," such as "function" and "utility," "has had the effect of mystifying the nature, or dynamics, of their value."[37] Greenberg's "disinterest," as a sign of eternal, universal truths, betrays the fantasy of "noncontingent value," whereas her account stresses the determination of aesthetic value by the subject's contingent interests, desires, aims. But if the content of the subject's particular interests is contingent and variable across populations, the mechanics of interest is anything but. "We are always, so to speak, calculating how things 'figure' for us – always pricing them, so to speak, in relation to the total economy of our personal universe."[38] "We perform a continuous succession of what are, in effect, rapid-fire cost-benefit analyses, estimating the probable 'worthwhileness' of alternate courses of action in relation to our always limited resources of time and energy."[39] "Most of these 'calculations,' however, are performed intuitively and inarticulately … so recurrent that the habitual arithmetic becomes part of our personality and comprises the very style of our being and behaviour."[40] Despite her disclaimer that "any particular subject's 'self'… is also variable," she ends by suggesting that subjects are, in effect, products of their own calculations.[41] In articulating an extremely strong version of the rational, self-transparent, and self-interested neoclassical subject, Smith's account of contingent values thus appears rather determinate from O'Hara's perspective. The difference of his version of interest from Smith's reproduces the difference of his vision of America from that of the liberal free-market discourse of the fifties.

O'Hara's aesthetic, as a space where free choice substitutes for disinterested judgment, runs in a surprising parallel to Greenberg's. If Greenberg's abstraction cultivates a state of attention without interest, O'Hara's "true abstraction" elicits a state of being interested without being self-interested. The aesthetic teaches us to remove economic interest from the nexus of the subject's beliefs, interests, and values. The aesthetic frees economic interest, economic choice, economic agency. Calculation of the kind proposed by Barbara Herrnstein Smith or Milton Friedman is simply unimaginable for O'Hara. Since one's choices are not oriented towards personal preference but towards personal environment, one can never know exactly why one chooses as one does, or predict how one will choose in the future.

The use of figuration in Rivers' works illustrates how this interest works. "As far as I'm concerned *nothing* makes an invented shape more moving or interesting than a recognizable one."[42] Abstraction here is not a matter of form, as it is for Greenberg. Making new things is not interesting. Rivers' works are a "smorgasbord of the recognizable."[43] The objects he paints, Camel cigarette packs, bits of ribbon, street signs, are recognizable; the method of choosing them, of picking them out, is abstract. In the interview conducted by O'Hara, Rivers said of his "trivial" subjects: "I may have a private association with that piece of ribbon, but I don't want to *interpret* that association, it's impossible, it doesn't interest me. Some painters think that associations with real images are terribly strong, and that people in general identify the same meaning with them as they themselves do. I don't think so."[44] There is nothing much to say about the meaning of the object, he just likes it. O'Hara's reaction to this work is not to try to ferret out the secret of Rivers' "private association"; he knows there isn't one. Rather, he treats Rivers' work as an encouragement to form his own instant, contingent "private associations." "What his work has always had to say to me, I guess, is to be more keenly interested" (*CPO'H* 515).

Rivers' art transforms the symbols of the public world into interesting objects. "This goes for the father of our country as well as for the later Camel and Tareyton packs. Who, he seems to be saying, says they're corny? This is the opposite of pop art" (*CPO'H* 514). O'Hara is writing in 1965, at a time when the critical consensus on Rivers is that his work constitutes an important precursor to pop art. Nothing, for O'Hara, could be farther from the truth. A bad kind of value is at work in pop art. Pop art presents the objects of mass society as artifacts of public space and general interest, encountered by everyone in the same way, and shining with social values. Commercial objects, in pop art, are social objects. The value of a pack of Camels, for O'Hara, should lie in how it happens to catch one's eye as one walks through a store. Just as Greenberg imagines abstraction as "training" us how to see nonaesthetic objects without interest, the function of art for O'Hara is to bring a pure, abstract interest into the world.

O'Hara sees poems and paintings as fictional spaces that set individual choices free from both the sovereign individual and society. In *The Lonely Crowd*, an enormously popular book published in 1950, the sociologist David Riesman imagines another way of eliciting abstract desire in relation to commercial objects. Riesman's thought experiment, like O'Hara's aesthetic, is designed to reduce the interference of the subject's belief in rational self-interest. This interference is more insidious and problematic than the external interference of advertising. "Although small children rapidly get over the stage of passionate belief in the advertising of the box top and its radar signal rings, there is ... one feeling they learn in that stage which they do not get over. This is the belief that they must have a reason for consuming anything."[45] If, as Galbraith argues, consumer choice is manipulated, Riesman argues that a mechanical interior, not the transparent machinations of advertisers, is to blame for the distortion of consumer choice. It is not enough to like something, one must know why one likes it, what desire it satisfies, what interest it furthers. This belief is perhaps the most "powerful barrier to or manipulator of consumer free choice."[46] Some of the money advertisers use for national promotion should be diverted "to a fund for experimental creation of model consumer economies among children."[47] The advertisers would set up booths where a wide variety of different objects were laid out, to see "what happens to childhood taste when it is given a free track away from gradients of taste or 'reasons.'"[48] There would be "private alcoves" where they could enjoy the products in "privacy." Each child should be provided with "a cubicle where he would have a key and complete privacy ... away from the peer group" and its tyrannical policing of self-identity and self-knowledge.[49]

Privacy here is neither the full experience of a concrete, authentic self nor the imaginary interior of a socialized, constructed self; privacy develops a focused gaze outward, to a context of commercial objects. Riesman's little booths, like O'Hara's and Jacobs' streets, are fictional spaces in which choice is set free. Private space for Riesman, like personal space for O'Hara, liberates the transforming principle of free choice from the unfree individual.

O'Hara's work occupies the far side of the fissure, first described by Karl Polanyi, between actual and fictional economics. The historical position of these poems can be discerned by observing the traces a reaction to the dominant discourse of the fifties has left in their form. Fifties realism described a world shrunk around the narrowly circumscribed, autonomous private sphere of the rational individual citizen. All choices were to be determined by private, stable, internal preferences. In the rational choice model, choice narrows to a funnel draining what the individual desires from society, evacuating collective life of its vitality. O'Hara's image of choice as an attunement to an urban environment reverses this dynamic, imagining a collective agency behind individual choice. The transformation of value in these works enables their most distinctive feature: contingent details of individual experience that open directly onto a common life.

Recall the collective body of "Ode to Joy," the merging of the speaker and Washington in "On Seeing Rivers' *Washington*," or the intimacy between the speaker and the "8,000,000" at the end of "Personal Poem." Figures of a novel collective are never far from the surface of poems so insistently devoted to the particular. In "A True Account of Talking to the Sun at Fire Island," this collective subject appears in the guise of the sun. The poem is derived from "A Most Extraordinary Adventure" by the Russian futurist poet Vladimir Mayakovsky, an important writer in O'Hara's personal canon.[50] The "fiery red" sun that visits the ardent communist Mayakovsky represents the collective power of the Russian revolution.[51] O'Hara's reworking of the poem reveals his discovery of a different revolutionary energy, a new route to collectivity, in the conditions of postwar America. As the speaker recounts, "The Sun woke me this morning loud / and clear, saying "Hey! I've been / trying to wake you up for fifteen / minutes" (*CPO'H* 306). The speaker wonders at the reason for the visit; "Frankly I wanted to tell you / I like your poetry." As they talk, the Sun and the poet find out they have a lot in common, and the Sun leaves with a word of encouragement. "Always embrace things, people earth / sky stars, as I do, freely … That / is your inclination, known in the heavens / and you should follow it" (*CPO'H* 307). Or, as O'Hara says in "Personism," "Just go on your nerve" (*CPO'H* 498). O'Hara's personal aesthetic follows this nerve up through the nervous system of a collective body, and directly into the unimaginable brain.

CHAPTER 3

William Burroughs' virtual mind

"When you cut into the present the future leaks out."
–William S. Burroughs[1]

What are literary experiments? They are, like scientific experiments, repeatable and regularized. But can we speak here of success or failure? At the very least we can expect, both in the experimental text's tendency to thematize its processes, and in the theoretical texts that typically accompany it, accounts of the conditions that would have to obtain in order for the experiment to be successful. The literary experiment (and this is perhaps what makes it "literary") has a virtual element. It shows us the kind of thing that would regularly happen if the world were different in some particular way. This appears to be especially true of those literary experiments that claim to be mimetic, to represent an aspect of everyday reality. These experiments show us ordinary artifacts suspended in imaginary laws; they show us the everyday processes of a world that manifests a principle of order that is not, or is not yet, recognizable in our own. William S. Burroughs' "cut-up" trilogy of the early 1960s is among the best-known and most influential of postwar experimental works. What happens in the virtual space of those novels has exerted a powerful attraction on the postwar imagination, but the principle of order defining that space remains to be articulated.

In the following I argue that Burroughs' experiment sets up a mode of synchronizing embodied knowledge across individual bodies. Crucial features of this experiment have remained invisible to the critics because this mode differs from alternatives often seen as exhausting the possibilities. In the space of his fictions, Burroughs erects an order that coordinates experience without reducing it to code. As I will show, this experimental order responds to the same problems in the same way as the most radical contemporary theory of the price system. Burroughs' trilogy represents a key transitional work in the evolution of the economic fiction.

In Frank O'Hara's and Jane Jacobs' writing of the late fifties, we saw examples of agents who take on striking new features through their orientation towards commercial urban environments. But the precise dynamics of this agency, and a detailed presentation of the order that supports it, remain outside the frame of those texts. By inventing a way to make such an order the immanent, organizing principle of a literary work, Burroughs develops a form that later writers like William Gaddis, Kathy Acker, and William Gibson will take up as uniquely fitted to the project of fictionalizing the market. Burroughs' novels set up a virtual space that begins to exert a gravitational pull on postwar reality, distorting everyday objects, pulling them into strange new shapes. In the tension between the virtual space of the cut-up trilogy and the actual space of postwar America, we can begin to see the social effects of an alternative to social life.

I.

The "cut-up" method by which Burroughs produced his experimental texts of the sixties involves cutting a text into pieces of various sizes, mixing them up, and rearranging them at random. Burroughs made a number of books through this method, the most significant of which is the trilogy that includes *The Soft Machine* (1961), *The Ticket That Exploded* (1962), and *Nova Express* (1965). The size of the cut-up pieces varies, from quarter pages at one extreme to the lengths of single phrases or sentences at the other. The pieces were never as small as a single word; this means that the cut-ups were assembled from semantically coherent elements selected or produced by Burroughs. In the composition of these books, the texts forming the material submitted to the cut-up method were primarily drawn from Burroughs' own writing, but also included literary (Rimbaud, T. S. Eliot) and nonliterary (newspapers, pop song lyrics) sources. Burroughs also employed the related "fold-in" technique, in which "A page of text – my own or someone else's – is folded down the middle and placed on another page. The composite text is then read across half one text and half the other ... For example I take page one and fold it into page one hundred–I insert the resulting composite as page ten."[2] In yet another variation, he sometimes read a text he had written into a tape recorder, then cut the tape up, spliced it together, and transcribed the result. Finally, the cut-up texts were interspersed with un-cut-up passages to form the published novels.

Critical accounts of the cut-up method have typically understood it, along with formally similar methods practiced by John Cage and

Jackson Mac Low, as manifesting what has come to be seen as a familiar postmodern concern with randomness, chance, indeterminacy.[3] But while Burroughs uses chance to determine the order of the pieces making up the final text, he insists that he employs randomness to represent a different principle of order. He claims that a desire to produce "spontaneity" motivates the cut-ups. "You cannot *will* spontaneity. But you can introduce the unpredictable spontaneous factor with a pair of scissors."[4] Burroughs asks us to distinguish between a thematics of chance, and a method that uses chance to mimic, in a literary text, a kind of order that cannot otherwise be shown. This "unpredictable spontaneous factor" does not introduce randomness, but a "surprising" order. "The arbitrary cuts ... are appropriate in many cases and your cut up tape makes surprising sense" (*TTE* 207). "What appears to be random may not, in fact, be random at all."[5]

Randomness is virtual here. It stands in for something else: a kind of order Burroughs thematizes in his choice of the elements submitted to chance operations, in the non-randomized passages, and in the trilogy's supporting theoretical texts. When, for example, Burroughs writes that "'The Waste Land' was the first great cut-up," he implies that the cut-up method represents an analogous principle of juxtaposition.[6] Rather than contrasting modernist order with postmodernist indeterminacy, Burroughs suggests we explore his own texts for a principle corresponding to Eliot's "mythic" principle of juxtaposition. What logic determines the juxtaposition of Burroughs' cut-up phrases? What kind of order, "not ... random at all," does Burroughs' random use of the scissors represent?

We need not look very far or hard for the answer to this question. He tells us, repeatedly. But his answer is so strange that none of his readers have pursued it. What Burroughs tells us is that the cut-up text represents an individual's immediate environment. The cut-up is a mimesis of the immediate context, the background, of individual embodiment, action, perception, and thought.

Cut-ups make explicit a psycho-sensory process that is going on all the time anyway. Somebody is reading a newspaper, and his eye follows the column in the proper Aristotelian manner, one idea and sentence at a time. But subliminally he is reading the columns on either side and is aware of the person sitting next to him. That's a cut-up. I was sitting in a lunch-room in New York having my doughnuts and coffee. I was thinking that one does feel a little boxed in New York, like living in a series of boxes. I looked out the window and there was a great big Yale truck. That's a cut up ... Most people don't see what's going on around them. That's my principal message to writers: for God's sake, keep your *eyes* open. Notice what's going on around you.[7]

The cut-up is Burroughs' solution to the literary problem of representing "what's going on around you." Burroughs' original title for *The Soft Machine* was *Right Where You Are Sitting Now.*[8] In *Naked Lunch* (1959) he writes: "There is only one thing a writer can write about: *what is in front of his senses at the moment of writing.*"[9] Chance operations provided Burroughs with a new way of representing this immediate context, the background of human embodiment. He offers the following writing exercise as an analogue to his chance operations. "Now try this take a walk a bus a taxi do a few errands sit down somewhere drink a coffee watch TV look through the papers now return to your place and write what you have just seen heard felt thought with particular attention to precise intersection points."[10] The cut-up method is intended to reproduce the juxtapositions, the "precise intersection points," encountered by a body moving through the world. "Cut-ups make explicit a psycho-sensory process that is going on all the time." Cut-ups represent the process, "not … random at all," that determines the juxtaposition of elements in the immediate context of human being in the world.

One has only to turn to examples from the trilogy to understand why Burroughs' ideas have been so consistently ignored in the interpretation of his cut-ups. At first glance, the kinds of juxtapositions we find there don't look like the immediate context of embodiment so much as its opposite: bodies, places, perceptions, and actions ripped out of context and recombined according to a cyborg logic. Consider the following examples, which provide a characteristic sample of the trilogy's juxtapositions. "Erogenous cotton flesh lying there streaked with phosphorous – someone walking" (*TTE* 130). "From a headline of penniless migrants electric storms of violence" (*TTE* 149). "Permutated fucking shadows through ceilings of legs and sex hairs, black spirals of phantom assholes lifting and twisting like a Panhandle cyclone" (*SM* 141). "Someone walking trails my Summer dawn flesh" (*TTE* 67).

Passages like these, with their stark juxtapositions of heterogeneous body images, their fusion of organic and artificial material, and their violation of the norms and the scale of human embodiment have seemed to many readers to reflect contemporary technological discourses that treat the body and the artificial as information systems that can be articulated together. Along with the tendency to read Burroughs as thematizing randomness, the tendency to read him as engaging cybernetic discourse emerged early in the criticism, and has continued to dominate it. Marshall McLuhan, in an essay published in 1964, sees Burroughs as representing "the new electric environment." The cut-up works are devoted to supporting Burroughs' "proposition" that "the nervous system can be reprogrammed biologically as readily as any radio network can alter its fare."[11]

More recently, N. Katherine Hayles, in her 1999 book *How We Became Posthuman*, takes Burroughs' cut-up works as central examples of the representation of a cybernetic order where "information [is] a (disembodied) entity that can flow between carbon-based organic components and silicon-based electronic components to make ... a single system."[12] Burroughs "suggests by [his] cut-up method a textual corpus that is ... artificial, heterogeneous, and cybernetic."[13] For Hayles, Burroughs is among the earliest and most important inventors of what she calls "posthuman" forms. They are predicated on the "erasure" of human embodiment, which is replaced by an understanding of "human being as a set of informational processes."[14] "The posthuman appears when computation ... is taken as the ground of being, a move that allows the posthuman to be seamlessly articulated with intelligent machines."[15] In the cybernetic world Burroughs imagines, it is "no longer possible to distinguish meaningfully between the biological organism and the informational circuits in which the organism is enmeshed."[16] In his cut-ups Burroughs "create[s] mutated posthuman forms that both express and strive to escape from the conditioning that makes them into split beings."[17] Instead of representing the context of embodiment, as he inexplicably insists, Burroughs represents the dissolution of that context into streams of information, which can be cut up, spliced together, recombined to make such bizarre mutations as "Erogenous cotton flesh lying there streaked with phosphorous – someone walking."

This account has, at least at first, much to recommend it. We have a good sense of what cybernetic orders look like, and Burroughs' juxtapositions, such as the one quoted above, look a lot like cybernetic fantasy. In addition, this view is compatible with the other major trend in the criticism, the literal reading of Burroughs' random operations. As Hayles notes, cybernetic theorists considered randomness or "noise" an essential property of information systems, and constitutive of their formal, systematic coherence.[18] But when we search these texts for the principle that enables cybernetic fusions we will not find it. What allows different bodies, or organic and inorganic matter, to be articulated together is the idea that everything is composed of information. Every aspect of existence and reality can be formalized, made fully explicit, resolved into information which can then be manipulated. There is nothing like this in Burroughs. His forms *look like* the forms produced by cybernetic processes, but representations of these processes are conspicuously absent.

Still, Hayles might argue that Burroughs is producing descriptions of cybernetic processes even if he never articulates them. When Thoreau, for example, writes about a locomotive in *Walden* without describing its mechanism, there is no reason to doubt that he has a steam engine in mind, or to think that he is imagining a new kind of power that merely looks like a steam engine. But when we look closely, Burroughs' practice of juxtaposition reveals features that are inassimilable to cybernetic orders. Not only does he not represent the formalization of the world into information that underlies cybernetic transformation, his juxtapositions highlight elements that are absolutely resistant to formalization, to reduction to information.

The smell, a typical element of the cut-ups, foregrounds this resistance. From a single page of *The Soft Machine* we get the following smells: "stale summer dawn smell," "smell of carbolic soap," "swamp smells," "whiffs of raw meat," "genital smells," "belches of institution cooking," "spectral smell of empty condoms" (*SM* 61). This page has been produced by the cut-up method, and we find these various smells more or less starkly juxtaposed with other kinds of images: a "kerosene lamp," "penny arcades and mirrors," "a brass bed in Mexico" (*SM* 61). Leaving aside for the moment the ultimate question of the particular *kind* of embodiment the page is mimetic of, it seems clear that these smells occur in a context of embodiment. They are ineluctably oriented to a body, and are intelligible only in the context of a certain kind of body (i.e. one capable of smelling). Further, unlike the composition of a metal chair or a human arm, the experience of a smell can never be entirely formalized, made fully explicit, completely reduced to information. Certainly a lot can be said about a given smell, but it can never be given the kind of total articulation imagined by cybernetic theory. There is a certain non-explicitable horizon (the kind of being capable of smell) that bounds everything that can be made explicit about the "smell of carbolic soap." As Hayles constantly emphasizes, the elements in a cybernetic system are iterable, transferable across contexts. But this particular element, this smell, is ontologically dependent on the context of a certain kind of embodiment. It is nothing without it. In the space of cybernetic fantasy, the molecules that give rise to a particular smell can be synthesized, a human arm can be grafted onto metal. But it is much more difficult to see how the experience of the "smell of carbolic soap" can be fused with a "kerosene lamp." If one looks closely, the cut-ups don't even look cybernetic.[19]

Burroughs' choice of elements that foreground embodied experience is consistent with his claim that the cut-up is a mimesis of "right where you are sitting now," that it represents the juxtaposition of elements in the context of human embodiment. But if we can't imagine the cybernetic circulation of the experience of a certain smell, neither is it easy to see how the smell of carbolic soap, whiffs of raw meat, a bed in Mexico, and a boy in Panama are all elements in a single context of embodiment. It is not clear, at this point, to what in the experience of embodiment the heterogeneity of scale, time, and space of the juxtaposed elements in the cut-up could possibly correspond. We can therefore be certain at the outset of a limit to this line of pursuit, in the features of the cut-up page that render it unrecognizable as an image of where we are sitting right now. But where and what is this limit exactly? We will want to clarify our intuitive sense that if the elements Burroughs shows us have a relation to some kind of embodiment, it looks rather different than any familiar version. With a view to defining the boundaries of the space created by these fictions, it will be useful to see exactly how far an account of the context, the background, the situation of ordinary embodiment takes us in understanding Burroughs' experiment.

The idea that the "smell of carbolic soap" is ontologically dependent on a certain nonformalizable context derives from the phenomenological account of intelligence and embodiment developed by thinkers like Heidegger and Maurice Merleau-Ponty in the early and mid-twentieth century. By the 1960s, philosophers in the Anglo-American tradition, led by Hubert Dreyfus and Charles Taylor, began to see in this account a powerful alternative to the representationalist theory of mind reflected in cybernetic theory and contemporary artificial intelligence research. The experience of a smell is thus a vivid example of what Taylor calls "engaged agency."

Engaged agency ... is that agency whose experience is made intelligible only by being placed in the context of the kind of agency it is. Thus, our embodiment makes our experience of space as oriented up-down understandable ... The first term – the form of agency (e.g., embodiment) – stands to the second – our experience, as a context conferring intelligibility.[20]

The context, or background, of this kind of agency is what Heidegger calls "preunderstanding." It is not composed of representations or mental states, but is an actual context in the world. "This background sense of reality is nonrepresentational, because it is something we possess in – that is inseparable from – our actual dealings with things."[21] Thus the idea that our sense of reality, our ability to move around and experience smells, could be made entirely explicit, could be "translated" into information, is "misconceived in its very nature ... Why can't it all be articulated? Because it isn't a matter of representations, but of a real context conferring sense."[22] Our experiences cannot be reduced to an iterable string of code; they can't be transferred outside the actual context in the world that makes them what they are.

While Burroughs' choice of smell experience as an element of his cut-ups presents a particularly clear example of engaged agency, this account is not limited to experiences obviously dependent on embodiment, but offers a general model of human thought, action, and perception. In the same way that the background of embodiment makes sense of up-down spatial orientation, our recognition of and interaction with things in the world depends on the background of our situation in the world. For example, when we encounter a stop sign, we don't encounter it as a bit of neutral sensory information (red octagon), which we compare against a database in our heads to decode as a stop sign. Rather, the object is encountered *immediately* as a stop sign; it occurs in a context of driving, drivers, cars, roads, etc., and is disclosed as a stop sign by virtue of its belonging to that context, that world. In the course of normal human functioning, it never shows up as a red octagon. Only when there is some disruption, some problem (no one else is stopping) does it show up as a "worldless" bit of information. The context the stop sign belongs to isn't "in our heads," it's not a representation of a world of unprocessed sense data. As Dreyfus wrote in his influential attack on the early, representationalist A.I. research program: "When we are at home in the world, the meaningful objects embedded in their context of references among which we live are not a model of the world stored in our mind or brain; *they are the world itself.*"[23] We come to awareness, we learn to think and act within this meaningful context. When we move, think, and act, the meaning and source of our actions is not to be sought in private acts of information processing, but in the actual context we find ourselves in.

Just as the context of embodiment constitutes the "preunderstanding" of smells or up-down orientation, particular things are disclosed first as part of a whole, part of a context. This whole, the context that forms the horizon of particular encounters with individual things, provides a structure of meaning for human activity. The entire human world is "prestructured in terms of human purposes and concerns."[24] "What counts as an object or is significant about an object already is a function of, or embodies, that concern."[25] When one sees a chair, one sees something one sits on. What one notices in noticing the chair is the "concern," the meaning it has as a part of the context of a human world. This context prestructures action, and shapes and defines the intentions of the engaged agent. Note, for example, how context shapes action and intention in Merleau-Ponty's description of a soccer field.

For the player in action, the football field is ... pervaded with lines of force ... and articulated in sectors (for example, the "openings" between adversaries) which call for a certain mode of action and which initiate and guide the action as if the player were unaware of it ... The player becomes one with it and feels the direction of the "goal," for example, just as immediately as the vertical and horizontal planes of his own body.[26]

Here we seem to have reached the limit of the phenomenological account as an aid to understanding Burroughs' representation of context. For the structure of meaning that supports one's awareness of a chair in a school classroom or a goal on a soccer field appears to have no parallel in a cut-up passage like the following: "Went down off England with all dawn smell of distant fingers ... About this time I went to your Consul" (*SM* 10). If this is a context, how is it a meaningful whole? What structure could possibly disclose what Burroughs insists in calling the "surprising sense" of such passages? We began by attempting to take seriously Burroughs' claim that the cut-up page represents the context of embodiment. We now see that if the "smell of carbolic soap" appears to be dependent on some kind of embodiment, the principle structuring this embodiment must be quite different from any we find in the actual world. But before pursing this fictional principle, we should pause to note that our detour through phenomenology has produced a second result. For we are now able to modify our initial question about Burroughs' experiment in an important way.

We began by looking for the principle of juxtaposition in the cut-ups, and we can now see what it is we are really looking for. Or rather, we can now see that *what* we are looking for is also a *who*. The principle of juxtaposition that structures the elements of the context of "right where you are sitting now" is also the structure of subjectivity. Knowing where you are sitting tells us who you are. Burroughs calls the subject that emerges in his cut-up experiments the "third mind."[27] If we don't yet know who this is, we can begin to see that this is who we are looking for when we look for the structure of the context. As Dreyfus writes, when we recognize a chair as something "one" sits in or a soccer ball as something "one" kicks, "the one takes the place of the individual subject as the source of significance."[28] Or in Heidegger's language, the one who is the "who of everyday Dasein ... The one is the realest subject of everydayness."[29]

The "one" expresses the public norms of the shared world of engaged agency. The one shows us where the chair is and tells us how to use it. It tells us how close to stand next to someone else on a bus, how to respond to a greeting, what smells are unacceptable in a kitchen. The one is identical to the "concerns" that define and order the elements of the context. These norms determine the links, the juxtapositions of elements: chairs belong in a classroom; stop signs belong with the activity of driving. Norms are not beliefs about the world that members of a society share; they bring individuals into a society and enable them to encounter the world as one does. These norms are what individuals absorb when they are socialized into a human world and become human agents. Thus individuals are "embodiment[s] of the one"; the subject of our embodiment is the one.[30] Without these norms, there could be no context; what one knows, how one acts, constitutes the integrity of the context, makes it a whole, makes it a world. The meaningful structure of the context is the ontological basis of the subject of human activity. So when we ask what structures the context Burroughs sets up, we are also asking who, what kind of subject, his experiment discloses.

But perhaps this line of questioning has taken us farther than it initially seems. Perhaps we move too quickly if we say that the ontology of the one is simply different from what we find in Burroughs. In the trilogy we don't find just an absence of norms as the principle that orders the context, but an intense assault on norms. Burroughs develops his principle of order in sustained opposition to the principle I've been sketching. To see this, we need to recall that a particular culture, the lifeworld of a certain society, forms the context, the "world" of phenomenology, and of the theories, like Taylor's and Dreyfus', derived from it. These kinds of explanations are marked by their continual reliance on cultural examples. One uses chopsticks in Japan, a knife and fork in the West.[31] Italians stand very close together on buses, Scandinavians stand farther apart. The "shared public world" of the context is the world of a particular culture; one is either Japanese or Western, Italian or Scandinavian.

Norms are social and cultural norms; culture is context. In this idea we recognize the principle of juxtaposition that underlies "the first great cut-up," Eliot's "The Waste Land." As is well known, Eliot believed modern life had eroded the coherence of the traditional culture of the west. In the celebrated line, "These fragments I have shored against my ruins," the "one" speaks in the first person, fearing its death.[32] By juxtaposing these "fragments" with the scenes of modern life, Eliot hoped to recreate the vanished context of the tradition, to restore a structure of meaning to the chaos. In contrast, the new cut-up, Burroughs' trilogy, represents culture, norms, "the one," as a sinister control system imposed on being in the world.

In the trilogy, Burroughs creates a variety of images of a lifeworld structured by social and cultural norms. Like Heidegger and Eliot, he shows a preference for using old, vanished cultures (ancient Egypt, Celtic tribes) as authentic examples of the lifeworld context. And like Heidegger especially, he employs the temple as a figure for the meaningful context that structures and supports the lifeworld of the culture. But rather than the necessary horizon of meaning and action, here the cultural lifeworld is invariably a space of the sadistic torture and brutal repression of human bodies and capabilities. The sacred space is the place of human sacrifice: "The Druid priest emerges from the Sacred Grove, rotting bodies hang about him like Spanish moss" (*SM* 109). In this space, rituals, the shared, normative practices one performs, present the degrading spectacle of human zombies going through empty, repetitive motions flogged on by sadistic, imbecilic priest-rulers. Here the cultural lifeworld is not the authentic context of human life; cultural norms are not the source of meaning, the one is not the "realest subject" of everyday existence. Burroughs shows the cultural lifeworld as a vast charade, a "racket" played out in Egyptian, Druidic, Mayan, or Christian costume. His novels thematize a method of unmasking the racket and revealing the actual context, the true subject of embodiment. The method for exposing the cultural lifeworld is the cut-up.

A chapter of *The Soft Machine* entitled "The Mayan Caper" and consisting mostly of straight narrative, shows the protagonist traveling back in time to visit Mayan civilization at its height. He finds a lifeworld regulated by a "control system" consisting of the rhythms of agricultural labor, a developed calendar, and "a continuous round of festivals" (*SM* 90). Burroughs makes his description of the festivals (one of which involves the priests dressing up in centipede costumes and castrating sacrificial victims) an elaborate parody of the kind of ritualized practice that so often serves phenomenology as a model for human behavior in general. Disgusted by the "control system" of this lifeworld, the narrator makes tape recordings of various scenes of everyday activity. He then cuts up the tapes, splices them back together at random, and plays the result back through a "control machine" found in the largest temple. This has the effect of destroying the cultural lifeworld and revealing a repressed natural world. ("Tidal waves rolled over the Mayan control calendar" [*SM* 93].)

Burroughs compares the cultural lifeworld to a narrative. Its structure of meaning is analogous to the sequential representations of a narrative, a linear stream of code, which is opposed to the structure of the context of embodiment. This context is represented by the "surprising sense" of the cut-up. "Somebody is reading a newspaper, and his eye follows the column in the proper Aristotelian manner, one idea and sentence at a time. But subliminally he is reading the columns on either side and is aware of the person sitting next to him. That's a cut-up." The moment when one imagines that the activity of reading is restricted to "following the column" corresponds to the subject who takes the cultural lifeworld for reality. It's the same mistake: culture isn't really a context, it's a narrative. And narrative, in turn, looks a lot like cybernetic code. Processed through "control machines," this code falsifies the nature, and the subject, of experience. Thus Burroughs' rejection of culture is not a rejection of the ontological priority of context, background, or situation for a representationalist alternative. It is rather that, from his perspective, culture itself is just a sequence of representations. Heidegger and Eliot misidentify culture as context. In Burroughs' experiment, a different awareness of context propels one out of the cultural lifeworld and into reality.

The representation of temporality in "The Mayan Caper" reveals a crucial feature of Burroughs' concept of context. The phenomenological model, in identifying the subject of human existence with a set of cultural norms, has a hard time accounting for change, particularly rapid change. As Dreyfus writes, "The sociocultural background too can change gradually, as does a language, but never all at once."[33] But this emphasis on gradual change finesses the conceptual problem here. Who is the agent of change? How does change happen? Doesn't the ontology of the one preclude it from making changes? And if the one isn't making changes, then who is? Individual subjects? In his more recent writing, Dreyfus returns to this problem in ways that highlight the limitations of the theory. He suggests that individuals can experience rapid change by physically moving from one cultural context to another.[34] Here we see the return of the idea the phenomenological model was designed to overcome. A subject free to invent private meanings becomes a body free to visit different worlds.

The "Mayan control calendar," which founds a regular, cyclical temporality, represents a key feature of the cultural lifeworld for Burroughs, and recurs as a symbol of control throughout his writing. The temporality of the cut-up trilogy, in contrast, is characterized by rapid and continual change. Burroughs expressed this feature in a striking sentence from his recording "Origin and Theory of the Tape Cut-Ups": "When you cut into the present, the future leaks out." The context as Burroughs depicts it is temporally, as well as spatially, heterogeneous. The cut-up page juxtaposes moments of the distant past with moments of the distant future. Change is not gradual; this temporality isn't amenable to narrative form. The causal structure isn't the slow evolution of a language or the gradual erosion of a landscape. The subject that emerges in this context is the agent of constant, unpredictable changes that wreck the historicity, the glacial pace of change of the cultural lifeworld. The sequential time of the one belongs to the sequential narrative of a culture, while awareness of the immediate context of embodiment propels us into a novel time-space.

Burroughs' experiment tests neither the sequence of a code nor the context of a society or culture, forms that turn out to be identical for him. The scientific formalization of life processes and phenomenological embodiment are not only theoretical alternatives to Burroughs' concept, they are the historical alternatives that bound the space of possibility of literary realism in the 1960s. Marshall McLuhan demonstrates one side of this when he sees the cut-up trilogy as a mimesis of contemporary cybernetic technologies. In seeking to reestablish a culture, the authoritative examples of Eliot, Pound, and Joyce – Burroughs' predecessors in the art of juxtaposition – define the other side. By critically engaging these alternatives, Burroughs' practice marks out the near boundary of a virtual space. This space is not Burroughs' private invention. I am interested not only to show what he meant actual randomness to represent, but also to demonstrate the actuality of the virtual space he is representing, this world beyond the real world. This literary experiment shows us that when Burroughs sought to go beyond realism, it was inevitable that he would end up in *this* space. This is the outside of postwar American realism. Having defined this boundary, we can now proceed to examine the features of the space on the far side. What principle replaces cultural norms in structuring the background of action and perception? Who is the context of "right where you are sitting now"?

2.

A "spontaneous factor," represented by Burroughs' use of scissors, structures the context. This factor is the principle of juxtaposition that corresponds to the norms that place stop signs with roads and cars in the context of driving. But if the literal use of scissors stands for this still-mysterious spontaneous factor, then what do the elements of the cut-up text stand for? In one sense, of course, they follow the ordinary semantic logic of the English language. There is nothing special about Burroughs' use of language in this sense. Unlike language poets, for example, who intend to attack conventional notions of reference, Burroughs takes care to preserve the semantic coherence of his elements. Thus the "smell of carbolic soap" represents a certain sense experience; "kerosene lamp" in a cut-up sentence has the same referential structure that kerosene lamp has in this sentence. And when he says that the cut-up is a mimesis of context, he means that when he juxtaposes these elements through random operations, he represents the juxtaposition of their referents in a context of embodiment.

But there is another, virtual feature of the symbols that make up the cut-up. While one sees how a text can be cut up and rearranged, it is not so easy to see what feature of contexts of embodiment is amenable to an analogous process. To understand what the action of rearranging the elements of a novel at random stands for, we need to identify this feature. Burroughs intends the letters on the cut-up page to stand in for a different kind of symbol, one that manifests strange properties in the experimental space of the trilogy, and that, as we shall see, we misdescribe in calling a "symbol" at all.

Burroughs has no theory of language. Language in the trilogy stands for something that is not language.[35] He borrows the terms of Arthur Rimbaud's famous sonnet "Voyelles" in using colors and letters to indicate a certain symbolic quality of the objects of experience. "Vowel colors: I red / U green / E white / O blue / A black" (*SM* 136). A sequence towards the end of *The Soft Machine* gives this theme its fullest development. The pornographic content of this passage, like the constant use of smells throughout the trilogy, highlights both the context of embodiment, as well as the jarring reorganizations of that context made possible by these virtual symbols. The first half of the sequence depicts a couple meeting and having sex, divided into five sections each labeled with a color (white, black, green, red, blue), and each containing elements of the corresponding color. Then the sequence of colors repeats, but this time in a different order. The text in this second sequence has been cut-up, and manifests the usual stark juxtapositions: phrases cut from the preceding narrative and representing the couple having sex now lie next to "smell of subway dawns and turnstile. tarnished pub mirrors" (*SM* 143). The order of the color symbols has been shuffled, along with the order of the objects and actions with which the colors are associated. A recognizable context of embodiment, and a legible narrative sequence, cedes to a context that is not recognizable, and a sequence without narrative form. If the representation of cut-up in "The Mayan Caper" thematizes Burroughs' rejection of norms for a different principle, in this cut-up the symbolic colors associated with represented experience are identified as the element that enables the radical restructuring of the context.

"I red / U green / E white." We must develop our understanding of this most difficult feature of Burroughs' text by cataloging its contradictions. In the first place, these virtual symbols are not representations. They do not convey information. "I" does not represent the color red; the letter doesn't stand for the experience of the color. Neither is it analogous to a code, to information: the vowels aren't an underlying set of representations that constitute the appearance of the color. The two terms aren't distinct: the color is a symbol, and the symbol is a color. In the world of the novel, the color-vowel indicates an *additional* feature of the experience of objects. In the space opened by the cut-up novel, an object has all the features that it has in our world, and one extra feature: it is associated with a particular vowel-color. This vowel-color is that feature of things that structures their juxtaposition in the context of experience.

As we have seen, theories of embodied experience point to a thing's place in a context as what enables the thing to be experienced at all. We don't experience the world as context-free bits of information that we must continually process into meaningful wholes. In the phenomenological example, what one notices in noticing a chair is something one sits on, that belongs with tables, in rooms, in buildings. The chair is "pre-structured" in terms of its place in a meaningful context. In Burroughs the context is still the horizon of meaning, but the structural principle of the context has changed. The virtual symbols, the vowel-colors, replace the norms that structure the context for phenomenology. These symbols have a self-organizing property that Burroughs represents by using scissors to cut up pages and recombine them. As we have seen Burroughs emphasizing in the theoretical accompaniments to the cut-ups, he does not intend for us to approach these texts as a random string of letters, but as a fictional world of experience. When the "smell of soap" is juxtaposed with other words and sentences through the operation of the author's scissors, what has been created is a fictional world where now the smell of soap belongs in a bathroom, on a sink; now it belongs in a subway, next to a lamp.

The action of Burroughs' fictional symbols does the work performed in our world by norms. These virtual symbols continually structure and restructure the context in which objects appear. Unlike a language or a code, there is no grammar, no rules of combination for these symbols.[36]

They manifest an "unpredictable," "spontaneous" process of juxtaposition. The random use of scissors represents this process, a process that structures the availability of what is immediately available to experience. To say these shifting symbols do the work of norms appears contradictory. Either the world Burroughs sets up is context-dependent and norm-governed, or it is composed of iterable code and its reconfigurations are determined by formal rules of combination. The possibility of an alternative to these options depends on the nature of these strange symbols that behave like both and like neither.

To help us to better understand the shape and function of these symbols, I want to turn to a formally identical representation of a different kind of symbol in the work of F. A. Hayek. In my introduction, I briefly argued that Hayek's theory of the price system illuminates aspects of JR's economic decision-making. To approach the basic questions opened by Burroughs' experiment, I want now to return to Hayek's work more fully. In describing a purely economic world, it turns out that Hayek produces a useful description of Burroughs' fictional world.

Many readers will associate Hayek with an individualist, rights-based defense of the free market of the kind surveyed in the introduction.[37] This still-widespread association reflects the attempt by Milton Friedman and neoclassical economics to co-opt Hayek in the sixties and seventies. But careful readers of Hayek have noticed a twist in his thinking that distinguishes him rather sharply from neoclassicism. Phillip Mirowski notes that Hayek "renounced ... formal theory" but "clung to the language and metaphor of the nascent cyborg sciences."[38] "On the one hand he can sound so very modern – 'the price and market system is ... a system of communication, which passes on ... the available information that each individual needs to act, and to act rationally' – and yet, on the other, continue to treat this 'information' as something ethereal, impervious to all attempts at codification, analysis, and control, and in the end, fleetingly evanescent."[39] Mirowski is right to put "information" in scare quotes. Hayek's prices, like Burroughs' vowel-colors, are virtual symbols: they look like information and work like norms.

Hayek's project, especially in the groundbreaking essays of the late 1940s, was to analyze what would happen in a world where market prices are left to organize things without the interference of other kinds of order. His work thus belongs with Arendt's and Polanyi's as an early exploration of the prospect of what Arendt calls the "communistic fiction" of an entirely economic world.[40] Hayek's confidence in the possibility of giving this utopia a rational and coherent analysis derives from his perception of an unacknowledged capacity of the price system. For Hayek, prices can solve the problem of coordinating embodied knowledge across the human world, the problem of coordinating a kind of knowledge that cannot be formalized.[41] Hayek refers to a knowledge "which by its nature cannot enter into statistics" (UK 83). "One kind of knowledge, namely [formalized] scientific knowledge, occupies now so prominent a place in public imagination that we tend to forget that it is not the only kind that is relevant" (UK 80). There is "a body of very important but unorganized knowledge which cannot possibly be called scientific in the sense of knowledge of general rules: the knowledge of the particular circumstances of time and place" (UK 80). As with Burroughs' representation of engaged agency, Hayek is interested in knowledge that is ontologically dependent on the context of embodiment, and that cannot be taken out of that context. Knowing "how" (unlike knowing "that") cannot be translated into code and conveyed to some central planning authority that can then coordinate all the knowledge across society.

But without some way of accomplishing this coordination, the context of the individual agent will lack the structure necessary for that individual to become the agent of collectively meaningful actions and perceptions. In order for individuals to become engaged agents, the immediate context of embodiment must be structured in terms of society as a whole. "The 'man on the spot' cannot decide solely on the basis of his limited but intimate knowledge of the facts of his immediate surroundings" (UK 84). We must somehow "fit his decisions into the whole pattern of changes of the larger economic system" (UK 84). The kind of gradually evolved norms that cause a chair to show up as something to sit in across an entire culture cannot be calibrated to constantly changing conditions. The collective needs the knowledge disclosed by the context of the embodied individual. The individual needs to know what counts as collectively important, valuable, useful, or necessary. Yet the kind of knowledge the collective needs from the individual is not available in a form that can be transmitted out of the immediate context that makes it what it is. And the knowledge the individual needs from the collective doesn't exist in the centralized, systematic form that would enable it to be transmitted to the individual.

This is the economic problem for Hayek: How to prestructure the context of embodiment in terms of a collective system? How to coordinate unformalizable, context-dependent knowledge? How to make something that looks like information (a scarcity of oil in New York) do the work of a norm (oil shows up in a field in Texas as something to be extracted)?

"This problem can be solved … by the price system" (UK 85). Price "attach[es] to each kind of scarce resource a numerical index which cannot be derived from any property possessed by that particular thing, but which reflects, or in which is condensed, its significance in view of the whole means-end structure" of the human world (UK 85).

Prices place a thing in the context of the entire market without the individual having to "go explicitly through all the relations between ends and means which might possibly be affected" (UK 85). They do this not by giving individuals information about a given object of experience, a representation of how it relates to something out of the individual's immediate context, but rather, price effectively *expands* this immediate context. It does this by adding an element to an individual's experience of a thing that is connected to every other object of experience in the world. The "meaning" price conveys cannot be derived from any property of the thing itself, considered in isolation. Rather, price shows the *place* of that thing in the context of a constantly changing world. Price "places" the elements encountered in the immediate context of embodiment in terms of the context of the entire market, considered as the aggregate of all exchanges across the world. A thing with a price "shows up" in terms of its significance within this total context. Price does not represent information, it "places" things: less than, or more than, closer to or farther from, easier or harder to get, ready to hand or not ready to hand. For the individual, "it does not matter for him *why* at the particular moment more screws of one size than of another are wanted, *why* paper bags are more readily available than canvas bags … All that is significant for him is *how much more or less* difficult to procure they have become compared with other things" (UK 84).

"The most significant fact about this system is the economy of knowledge with which it operates, or how little the individual participants need to know in order to be able to take the right action" (UK 86). When, in the context of an activity of making, the price of one element rises, something else might now show up as taking the place of the scarce item. This happens without any part of the process becoming explicit anywhere, to anyone. "The whole structure of activities tends to adapt, through these partial and fragmentary signals, to conditions foreseen by and known to no individual."[42] This novel form of temporality is generated by the principle that structures the context. "Cut into the present [and] the future leaks out." The central elements of Hayek's description of a world ordered by the quasi-symbol of price can be applied to the fictional world ordered by Burroughs' quasi-symbolic vowel-colors. At every moment in the trilogy the "spontaneous factor" coordinating all the vowel-colors shuffles the context to yield the next, unpredictable configuration. Nothing is left to norms, to the one. Burroughs' experiment shows objects of experience that have been imbued with this strange symbol. The context of embodiment is ordered by these symbols.

For Hayek, price structures the context in the same way the body structures up-down orientation; it juxtaposes things, brings things nearer or moves them farther away in relation to other things, associates a thing now with this purpose and now with that purpose. We can construct our own small economic fiction to demonstrate how this might work. When oil becomes scarce in the Middle East, price makes gas harder for me to get in Ann Arbor. I might not know why gas is more difficult to get. But I will simply and immediately see that it is. What feature of gas makes it harder to get? What feature connects the gas before me to the oil in the Middle East, the refining plants in the gulf, and the gas before every other human body? The price attached to it. That price connects it to all these other things. Depending on how all those things change, price makes it easier or harder for me to get. If it makes it really hard to get, something else (a bicycle, perhaps) might show up as associated with the job of getting me to my office. It's not that cost causes me to juggle between things for which I have already developed preferences. It's that before I see the price, I simply don't know how much or whether I want the gas or the bike.[43] Price determines my relation to things. By making something easier or harder to use than something else, it associates a thing now with this purpose, now with that purpose.

At one price, a tank of gas is easy for me to get, my sense of distance shrinks, the SUVs at the auto-dealer draw my eye, bikes and walking disappear. At another price, gas becomes associated with some rare and unusual use, or it disappears altogether. Walking, tennis shoes, used bikes show up, my sense of distance changes. Perhaps I work as an engineer, and in the lab, the high price of gas illuminates interesting properties of hydrogen batteries that I never really noticed before. The determination of my relation to gas, the association of gas with this or that use, the formation of my desire for SUVs or bikes, the shaping of my interest in hydrogen cells, doesn't occur either in my head or in society. It occurs in the price system.

For Hayek, price is "a kind of symbol," "An index," "Reflects, or it condenses." Hayek doesn't quite know what term to use to describe this curious symbol. Like Burroughs' vowel-colors, it is a *feature of the immediate experience of a thing*, not a representation of the thing experienced. This feature has special properties. All the vowel-colors are submitted to the same "spontaneous factor." The change of one price is coordinated with the changes of every other price. The "indications" of price "are at the same time the resultant of, and the guide for, all the individual decisions" made across the whole society.[44] The spontaneous coordination of prices means that a decision made in place A defines the context, "guides" and forms the intention, of a decision made in place B. Insofar as everything that shows up in the immediate context show up with a price, the immediate context of the body is also the total context of the collective.

The "who" of this context, the subject of embodiment, is collective. This undoes the epochal modern split between individual intentions and the collective effect of actions first articulated by Adam Smith and repeated by contemporary neoclassical economic realism. Here, no invisible hand is needed to turn private vice into public good, to coordinate private intentions with systematic effects. This crucial aspect of Hayek's thought has not been adequately recognized in the literature. Recall the two parts of Hayek's economic question. The first part asks: How can individuals' knowledge of their immediate context be communicated to the collective? The second part asks: How can the collective knowledge individuals need to make sense of their immediate context be communicated to them? The collective is incomplete without the embodied knowledge of the engaged agent carried by the price system. Individual perception and knowledge is incomplete without the collective knowledge carried by the price system. Committed to a Cartesian model of the individual subject, the vast literature on Hayek has focused primarily on the first part of his question. Knowledge is created by private individuals. It is then circulated through the collective by the price system. But by asking only how the price system coordinates the knowledge of separate individuals, they often miss Hayek's account of the way price shapes individual knowledge. This has led many writers to identify a "Hayek problem" in that sometimes Hayek seems committed to individual subjectivity, while at other times he appears to leave no role for the individual agent.

But there is no Hayek problem. He describes a new form of individual subjectivity, one in which the price system plays a basic role in framing individual knowledge and perception. As in the phenomenological model, intention here is immediately collective in the prestructuring of the context of the engaged agent. But the principle of this prestructuring isn't a set of norms; the collective subject isn't projected into the third person. Here society perceives, thinks, and acts in the first person. In Hayek's model, price is not an "objective" measure which individual subjects use to make calculations.[45] Similarly, in Burroughs' model, vowel-colors are not a set of representations to be decoded by individual subjects. The spontaneous organization of these quasi-symbols is the structure of subjectivity itself.[46]

Hayek's account of price provides us with a good description of Burroughs' vowel-colors. But why is this? What is the relation of the social scientist to the writer of fiction? The theory and practice of literary criticism suggests three possible forms of this relation. (1) Hayek provides an accurate description of how prices actually work, and thus an accurate description of the actual economic context of Burroughs' fiction. (2) The social context inhabited by both Hayek and Burroughs is characterized by an ideological account of how price works, which both writers exemplify. (3) Hayek has an interestingly unusual or original account of price, and Burroughs is influenced by Hayek's thought.

But Hayek's work is relevant here for none of these reasons. While Gibson, Acker, and others will place the trilogy's innovations in the service of explicitly economic fictions, Burroughs never identifies his vowel-colors with price. What we confront here is the intersection of (1) an organizational mode derived from pressures immanent to literary form and complete with literary (Rimbaud) predecessors, with (2) an organizational mode derived from an economist's observation of the price system, and his imagination of how price would operate if given total scope to order the human world.

It would be tempting to understand this intersection as the response on the part of two different writers to a feature of the world shared by both. The actual price system, the ubiquity of market exchange that has seemed to writers from Marx to Simmel to be the great modern fact, lies before both Burroughs and Hayek as an object of interest. One might suggest that *actual* features of the price system account for the resemblances in the *virtual* ways Hayek and Burroughs imagine their quasi-symbols working. Given basic, readily observable features of the actual price system – such as the way it connects a thing in one place with a thing in another, or how it arranges things in terms of the difficulty of getting them – one can see how these features *would* work *if* they were set to work organizing experience. So one might argue that Burroughs and Hayek are both, in their different ways, following the actual price system to a kind of logical conclusion.

But there is another, perhaps ultimately more plausible way to approach this problem. I just sketched out how one might erase the difference between the economist and the novelist by describing their imaginative engagement with a shared environment. But one might instead see their work as fundamentally circumscribed by the boundaries of their respective discourses. Hayek is concerned with economic problems; Burroughs, with literary problems. Their unexpected intersection in an identical organizational model would then not provide evidence of a concern that transcends disciplinary boundaries. Rather, the juxtaposition of Hayek and Burroughs would provide evidence of how two separate, immanently evolving discourses happen to arrive at identity and compatibility. The postwar fusion of the economic and the literary – a fusion we've explored in Gaddis and O'Hara, and will soon study in Acker and rap – would then not be caused by any actual social or economic conditions. Rather, this fusion would have two causes: a literature that refers primarily to earlier literature, and an economics that refers primarily to earlier economics. While *caused* by dynamics immanent to these discourses, the fusion made possible by the new compatibility of the economic and the literary could nonetheless come to have social *effects* by circulating a fascinating new image of collective life.

I will return to these issues in my conclusion. For now, we can see that the peculiar formal identity of Hayek's prices and Burroughs' vowel-colors points to developments not perceptible in the vicinity of the works with explicit economic content explored in my other chapters. We can understand this relation through either of the alternatives sketched above. But I think the simple fact of the formal identity of the two writers' systems enables us to alter our sense of the status of the trilogy. By reading Hayek next to the cut-ups, we can see the extent to which Burroughs' literary experiment constitutes a *discovery* rather than an *invention*. He is showing us something that is there to be seen by others, something that has in fact been seen by others, in different places, with different tools. At the risk of putting too much pressure on the scientific metaphor traditionally applied to avant-garde writing, I will suggest that the results of Burroughs' experiment have been reproduced by an independent investigator. The principle of order tested in the cut-up trilogy defines the trajectory of thought as it leaves the bounds of postwar actuality. In postwar America, this order isn't what we can't get outside of; it is the outside of where we are.

3.

To find an adequate figure for the collective subject of his fictional order, Burroughs obsessively returns to the passage in "The Waste Land" depicting the journey of the disciples to Emmaus.

Who is the third who walks always beside you?
When I count, there are only you and I together
But when I look ahead up the white road
There is always another one walking beside you
Gliding wrapt in a brown mantle, hooded
I do not know whether a man or a woman
–But who is that on the other side of you?[47]

Who is on the other side of you? Who is on the other side of "you" and "I," on the other side of the one? Who is the subject of the virtual world that lies on the other side of our world? Burroughs cites this passage in many places and in many forms. He titled the book containing his most extensive theoretical writing on the cut-up method *The Third Mind*. In the trilogy itself, this passage is cut-up and folded into the sections representing "right where you are sitting now," becoming a key element of the experiment's auto-thematization. "Who is the third that walks beside you to a stalemate of black lagoons and violet light?" (*SM* 37) "Forgotten shadow actor walks beside you" (*SM* 61). "Someone walking – won't be two" (*TTE* 47).

In Burroughs, the relation between individuals, between bodies, is a "third mind."[48] Subjectivity here is not a matter of private beliefs that may or may not be shared, may or may not be communicated or argued. As we have seen, the basis of the "who" of the context of embodiment represented by the cut-up is a process of auto-coordination defining the place, meaning, and being of things in the world. This process is the structure of virtual subjectivity, the ontology of virtual mind. Burroughs takes the "hooded" image of the resurrected Christ in Eliot's poem as a figure of this mind. Like Burroughs' own pseudonym, "El Hombre Invisible," the subject of "right where you are sitting now" is invisible.[49] Invisibility is an essential feature of this subject, part of its being. The subject cannot be taken as an object by any other subject simply because there is no other subject. Intelligence is not mine, or yours, or ours. In this context, the subject of my action, the agent of my agency, is immediately collective.

The difference between the individual subjects of intersubjectivity and the singular, collective "who" of the cut-up is also a difference between language and the quasi-symbol that language stands for in the trilogy. Burroughs distinguishes the spontaneous order of the vowel-colors from what he calls "the noxious human inter language."[50] Like Plath and Laing, Burroughs sees in the intersubjective relation the elemental principle of control, oppression, domination. The linear narrative of the cultural life-world, the interpellating discourse of advertising, the subjecting of bodies by state power: all these forms are variants of the "word lines" stretched between individual subjects. To take one of many examples, the trilogy depicts an alien organization, "Trak," half corporation, half shadow government, that employs the "word lines" of intersubjectivity as bonds to subordinate and control individuals. "SMOKE TRAK CIGARETTES. THEY LIKE YOU. TRAK LIKE ANY YOU. ANY TRAK LIKE YOU" (*SM* 39).[51]

The intersubjective form of address of the advertisement is alien to the spontaneous ordering of Burroughs' vowel-colors. Control is founded on these alien, intersubjective "word lines." Looking back at postwar reality from the perspective of the fictional space inhabited by the trilogy, Burroughs says, "I feel that the change, the mutation in consciousness, will occur spontaneously once certain pressures now in operation are removed. I feel that the principal instrument of monopoly and control that prevents expansion of consciousness is the word lines controlling thought, feeling, and apparent sensory impressions of the human host."[52] Intersubjectivity is not natural, but an "instrument of monopoly and control"; "inter language" is an alien attempt to twist the spontaneous order of the vowel-colors into word lines between subjects.

Humanity has become the host of the parasitic, viral logic of intersubjectivity introduced by malevolent outsiders, alternately and interchangeably figured as the state or as aliens. As in "The Mayan Caper," humanity recovers the true context, and the true human subject, from the alien imposition of the "noxious human inter language" through the cut-up method. "Cut word lines, cut time lines ... Cut the Trak Service Lines" (*SM* 39–40). A particularly memorable cut-up in *The Ticket that Exploded* thematizes this process. Burroughs cuts up a series of popular love song lyrics with his own texts and "The Waste Land": "Love skin on a bicycle built for two-like a deflated balloon – your cool hands on his naked dollars, baby – You were meant for me ... someone walking – Won't be two" (*TTE* 48–49). Here the me-you lines of the love lyric are cut up and cut into the third mind. The self-coordinating order of Burroughs' virtual symbols replaces the "word lines" of a "noxious human inter language."[53]

What is striking is that the trilogy's representation of mind makes it look as if there can be no natural explanation of intersubjectivity. By contrast, the kind of auto-coordination envisioned by Burroughs and by Hayek has traditionally been seen as an alternative to genuine cooperation. The classic example is Adam Smith's account of the market as a self-organizing system. As Smith wrote in 1776, "[The individual driven by self-interest] intends only his own gain, and he is in this, as in many other cases, led by an invisible hand to promote an end which was no part of his intention."[54] This sense of a basic split between the individual's intention and the systematic effects of that intention continues to structure so influential an account of the market in postwar literature and thought as Frederic Jameson's, who writes that the impersonal market process "replaces human decisions," and that the market cannot be a "collective project."[55]

In contrast to these traditional accounts of self-organization, in the literary order set up in the virtual space of the trilogy there is no trace of the split between human decision and impersonal process, between coordination and cooperation. Jurgen Habermas provides perhaps the most famous contemporary account of this split when he describes what happens when language gets replaced by a different "kind of symbol," money. For Habermas, there are "two forms of integrating action contexts, one that takes effect, so to speak, with the consciousness of actors and is present as a lifeworld background, whereas the other silently penetrates right through actors' orientations."[56] He contrasts cooperative "communicative action" through language with the "objective" adjustment of actions through money and the market. Habermas opposes the "objective harmony of action plans – as in the case of the market" to "the possibility that the *subjects themselves* undertake to harmonize their plans, as is the case with language as a medium of reaching understanding."[57] Thus when money "replace[s] mutual understanding in language as a mechanism of co-ordination," an objective organization of actions replaces the cooperation of different intentional agents.[58] Individual intentions still exist in the market order, but they are cut off from the systematic coordination of actions, and imprisoned as a reflexive self-interest with no way of reaching the other. We find here an echo of the distinction between cybernetic order and cultural lifeworld when Habermas discusses "the division between intentional and non-intentional action co-ordination" in terms of "the separation between a system and a lifeworld perspective."[59] The ethical, norm-governed use of language organizes the lifeworld. Money, conceived of as a formalized, systematic code, has "the effect of uncoupling interaction from lifeworld contexts."[60] True collectivity, cooperation, and the coordination of intentions are accomplished through language; the systematic, objective coordination of actions in the market runs on money.

This opposition disappears for Burroughs and Hayek. In their texts, self-interest and an interest in the collective cannot be separated; there is no need for an invisible hand to reconcile "private vice" with "public good." These quasi-symbols are not an objective code penetrating through individual intentions. *The spontaneous coordinating action of these quasi-symbols is the ontological basis of intention itself.* In prestructuring the immediate context of embodiment in terms of the entire human world, Burroughs' vowel-colors and Hayek's prices undo a string of oppositions fundamental to the order of postwar realism: language/money, intention/effect, cooperation/coordination, socialism/capitalism, lifeworld/system, collective/individual, embodied/cybernetic.

Here intersubjectivity is not an alternative to collective coordination. Intersubjectivity is insubstantial, or as Burroughs writes, it is a "veil" thrown over human perception, action, and thought. It is a veil thrown over the true nature of mind. When the phantom "word lines" that run between illusory individual subjects are cut, "you will begin to see sharp and clear" (*TTE* 209). The "word lines," the "noxious human inter language," are a ruse, a trick cooked up on some "control machine" that cuts off experience from reality. "There was a grey veil between you and what you saw or more often did not see that grey veil was the prerecorded words of a control machine once that veil is removed you will see clearer and sharper ... whatever you do you will do it better" (*TTE* 209). When cut-up, the "unpredictable magic" of the real context appears, and we undergo a "physiological liberation" as the poison is purged from the experience of embodiment (*TTE* 208).

From a perspective lodged in fictional space, Burroughs gazes back at the social world, developing an elaborate critique of contemporary conditions.[61] Critics such as David Lodge have noted and deplored the curious didacticism of this critique, which almost completely dominates *Nova Express*. And compared with the passages exhibiting the virtual dynamics of the cut-up that provide the trilogy's chief interest, these didactic sections can seem dull and repetitive. But this material fascinates less for its content than for the relation its existence proves. The disruptive energies feared by Arendt and Polanyi vibrate in the relation between the virtual space of the cut-ups and the actual space of postwar America. In the didactic passages of *Nova Express*, Burroughs tries to show us the deep contradictions, the malevolent, viral codes, and the immanent promise of a reality flooded by virtual light. One might want to locate the value of this literary form in the content of the social critique it makes available. But I find it hard to do this. The details of what Burroughs sees in the social world grow dim and distant compared with the alien, impossible light he sees by.

CHAPTER 4

Blood money: sovereignty and exchange in Kathy Acker

> I thought that, one day, maybe, there'ld be a human society in a world which is beautiful, a society which wasn't just disgust.
>
> –Kathy Acker (*ES* 227)

I.

In 1989, as the institutions of an earlier radicalism began to crumble in Eastern Europe, Kathy Acker reflected on her sense of the possibility of a new radical literature. "Perhaps our society is now in a 'post-cynical' phase. Certainly, I thought as I started *Empire*, there's no more need to deconstruct, to take apart perceptual habits, to reveal the frauds on which our society's living. We now have to find somewhere to go, a belief, a myth. Somewhere real."[1] In that novel, Acker represents this "movement from no to yes" as the transformation of terrorists into pirates. The scene of this transformation is a multinational, posthistorical Paris, a city where forms of domination and oppression from every period, from slavery to a futuristic form of mind control, are wielded by shadowy masters against the alienated and dispossessed multitude. This is a world where "the right-wing owns values and meanings," where every aspect of society, every form of social relation, has been infiltrated and thoroughly polluted by a malevolent, multiform sovereignty (*ES* 73). The oppressed masses, represented by Acker as the postcolonial Algerians, turn to terrorism in protest against these conditions, "arrang[ing] for the poisoning of every upper-middle and upper-class apartment in Paris" (*ES* 77). The blank nihilism of these terrorists, who advance no positive program but seek only "to kill the city of perfection," anticipates Michael Hardt and Antonio Negri's description of contemporary Islamic terrorism not as the attempt to re-create a premodern world, but rather as a "powerful refusal" of sovereignty.[2] The Algerians' goal is not to reform society, but to enact a total refusal of the social order: law, family, religion, even language. But unlike Hardt and Negri's fundamentalist bombers, for Acker's Algerians this is only the beginning; "revolutions usually begin by terrorism" (*ES* 75). Once the social norms and rules that hosted an oppressive sovereignty have broken down, no new structures are proposed; instead the Algerians' revolution rapidly assumes the character of a corporation engaged in an anarchic version of capitalist competition, a pure war for ownership. Nihilistic refusal cedes to a new, positive motive: "The Algerians had taken over Paris so they would own something" (*ES* 83). In a radical inversion of the socialist vision, Acker's Paris is reborn not as a society without a market, but as a market without a society.

At first, this doesn't look like a happy ending. But throughout Acker's late work free-market profiteers, operating outside and in defiance of society, appear as the specters of a radical liberation from a postmodern society of control. When "sovereignty, be it reigning or revolutionary, disappear[s] ... all my dreams ... would be shattered. 'And then,' the fortune-teller said, 'you'll find yourself on a pirate ship.'"[3] For Acker, the pirate is the revolutionary avatar of an entirely economic world, with the free market imagined as the open sea, the horizon of the possible. Subjective desire is freed from any limit but the economic, and all interpersonal relations become market relations: "They're on the march; as much as they ever do anything together; they're after booty. Ownership."[4] Acker's vision of a pirate ship as the "myth and the place" of a new radical literature reflects her realization, "as I put these texts together ... that the hippies had been mistaken: they had thought that they could successfully oppose American post-capitalism by a lie, by creating a utopian society."[5] By 1989, the sad failures of the "hippies," from her old teacher Herbert Marcuse to the elderly children in the Kremlin, prove "it is impossible ... to live in a hypothetical, not utopian but perhaps free, society if one does not actually inhabit such a world. One must be where one is."[6]

Early in *Empire of the Senseless* Acker develops a creation myth for piracy that reveals her sense of where we are, and where we can go. In the sixteenth century, she writes, there was a halt to all national wars, and when the soldiers of the various nations turned to piracy "the modern economic world began" (*ES* 26).[7] "Being free of both nationalistic and religious concerns and restrictions, privateering's only limitation was economic. Piracy was the most anarchic form of private enterprise" (*ES* 26). The end of national wars also brought an end to the "credo of those who are liberals," that "*Human beings are good by nature*," and allowed the vast private and anarchic war of the market to begin, the "hope of all begetting and pleasures. For the rich and especially for the poor ... the mirror of our sexuality" (*ES* 26). In the context of the novel this story tells the characters both where they are, and how they can get there. The free market with its fabulous possibilities already exists, but it is covered over by the tentacles of the society of control, the "concerns and restrictions" of a sinister sovereignty that has penetrated and polluted all social relations. The "hippies" had failed to see that "sovereignty, [whether it be] reigning or revolutionary," is the real threat to freedom; they had also failed to see the possibilities of an alternative to any form of sovereignty. A world that is the "mirror of our sexuality," where there is "no limit but the economic," remains just below the surface.

Acker's vision of the market as the "myth and the place" of a new American literature emerges at a time when the resurgent free-market discourse in the west received what appeared to be its ultimate vindication with the worldwide collapse of the alternative of state communism. Some of the tenets of what Milton Friedman calls "true radicalism" resonate with Acker's fable: the free market is the best of possible worlds, the space of real individual freedom and happiness, and it must be protected from totalitarian impulses of all kinds. However, the new laissez-faire movement also embraced a range of commitments, from the statism and traditionalism that famously accompanied the Adam Smith neckties of the Reagan revolution, to the enlightenment model of the individual subject characteristic of its libertarian wing, that Acker sees as extensions of the multiform sovereignty opposing freedom. Her commitment to the "most anarchic form of private enterprise" is total, unlike partisans of the new right for whom fundamental values are not subject to the market, but are guaranteed by a variety of autonomous social spaces such as religion, the family, and the state. At stake in these differences are opposing conceptions of the market itself. On the one hand is an image of the market subordinated to and restrained by various noneconomic rules and values; on the other is the vision of a radically free market. After 1989, right versus left becomes, in Acker's terms, sovereignty versus piracy. This opposition emerges most clearly as two ways of thinking about money.

If at one time everyone was a Keynesian, by 1989 it seemed as if everyone was a monetarist. This shift from an emphasis on fiscal policy to the "scientific" manipulation of interest rates as a means of imposing balance on market fluctuations was accompanied by rhetoric proclaiming a return to the free market, and the final victory of the invisible hand over the meddling fingers of social planners. But the claim that this was a radical change amounting to the abandonment of political control over the market was challenged by those who saw it merely as a change of the form of state control, and accused its sponsors of a false and dangerous understanding of the nature of money in capitalist society. After winning the Nobel Prize in 1974, F. A. Hayek emerged as the most prominent of the critics of monetarism, declaring money is the "loose joint" in contemporary economics. In 1976, a year before the monetarist policies he despised were officially adopted by the Federal Reserve Bank, Hayek famously proposed that "government should be deprived of its monopoly of the issue of money," and money creation should be opened to the free market by allowing the circulation of private currencies.[8] As John Gray notes in his study of Hayek, this radical proposal follows directly from Hayek's belief that "money is not the sort of social object that we can define precisely or control comprehensively."[9] The attempt to abstract macroeconomic processes from their microeconomic foundations in actual exchanges between individuals, epitomized by the monetarists' attempt to stabilize the economy by controlling the creation of money, is fraught with methodological and epistemological dangers. He draws a distinction between the concept of an "economy," such as the finances of an individual organization, and the "catallaxy," the aggregate of all the exchanges across a society. For Hayek, as Gray writes, "The demand that the domain of human exchange taken as a whole should be subject to purposive planning is, therefore, the demand that social life be reconstructed in the character ... of an authoritarian organization."[10] It is impossible to achieve the kind of rational control imagined by both the monetarists and the Keynesians they replace since the "tacit knowledge" embodied in actual microeconomic choices is of a different kind than the systematic knowledge derived from these choices. In fact, for Hayek it is the government's control of money creation that prevents the "spontaneous order" which would otherwise obtain across the catallaxy by alienating money from the market, from the actual exchanges between individuals.

This sense of money as the "loose joint," the alien and alienating factor in the economy, is also central to contemporary leftist critiques of the new free-market ideology. In *Empire*, Hardt and Negri advance the paradoxical concept of "capitalist sovereignty" against claims that the rise of globalism and the decline of fiscal intervention by governments herald a world market truly free of the constraints of sovereignty. No longer taking the form of a transcendent power that rules from above and is localized in the institutions of the nation-state, postmodern sovereignty has become immanent to the processes and exchanges of contemporary life. It rules from within, and is more oppressive and omnipresent than ever before. For Hardt and Negri, the monetary regime is a principal example of "capitalist sovereignty." "Money is the second global means of absolute control … Monetary mechanisms are the primary means to control the market."[11] Here it is not the market itself that is the problem, but the "control of the market" secured by control of the money. Importantly, exchange-value in itself is not implicated in capitalist sovereignty; the authors argue that the disappearance of the use-value/exchange-value opposition is an inescapable and politically neutral fact of postmodernism.[12] Sovereignty enters into market processes through the imprisonment of exchange-value in the form of legal tender. The global monetary regime arises not in response to the market's needs, as the monetarists claim, but as its ruler: the new "monetary construction [is] based purely on the political necessities of Empire."[13] In a situation where oppressive power is defined by the new immanence of sovereignty to economic life, their separation begins to look like a revolutionary goal. This leads them to reverse the traditional leftist stance and ask, "Why should that slogan ['big government is over'] be the exclusive property of the conservatives? … Where would capital be without a big government capable of printing money to produce and reproduce a global order that guarantees capitalist power and wealth?"[14] Unlike the old socialists, for the new revolutionaries the source of the oppressive global order is not in market processes per se, but in the pollution and corruption of those processes by sovereignty.

Michael Shapiro, in his book *Reading "Adam Smith,"* is even more explicit in taking money, as opposed to the market exchanges it mediates, as the real problem. He celebrates the progressive and liberated character of "the Smithian individual," who "is not the sovereign, self-contained owner or author of actions, but, rather, a dynamic, reflective, immanently social system of symbolic exchanges."[15] This individual is poisoned not by the exploitative character of the system of exchanges, but by the money that regulates it from within. Shapiro focuses on money's abstract character, citing Don DeLillo's description in *Players* (1977) of "the paring away of money's accidental properties, of money's touch" as a metaphor for how Adam Smith's vision of an "immanently social system of symbolic exchanges" is transformed into an alienating code.[16] Quoting Jean-Joseph Goux, Shapiro describes money as "depersonalizing exchange," and transforming exchange relations into "rather abstract relations between positions."[17] In a telling moment, Shapiro contrasts this process to "tribal" exchange relations that "were connected so closely with intersubjectivities that there were actual exchanges of body substances accompanying the exchange of goods."[18] Individuals in this model "do not have their reciprocity deferred through money which ... depersonalizes exchange."[19] This sense of the abstraction of money from actual exchange relations and its identification with shadowy agents of control is precisely what Hayek wishes to overcome with his radical call for the replacement of legal tender by privately printed money. By removing the "loose joint" in the system we fold the monetarists' economy back into the catallaxy, revealing "a whole society [that is] more like a forest than it is like any organization."[20] Hayek, as Gray notes, "in no way claims to be able to predict the forms in which private money creation will develop," confident that the "result will surpass anything that the conscious contrivance of social life can achieve."[21]

Kathy Acker imagines this form as blood money. "The trading arena, the market, is my blood. My body is open to all people: this is democratic capitalism. Today pleasure lies in the flow of blood" (*ES* 55). Her fictional combination of blood and money erases Shapiro's distinction between the immediacy of "tribal" exchange and the universal value-form of free market exchange, enabling Acker to imagine the human world as a market without an outside. For Acker, as for Hayek, value is not objectively measurable; it attains stability through the "spontaneous order" of the catallaxy, which both writers describe in metaphors drawn from nature and biology. Individual exchanges are the microeconomic cells of the catallaxy. Interference with the functioning of this market, any attempt to administer market relations, is for Acker, as it is for Hayek, a transparent effort to "demand that social life be reconstructed in the character of a factory, an army, or a business corporation – in the character, in other words, of an authoritarian organization."[22] The authoritarian impulse takes many forms in her late novels: traditional morality, the nuclear family, gender identity, the police. But the form of control most feared by Acker, and most revealing of her commitments, is represented as the attempt of a government agency to pollute the bloodstream and disrupt the exchange and flow of blood by introducing an alien code, a virus into it. In *Empire of the Senseless* once the Algerians turn themselves into pirates, establishing a society where there is "no limit but the economic," they tell the deposed rulers "no longer will you work ... creating herpes and AIDS," and "by doing so controlling all union" (*ES* 71). Of course, in the real world AIDS can be seen as corrupting or preventing union, but the special horror of the virus as a governmental instrument of *controlling* union depends on a fictional context where blood is money. In this image of legal tender as conspiracy, Hayek's concern with private money is reproduced by Acker's concern with pure blood. What is at stake is the possibility of a radically free market, "the most anarchic form of private enterprise," where universal values and undistorted forms of exchange are founded within rather than without the body, and where free individuals encounter no "limit but the economic."

2.

In *In Memoriam to Identity*, Acker writes: "People either do what they're told or they go outside the law, find something else, maybe themselves" (*IM* 155). Transgression is central to Acker's work and operates at all levels of her novels, from the trademark obscenity of her style to the criminality of her characters. Acker's critics have noticed the rigorous consistency of this transgression, directed, as in the quote above, at "law" rather than specific laws, at society rather than certain social norms. Larry McCaffery, for example, argues that her texts "are designed to force a confrontation between readers and *all* conventions."[23] Acker conceives the "mythic" project of her late novels as an attempt "to find a way to live in taboo," to imagine a collective space without any conventions at all.[24] Frederic Jameson's description of utopic novels as imagining "a mechanism" that "neutralize[s] what blocks freedom" is appropriate to the scope of transgression in Acker's late work.[25] The novels are an assemblage of transgressive gestures; various, disjunctive scenarios set up norms so they can be immediately violated, and the repetition of these gestures across the text constitutes a method, a "way to live in taboo," and a means of rejecting every form of sovereignty, every limit and control imposed on human life. Like Hayek, who imagines that the destruction of artificial controls over the market will reveal "a whole society that is more like a forest than it is like any organization," Acker represents "liv[ing] in taboo" as a way of recuperating a repressed nature.[26] In escaping from the law, you find something, maybe yourself; when every form of sovereignty disappears, "you'll find yourself on a pirate ship." Sovereignty constitutes alienated relations, it blocks natural relations. In these novels revolt is consistently figured as a purification, as a return, a rediscovery of "nature" as a spontaneous system of exchanges and flows between individuals. Two related themes, Acker's treatment of the incest taboo and her celebration of masochism, show her transgressive machine in action, cutting away the malignant apparatus of sovereignty and revealing the positive and natural freedom of the market underneath.

The taboo on sex with one's relatives is the mark of the alienated society for Acker, the original prohibition from which the social systems of a sovereign culture develop. In a late essay, Acker underlined the importance of incest to the central event in *Empire*: "When the Algerians take over Paris, I have a society not defined by the oedipal taboo."[27] Acker thinks of her myth as representing a world where the incest taboo does not exist, and much of the sexuality in the novels is incestuous. Abhor's most important sexual relationship is with her father, while Capitol (the "translation" of Faulkner's Caddy) has her only fulfilling sex with her brother Quentin. Though Abhor at times deeply resents and flees from her father's advances while Capitol actively pursues Quentin, the absence of the incest taboo is constitutive of both characters' view of the world.

Acker's sense that incest constitutes a radical move "outside the law" derives from an anthropological discourse that sees the incest taboo as central to the formation of society itself. In Claude Levi-Strauss' famous formulation, the incest taboo is the "fundamental step because of which, by which, but above all in which, the transition from nature to culture is accomplished."[28] In his account, a man's desire for the closest woman is tempered by the group's refusal "to sanction the natural inequality of the distribution of the sexes within the family."[29] Society emerges with this appropriation of a valuable and scarce resource for the common good; the circumscribing of the individual's desire forms the basis for a system of reciprocity Levi-Strauss sees as fundamental to developing social ties. "The woman whom one does not take ... is, for that very reason, offered up ... The prohibition ... is instituted only in order to guarantee and establish, directly or indirectly, immediately or mediately, an exchange."[30] Thus in limiting the range of possible partners, the use-value of a woman as "natural stimulant" is transformed into a "sign" in general circulation, and this process defines the "transformation from nature to culture."[31] Levi-Strauss goes on to claim that "it is thus the same with women as with the currency," which resembles "the action of the needle ... weaving in and out" of the disparate "closed systems" of families into a "social fabric."[32]

Feminist anthropologists have criticized this view of the incest taboo as initiating exchange by transforming women into the first legal tender. Gayle Rubin, a member of the SAMOIS[33] group with whom Acker was affiliated earlier in her career, attempts a feminist revision of Levi-Strauss in her influential essay "The Traffic in Women." For Rubin "it would be a dubious proposition at best to argue that if there were no exchange of women there would be no culture," no exchange of any kind.[34] Rather, what is important about Levi-Strauss' analysis of the incest taboo is that it "enables us to isolate sex and gender from 'mode of production,' and to counter a certain tendency to explain sex oppression as a reflex of economic forces."[35] The incest taboo demonstrates the separability of exchange from what Rubin calls (interchangeably) "the sex-gender system" or the "kinship system," which has "no economic function," and can therefore be dispensed with independently. The crucial difference between Levi-Strauss and Rubin is that Levi-Strauss understands taboo as the necessary precondition for economic relations, while Rubin sees the incest prohibition, and the complex social systems deriving from it, as fundamentally extrinsic to exchange. For Rubin, as for Acker, the sex-gender system is inaugurated by a taboo, while the market is not. When she describes herself as representing a society not bound by taboo, Acker opposes the artificial limitations of the social world to the free market, "piracy," where there is "no limit but the economic." Economic limitations are of a different kind from social limitations; the latter are the arbitrary distinctions of a nightmarish sovereignty, whereas the former define the space of relationality itself, and the borders of human reality.

We can observe the distance of Acker's view of nature from traditional, conservative conceptions in the force of her insistence that the family structure comes after the market, and constitutes a kind of regulation imposed on it. In removing the incest taboo from her mythic society, Acker imagines that the weeds of sovereignty can be pulled out by their roots. By representing an exchange economy that continues to function in the absence of the original sovereign command, her novels naturalize the exchange process. Thus in *Pussy*, incest marks "the beginning of the world of pirates."[36] "Incest begins this world" by separating exchange from the sex/gender system, and inaugurating the entirely economic world of piracy. For Acker, we don't need to prevent incest in order to have currency; in fact we don't need to do anything at all. The process of transforming nature into currency has always already taken place, and a circuit of exchange flows between people without the mediation of limits, disciplines, and rules.

This impulse to remove artificial regulations and systemizations from a free and natural, "spontaneous" system of exchange informs Acker's understanding of the individual. In *In Memoriam to Identity*, one of the characters, a prostitute, dismally reflects on her prospects for a new life in terms that illuminate Acker's reworking of the categories of purity and impurity: "Perhaps I had become too polluted, not down there [sexually], but socially ... to be pure, *even down there in the blood*" (*IM* 133). Images of the bloodstream infiltrated and polluted by social codes haunt Acker's late work; liberation from the insidious web of social control is figured as a purification of the blood, and the restoration of a natural, true self. But if Acker's emphasis on the purity of blood implies an authentic identity that transcends the social order, her equation of blood with money situates this identity within the flux and continuous circulation of the market. Although "blood is who I am" (*IM* 117) my blood is never really mine. Acker wants an authentic identity that makes potent claims against alienation and assimilation, and works as a site of resistance to social disciplines. However, her commitment to the market as a natural social order based on universal and uninhibited exchange inspires a fear of any identity that might limit the kinds of exchanges available to the subject. The ideal qualities of the market actor – freedom of choice, the ability to keep all options open, and unfettered desire – come into conflict with the structuring limitations of stable identities. Acker writes of "individualism as the closing down of energy," while celebrating radical individual freedom from social norms.[37] She seems to endorse a biological essentialism ("blood is who I am"), even as she suggests that the relevant body is the collective body of the market ("the market is my blood") (*ES* 55).

A passage early in *Empire of the Senseless* illustrates this dynamic tension between authentic identity and exchangeable blood. A certain "Dr. Schreber" analyzes the protagonist, Thivai, who listens intently, thinking, "finally perhaps I'd learn something about myself" (*ES* 31). The good doctor points to the subject's evident masochism as the key to his true identity, when Thivai interrupts him: "I don't give a damn … about psychology. About myself … Psychology and my psychology's a dead issue … All I want to know from you is what you want from me … Because, for me, desire and pain're the same" (*ES* 32). Thivai's desire to "learn something about myself" is replaced by the desire "to know from you what you want from me." The doctor is mistaken in thinking of his masochism as the key to a deep, static identity. Masochism as a mode of interaction, a way of relating to oneself and others, substitutes for an identity claim: I don't know who I am, but I know what I want. The phrasing of the passage actually suggests a stronger claim: I know what I want *because* I don't know who I am. Desire, the "subjective preference of market actors," is here, as in Hayek, the reality underlying and funding the "catallaxy," which must not be confused with "a genuine hierarchical '*economy*' – such as that of an army."[38] Pain enables the subject to be sure that her desire is really hers, and it does this, as Acker writes in her article on de Sade, by "over-throwing our very Cartesian selves" pawned off on us as the genuine article.[39] In Acker's myth, pain legitimates and authenticates the subject's desire, and masochism emerges as the central modality of liberated subjects who choose a market that looks like a war over a society that looks like an army.

In the Algerians' revolution, as throughout Acker's work, an ideal of liberty is the primary, often the solitary, value. In the chapter entitled "Freedom" in *Empire of the Senseless*, Acker writes: "Liberty, shit. The liberty to starve. The liberty to speak words to which no one listens" (*ES* 163). These statements at first read like a version of the familiar attack on the liberal concept of negative liberties: liberty means starvation and isolation, abandonment to an unfair, unequal social world. But unexpected associations between Acker's view of liberty and some of her deepest commitments emerge in another passage from the same chapter. "Liberty's a nail which was thrust into my head. It's also a nail they stuck into my cunt. Only I know my cunt is my diseased heart" (*ES* 163). Liberty as a nail piercing her heart, opening her body, and releasing her blood, takes on the positive value with which wounds are generally endowed in Acker's work. In fact it turns out that "the liberty to starve" is valued by Acker not as an unfortunate consequence of the free market as per the usual conservative apologies, but as a sign of the "vulnerability" to reality and to real experience that gives liberty itself its value. To be vulnerable is to have no false security in the world, none of the deadening alienation from the risk of desire that results from entombment in one's social identity. This celebration of liberty as "a nail ... thrust into my head," of freedom as a state of both psychic and physical vulnerability, is an aspect of Acker's general celebration of masochism in the process of divesting the self of its social skin. Acker consistently presents participation in the market as a form of masochism. Arthur Redding observes that Acker's masochism seems to derive much of its force from literalizing and embodying contract. He argues that in these novels masochistic pain emerges out of "contractual relationships" between consenting partners, thus imitating the defining exploitative relationships of capitalism, and problematizing what he calls her "emancipatory politics."[40] While Redding is right to note the way Acker's masochism is modeled on the contract, for her there is no contradiction between the masochistic contract and a sublime emancipation. In fact, masochism for Acker is a means of guaranteeing the legitimacy of freedom of choice and consent in the absence of a model of sovereign, self-identical individuality that gives freedom of contract meaning and defensibility in the liberal tradition.

Acker's interest in masochism dates from her involvement in the radical lesbian collective SAMOIS in the late seventies. SAMOIS defends the ability of the subject to know what she wants despite the judgment of external observers that masochists cannot really consent to acts that harm them. SAMOIS rejects the "marxist critiques of bourgeois contract theory," the argument that "just because someone voluntarily enters into an agreement to do something does not mean that they have not been coerced by forces impinging on the decision."[41] The fact that no one's choices are insulated from pressures of various kinds, and that the autonomous enlightenment model of the individual doesn't correspond to a reality of interpenetrating and flexible identities, does not vitiate free choice. Masochism demonstrates the legitimacy of subjective desire despite the incoherence of the subject. For Acker, as for SAMOIS, it is not the possibility that someone might desire something not in their own interest that is the real threat, but the attempt to define those interests objectively, and to outlaw some desires as "false consciousness." The enemy is "people who want to protect me" from tops and sadists, the attempt by society or the government to limit freedom of choice by defining the interests of real individuals according to a rational, coherent, and imaginary subject.[42] When, in *Empire of the Senseless,* Thivai proclaims his indifference to the doctor's attempt to explain his masochistic psychology "because for me, desire and pain're the same," he is asserting the authenticity and legitimacy of his conscious desires, his choices, against the doctor's idea of who he "really" is and what he "really" wants. The subject who desires pain performs the "liberty to starve. The liberty to speak words to which no one listens," Acker celebrates, rescuing the subjective preference of market actors from the wreck of "enlightened self-interest." As in O'Hara, Acker's fiction subtracts reflexivity from desire: choice here is a matter of being interested without being self-interested.

If masochism for Acker is about the separability of consent and freedom of choice from an ideal of full, rational, autonomous individuality, the equation of desire with pain also plays an ethical role as a kind of hygiene, purifying the individual of social pollution. Acker extends her representation of masochism in a curious passage nearly halfway through *In Memoriam to Identity.* In a chapter "translated" from Faulkner's *The Sound and the Fury,* Acker reflects on the despairing, self-obsessed Quentin and his flirtation with a literary career: "Writing is one method of dealing with being human or wanting to suicide cause in order to write you kill yourself at the same time while remaining alive" (*IM* 174). To this I would juxtapose a related moment: "When a human's dying, the human sometimes realizes that his belief in justice and society is ungrounded and that this death, and this life, is meaningless" (*IM* 145). If death reveals the final insubstantiality of society, then to suicide while remaining alive is a technology for stripping the individual of his oppressive social identity and beliefs, and drawing him into a "meaningless," mythic relationship to a subjectivity at once entirely personal and shareable with every human. The practice of committing suicide without dying is paradigmatically achieved in "real" writing for Acker, which is not "to record or represent a given action ... I lose myself ... but I don't escape the fatality of events, their weight and their irreversibility, merely because I cannot claim them for myself" (*IM* 256). The realization that "this death, and this life, is meaningless" resonates with a number of similar passages not only in its insistence on the desperation of disciplined social existence, but also in expressing a more elusive theme close to the heart of Acker's project.

"The only event which any human can know is the one event he or she can't perceive, that he or she must die" (*ES* 55). With a typically Ackeresque logic she goes on: "If the only event I can know is death, that is dream or myth, dream and myth must be the only knowing I have" (*ES* 54). For Acker one can have knowledge or experience, but not knowledge of experience. Life is "meaningless," and knowledge hovers mysteriously above experience as "dream or myth." "Reason" is always "in the service of the masters" (*ES* 12), and any attempt to abstract from experience, to generalize and categorize is always the attempt to institute a malevolent social discipline. This inability to know is compensated, for Acker, by the ability to exchange: "I've always wondered how some people teach other people ... blood transfusions teach" (*IM* 180). Exchangeable blood substitutes for corrupt knowledge. This is not simply an anti-epistemology, the anarchic skepticism usually attributed to Acker. Her insistence that knowledge cannot be extricated from experience is consistent with a commitment to market exchange as a "spontaneous order" threatened by attempts to impose a rational order on it. Her distinction between the inability to know and the ability to exchange reproduces Hayek's categorical distinction between systematic, "objective" knowledge *of* the market and the "practical," embodied and "subjective" knowledge at work *in* the market. For Hayek, the knowledge embodied in the choices of individuals faced with certain options is of a different kind than the systematic knowledge available at the macro level. As Gray writes, for Hayek "the impossibility of central social planning rests, firstly, on the primordially practical character of most of the knowledge on which social life depends."[43] The knowledge of market actors is so irreducibly specific, so contingent on the immediate context of embodiment, that it is "primordial," "inarticulate;" it is unknowable, but it circulates in the actual exchanges constituting the spontaneous order of the catallaxy. When I make a choice – to buy or sell something, employ or work for someone – I do so based on my "inarticulate" understanding of a concrete situation.

Acker's writing stresses exactly this difference between formalizable knowledge and the "primordial" knowledge underlying exchange. At the end of *Empire of the Senseless*, Abhor wants to learn how to drive, so she gets a copy of *The Highway Code* and just begins. The absurdity of trying to learn how to behave from "rules of behavior" becomes apparent when she reads, "Watch your speed; you may be going faster than you think," and pushes the pedal to the floor "so I was sure to not be going faster than I thought" (*ES* 218). Finally, she decides that the only valuable rules are those that simply express "commonsense," and she could therefore throw away the rule book "cause I know what commonsense is cause that's what commonsense is" (*ES* 214).

In articulating her sense that exchange consists of the circulation of an unformalizable kind of knowledge, Acker draws upon William Gibson's treatment of this theme in *Neuromancer*. About a quarter of *Empire of the Senseless* consists of a rewriting of Gibson's novel, which constitutes a key intermediary in the development of the economic fiction from Burroughs to Acker. A brief glance at it will help to clarify Acker's logic. The novel is perhaps best known for coining the term "cyberspace," but in reading it as a quintessentially "posthuman" text concerned with information technology, critics have obscured the meaning this term has for Gibson. With cyberspace, Gibson imagines a mode of negotiating a vast collective pool of information that looks rather different from the internet that emerged in the 1990s. In *Neuromancer*, navigating cyberspace is not a matter of the input and output of code. When Gibson's protagonists "jack in" to the network, they engage all their senses. This is not a matter of simply sitting before a computer screen, but of inhabiting a different kind of body in a different kind of three dimensional space. Characters move through the virtual world of cyberspace with a virtual body, physically navigating a "landscape" of information which takes a physical, three-dimensional form. They move through "valleys" and "peaks"; information becomes "faint glyphs of colored light that shimmered"; they notice the jagged border of a database; a security system bristles with threatening spikes.[44]

Cyberspace is space that reproduces the context of human embodiment. This is not a matter of ornamentation, but a critical feature of the human relation to information. For Gibson, the human body, moving through space, is a powerful way of organizing and accessing information. Think, to take Acker's example, of the enormous amount of information, the staggering array of rules and exceptions that would be required to formalize the process of driving an automobile. And yet people are able to drive, to navigate curves and stops, to accelerate and slow appropriately, without using any formal rules or processing any information. Embodiment transforms the "unthinkable complexity" of information into an easily manipulated form.[45] In Gibson the body, as Mark Hansen puts it in his description of analogous dynamics in new media, frames information.[46] Framed by the body, information becomes the kind of tacit "knowing how" described by Acker and Hayek. Information does not dispense with the body; cyberspace does not replace space with data. To be used most efficiently by human agents, information must enter the context of embodiment, it must become flesh. In Gibson's fiction, information possesses an "infinite intricacy that only the body, in its strong blind way, could ever read."[47] This is the original meaning of "cyberspace": not data replacing flesh, but "data made flesh."[48]

Gibson's model for cyberspace is a fictionalized market. The novel begins with a description of a densely populated, "interesting" market street that recalls Jane Jacobs. In this market, Gibson sees "the dance of biz, information interacting, data made flesh in the mazes of the black market."[49] Bodies moving through the shops and bars and arcades show "the intricate dance of desire and commerce," a free circulation of embodied knowledge that provides the template for cyberspace.[50] Acker's economic fictions extend and develop this view of the body as a mode of framing and manipulating knowledge. For her, the body is a space through which exchange flows without conventions, and knowledge circulates without rules. From this perspective, the artificial, systematized, and disciplinary social world looks as if it could simply be swept away from a natural market.

3.

Throughout Acker's novels she often refers to "real writing," "true writing," "pure writing." Writing is defined, thematized, and parodied to an extent that justifies the author's frequent claim that the real subject of her books is writing itself. Taking their cue from these statements, Acker's critics have approached her idiosyncratic style as a polemical manifestation of her political, social, and literary commitments; understand how she writes, and you will understand what she's trying to say. This criticism divides into two neatly opposed responses. Arthur Redding speaks for the more common view, arguing that that she "out-Burroughs Burroughs," referring to his cut-up method, and suggests that Acker's reductive and often hilarious versions of Faulkner and Twain "savage the lives and legends which might once have served ... as narratives capable of defining ... selfhood."[51] Martina Sciolino also focuses on Acker's characteristic method of "plagiarism" as participating in the quintessentially postmodern project of dismantling the self. She argues that Acker "typically includes the debris of an information age in a montage that forces associations between material culled from radically different registers."[52] Sciolino's observation suggests a pronounced element of abstraction in Acker's writing; reading her work as a "montage" stresses its status as representation. The project of dismantling the self is expressed in language that floats free of sovereign subjects, circulates between individuals, and is available to everybody because it is not identified with anybody. Kathryn Hume expresses the diametrically opposite view when she finds in Acker a remarkably consistent "voice" that unifies disparate sources in the author's powerfully individual idiom. This Acker is an old-fashioned "humanist," fundamentally committed to a "passionate defense of a remarkably stable core [of the individual] against the demands of society."[53] The abundant evidence from the novels supplied by both schools suggests that they are both right. Acker is explicit in expressing her belief that the truth about true writing is both that it is blood, the inalienable property of particular individuals, and that it is money, the infinitely exchangeable medium of relative and subjective values.

"I have always wondered how some people teach other people. Death and blood transfusions teach" (*IM* 180). The question of communication is a major problem for Acker. In a world where the codes mediating between individuals have either broken down or must be broken down, and in which linguistic expression is affirmed to be a matter that the speaker can't control, characters have a difficult time getting others to understand them. One chapter in *Empire of the Senseless* is devoted to Abhor's search for a crucial "code," which when retrieved reads: "GET RID OF MEANING. YOUR MIND IS A NIGHTMARE THAT HAS BEEN EATING YOU: NOW EAT YOUR MIND" (*ES* 38). Acker elaborates this imperative to "get rid of meaning" in an often-quoted passage on literature as the demystification of "Reason": "Reason is always in the service of the political and economic masters. It is here that literature strikes, at this base, where the concepts and actings of order impose themselves" (*ES* 12). Thus Acker's "literariness," her idiosyncratic style, has a partially negative project: writing here functions not only as expression, but as a process of robbing the speech of the masters of its illusory universality, dismantling the linguistic and logical structures that shield a condition of tyranny from sight. This project is manifest in a Nietzschean assault on the fundamental arbitrariness of causality: she routinely replaces the word "and" with "because," and shamelessly abuses "if x then y" chains. "Mark knew everything cause he was gay" (*ES* 197). "If you don't go anywhere, you don't go anywhere" (*ES* 217). Acker's style is characterized by sweeping reductions, nihilistic sarcasm, and a generally bad attitude. Persons become "gulags" (*ES* 40), or "shriveled cashew nuts" (*ES* 49), statements like "you don't matter and reality doesn't matter" (*ES* 34) are randomly distributed throughout the text, and obscenities are tacked onto the end of the rare innocuous sentence in an excess of nausea. ("Climactically Algeria is a sluggish country and cunt") (*ES* 48).

The characters themselves are often unable to understand the simplest speech-acts, while at another level they are utterly incapable of comprehending or responding to each other's needs for love and comfort. A tale of unrequited love is Acker's characteristic plot, and it dominates the intertwining stories of *Empire of the Senseless* and *In Memoriam to Identity*. Human relationships in these stories constitute a violent sentimental education for the protagonists, who are rejected, abused, and violated by virtually everyone they meet, until they arrive at a version of the resolution spoken by Cap: "Nothing made sense but feeling … I don't need to say anything to anyone" (*IM* 158). The primary function of interpersonal contact for Acker's characters is to receive wounds from others. When Cap declares in retrospect, "rejection in love creates a real and permanent (until death) wound in and below the flesh" (*IM* 81), she is relating a deeply satisfying experience, in many ways the consummation of her relationship with other people in general. This wounding functions as a consummation because trauma is central to Acker's understanding of the word as blood; in opening the body, the wound opens the possibility of a new and undistorted communication between individuals. If language as "code" or "meaning" is a mystified form of control by shadowy masters, Acker suggests the possibility that writing, under certain conditions, performs an authentic reference to the underlying reality of the subject. "All my senses touch words. Words touch the senses. Language isn't only translation, for the word is blood" (*IM* 90). In general, for Acker "identities are holes" (*IM* 115), meaningless categorizations of individuals according to obsolete and oppressive social conventions. However, as I noted in the previous section, she affirms the existence of a selfhood that is natural to the subject; free of the taint of convention and before language, it can't be directly expressed in words. When a character in *In Memoriam to Identity* remembers that "even" when she was a child, "I sensed that blood is who I am," she echoes a number of similar statements throughout the novels (*IM* 117). But what is the significance of an identity predicated so exclusively on blood? If your blood is who you are, how does your writing reveal you? What exactly is the relation between writing and the wound that exposes the body?

Over the last fifteen years a body of criticism has developed that seeks, like Acker, to move past "the need to deconstruct,"[54] by examining the relation between wounding and representation. Trauma theory has attempted to derive a theory of language from this relation, developing a logic parallel to Acker's own view of the word as blood as articulated in the novels. In *Unclaimed Experience*, Cathy Caruth argues that engaging with the experience of trauma, the puzzling, repetitive return of the catastrophic event to the mind of the survivor carries an imperative to develop a "new mode of reading."[55] This new orientation to texts reconfigures our sense of reference and representation in an attempt to grasp the truth of a "shadowy reality" that somehow resists direct understanding. In taking a form of de Manian deconstruction as the model for a kind of reading that offers access to this reality, Caruth takes issue with the familiar claim that post-structuralism disables historical reference. She argues that its ability to locate language's resistance to simple and direct referentiality exposes the fact that the extraction of clear meanings from texts always conceals the violent erasure or "betrayal" of an event that cannot be understood, and so clears a space for the authentic "witnessing" of an unsettling reality. In her account, the meaning of a text is produced by neither the author nor the code, but rather by a traumatic event that remains unassimilated, and inassimilable, both to the author's experience and to the apparent meaning that is mechanically generated by the functioning of the text's grammar. Caruth imagines the pure literalness of an event as embodying an integrity that is destroyed by situating it within a "history," a conceptual or figural framework. She thus distinguishes direct or simple reference, which is always a self-deceiving fiction about the effect of a mechanical system, from a kind of signification that in its brute, literal materiality bears the trace of the repressed event. Acker, in claiming "the word is blood," marks this distinction between ordinary reference and writing where "language and the flesh are not separate" (*IM* 89). In both authors, the unassimilated matter of the event produces a disruption in the figural system, and it is by attentiveness to this break or gap in the text's meaning that something like authentic reference becomes legible.

The model of interpretation offered by Caruth is most clearly expressed in her chapter on de Man, whom she reads as both presenting a theory of reading and as performing the fundamental insight of "a theory that does not eliminate reference but precisely registers, in language, the impact of an event."[56] For de Man, language is a "coded set of differences not based on any extra-linguistic reality."[57] But reference inevitably reasserts itself in these texts as a "disruption" that resists the system's workings by introducing breaks and discontinuities into its figurations. This reference is not identified with the author's intention, but rather with the "unredeemable *literality* of events" that escapes the control of both the author and the system. Thus de Man, in Caruth's reading, succeeds in the "paradoxical evocation of a referential reality neither fictionalized by direct reference nor formalized into a theoretical abstraction."[58] What is at stake for Caruth in de Man's theory of the return of reference as a break in figural meaning is the way an event that is erased or covered over by understanding touches us in the moment when understanding fails.

Caruth's argument that meaning is reducible to the "impact of an event" is identical to Acker's claim that "words touch the senses," and the critique of representation in her fiction is directed against what Acker describes as the repressive conventions that distance meaning from experience. The conventional belief that one can acquire an understanding of a text that is independent of one's experience of it, is precisely what must be overcome in order for language to function as transmission instead of as the site of oppression. In *In Memoriam to Identity* she writes that "the flesh must be the mind," and that "understanding can't be verbal" (*IM* 118). Experience and language are of different orders, and the breakdown of cognitive understanding not only threatens the repressive authority legislating "rational" interpretation, but as in Caruth opens a gap in which a person's true, defining experiences might appear in her discourse in all their opaque and uncompromised materiality. Thus the word becomes blood through the alchemy of the failure of conventional interpretive strategies. The accidental, the "unredeemably *literal*," and the materiality of overdetermined signifiers are represented here not as mere static to be tuned out in the reception of an author's intention, nor as the structural element that produces an infinity of meanings. Rather, they constitute a kind of "voice" privileged over the author's conscious intention, a voice that demands our *mis*understanding as an act of "witnessing" an event that will not go away, and that cannot be translated into other terms or assimilated to a system without being violated. Thus as Acker writes, stressing the transcendence of the "social self" through trauma: "To write is not to record or represent a given action ... I lose myself ... in writing, but I don't escape the fatality of events" (*IM* 256).

For the figures in Caruth's text, there is nothing "shareable" or translatable about the private, inassimilable, and unintelligible experiences that define them. Similarly, for the readers she presents, the encounter with the text of another either amounts to a mute "witnessing" of private events we can't know or talk about, or represents an opportunity to engage with our own pasts, to pierce their superficial intelligibility and uncover the persistence of our own repressed events. Caruth's representation of texts that are disrupted by events that can be owned by or identified with individuals but that can't be understood by anyone, suggests that what is ultimately at stake in the version of de Manian deconstruction she takes as a model of interpretation is the protection of intensely individualized identities from the eliding violence of understanding. The "new mode of reading" her book articulates thus produces texts that always refer, in spite of their meaning, to singular experiences as the principle of true identity and authentic difference. I linger over Caruth not to provide terms for reading Acker, but to demonstrate that the novelist's insistence that "understanding can't be verbal" is identical to the theorist's claim that texts "demand our misunderstanding" (*IM* 118). Here I want to stress the commensurability of Caruth's claims with statements in Acker such as: "It's possible to name everything and to destroy the world" (*IM* 123). To Acker, the mediation of ordinary linguistic reference is endlessly destructive, bound up with obsolete and oppressive forms of social organization that violate the purity of individual experience. The wound pierces the epidermis and opens the body, the locus of authentic and natural experience prior to language and to the accretion of the social. The body, and particularly the body that has been opened, wounded in intense, unsettling experiences, stains and distorts the subject's discourse, which spills into public spaces with the defiant, vivid, and disturbingly intimate quality of blood. This invasion of shared language by the incomprehensible and inassimilable truth about the self both violates the integrity of the public sphere and clears the way for what Acker imagines as a new, radically innocent community.

In attempting to demonstrate the identity of Acker's and Caruth's understanding of language, I would also like to mark a difference between the two writers' sense of the value of traumatic experience. Caruth ascribes to a version of the psychoanalytic belief that the mature personality is built up around a repressed event, like a pearl around a grain of sand. Her theory is partially invested in a generally therapeutic project, helping victims to rebuild their lives, to trust others again, and so forth. In addition, her discussion is committed to grounding group identities in historical events: the Japanese in Hiroshima, the Jews in the Holocaust, and so on. Acker, on the other hand, is utterly uninterested in maintaining the "holes" of social identities of any kind, and manifests a sarcastic disdain for both psychoanalysis and the mature personality. Whereas in Caruth, as in the postmodern context in general, the commitment to an identity based on blood is associated with the articulation of new versions of old group identities, Acker's aim is to rescue the individual from what she sees as the oppressive, deadening effects of society and convention. Trauma does not represent an epistemological key to the authentic difference between various groups and types of individuals; her theory of the wound is more radical in that it defines the ontological priority of individual experience over *all* social and conventional mediation. In these novels the metaphysical apparatus required to sustain racial or cultural identity is displaced in favor of the barest registration of subject position: "you are wherever you are" (*ES* 58). A stark analytic of class, of one's place on the owner/owned divide, substitutes for subjectively richer forms of identification. Even the term "class" is perhaps too loaded with the implication of broad social configurations to capture Acker's sense that the amount of money a person happens to have in her pocket can "place" her as definitely and as meaninglessly as her latitude and longitude.[59] Thus being an American designates the lack of national identification: "Money is a kind of citizenship. Americans are world citizens" (*ES* 39). The people that come closest to having a cultural identity in *Empire of the Senseless* are the Algerians, the oppressed migrant workers in Acker's revolutionary Paris. The revolutionary Algerian community is defined by the use of Arabic, a language that strikes Abhor as full of mysterious potential until the translation of characters spray-painted against a wall robs it of the cloak of exotic otherness: "Ali is pretty," but "anarchy always kills a kid off" (*ES* 54). Thus even the Algerians are ultimately defined by the common possession of a language that is affirmed to be meaningless even when translated: "it was a sign of nothing" (*ES* 53). Racial identity, and the "cultural" identity derived from it, is another "hole" for Acker: like everyone else, the Algerians have literally nothing in common.

Ultimately, for Acker all authentic experience is traumatic because it removes the comfortable, numbing shield of prescribed identities and exposes the person to real contact with the world. Thus while their commitments share a basic logic, Acker is relatively unconcerned with the specific character of the trauma: any wound will suffice to bleed through the subject's language and perform an authentic reference, and the more the better. I make this distinction between Caruth and Acker not simply to reward the latter for carrying the logic of identity to its "anti-essentialist" limit by grounding it in the contingencies of individual experience. In Acker the force of this move is to render an identitarian logic of difference compatible with an economic fiction. Thus she is opposed to giving an identity a name, to creating group identities, since she is ultimately committed to a radical individual difference that is compatible with a no-less-radical sameness.

Like Burroughs, Acker adapts Rimbaud's vowel-colors to express her fiction of the word as blood.

Language is alive in the land of childhood. Since language and the flesh are not separate here, language being real, every vowel has a color … All my senses touch words. Words touch the senses. Language isn't only translation, for the word is blood. (*IM* 89–90)

Later in the novel R. (Acker's "translation" of Rimbaud) expresses the other half of her fiction, the word as money. The historical Rimbaud famously abandoned poetry at the age of twenty-three when at the height of his literary powers to pursue a life of adventure in Africa. In the penultimate chapter of *In Memoriam to Identity*, Capitol reflects on R. after his lapse into silence: "We're all how this society makes us. R., in his way, was still pure, a poet. He didn't give a damn about God. About what people thought about him. All he cared about was money. He was the only one of us fit to live in this world" (*IM* 206). The possibility of this merely being another of the cheap, disposable jokes so characteristic of Acker's aesthetic is foreclosed by a passage later in the chapter in which R. pores "over his business books … figures accounts savings, every penny … counted again and again, sometimes he would fall asleep over what he called *real poetry*" (*IM* 211). These characterizations are striking in that rather than representing R.'s move from poetry to business as a basic shift on the order of turning from art to life, an interpretation offered by Rimbaud himself in his last works, Acker suggests that "figures" and "accounts" are simply a better kind of poetry, a language superior in its expressive and communicative potential to the language of his poems. To this I would juxtapose a passage from *Empire of the Senseless*, in which Abhor claims, "Being a whore means you separate sex and feeling. Sex is an activity as meaningless as is money" (*ES* 92). This equation of sex without feeling with the senselessness of money implies an alternative to the various broken-down codes littering the novel, from Arabic as the "sign of nothing" to the official gibberish of a government-issued driving manual. Money can become a privileged form of representation because it doesn't refer to anything, it is "senseless," unable to carry the subtle psychological or cognitive distinctions of the interpellated subject. To articulate sex as a desired good apart from its entanglement with law and morality Abhor, like the "pure poet" R., turns to money, which expresses value in degrees and quantities, and is therefore able to circulate as the only language minimal enough to be adequate to a social world where there is "no limit but the economic."

For Acker, *"real poetry"* is a mythic alternative to language (*IM* 211). Language is saturated with the virus of sovereignty, with social codes of all kinds, but if it could be replaced by a "substance which has a more direct, a more visceral capacity for expression, then all the weight that the current social, political, and religious hegemonic forms of expression carry will … become … lost."[60] Her thematization of writing is less an attempt to describe her own style than it is the project of her fiction, part of the effort to imagine "a myth," we can believe in. Writing is not like writing in these novels but it is like blood and like money. Acker's double assault on representation, with language giving way to blood on the one hand, and to money on the other, seems to reduce to a contradiction between an entirely private, subjective form of reference, and a mathematical notation of collective value. But in her fiction the process of transforming nature into currency has always already taken place. Throughout her late novels blood is equated with value and becomes the medium for exchanges between individuals. Blood is like "light"; through its agency objects are translated into values, "changed through that beauty which is blood into beauty" (*ES* 221). Acker's blood money, like Hayek's radical proposal to abolish legal tender, takes the vision of the market as "catallaxy" to its limit. The myth of sovereignty, what Hayek calls the "mystique of legal tender," the false idea that "the state … somehow confers value on money it otherwise would not possess," is confronted by an alternative myth.[61] The fiction of blood money shows collective value emerging directly from free choices and individual exchanges; the attempt to control the rate of money creation or to guarantee money's value through government power produces disequilibrium for Hayek, and for Acker, dystopia.

If the logic of the word as blood represents the purification of communication by eradicating the "nightmare" of meaning, the logic of money as blood represents the purification of market value by consigning the "flimsy paper" of government money to the garbage can of history (*ES* 32). Acker's fusion of blood and money encloses all human relations within a natural market without history, ideology, or code. "The trading arena, the market, is my blood" and there shall be no outside (*ES* 55). Her mythmaking project reaches its culmination in this move whereby the social order is displaced by an organic market, and the relations between sovereign individuals are replaced by an image of relations within a singular subject, such that contact with the other is achieved not by moving across bodies, but by going beneath the skin.

CHAPTER 5

"You can't see me": rap, money, and the first person

By the mid-nineties, popular American rap had attained a stable form that persists, though subject to a continuous process of refinement and simplification, practically unchanged in its central features. This form, sometimes described by critics as rap's "formula," essentially consists of two elements: the description of the speaker's money, and the development of a violently antagonistic relation between the speaker and a general, unnamed "you." Consider the following examples. "I'll rip your torso, I live the fast life / Come through in the Porsche slow."[1] "I'd rather bust you and let the cops find you / While I be dippin' in the Range [Rover] all jeweled / like Liberace."[2] "I know you better not open your mouth when I ride by / And I know you see this Lexus GS on shine."[3] "Ain't shit changed, except the number after the dot on the Range [Rover] / way niggaz look at me now, kinda strange / I hate you too."[4] "Nothin' but bling bling in ya face boy."[5]

This catalogue of the juxtaposition of money with a threatening stance towards "you" could be multiplied by the lyrics from virtually any popular rap album released over the past decade. Indeed, the "street credibility" or "authenticity" widely recognized as essential for a rapper's commercial success is largely a function of her[6] adherence to the form. The ubiquity of this form means that an earlier distinction between "gangster" and other subgenres of rap has become largely irrelevant.[7] Raps about money without even a gestural threat directed at "you," or raps threatening "you" without any reference to "my" money, practically disappear after 1995. In the following, I argue that the two elements of the rap form are integrally related, in that the opposition between the "I" and the generalized "you" provides the context in which the meaning of the money is established. My thesis is that the rap form constitutes an interpretation of money. The way this interpretation is carried out marks a transformation of the economic fiction. If works examined in earlier chapters of this study show the opening of aesthetic spaces in which the economic works differently, rap undertakes the aesthetic processing of actual economic forms. I will show how rap and its related cultural practices work as aesthetic interfaces with economic form, interfaces that function to separate economic value from social value. And I will show how the dynamics of rap's interpretation of money depend on rap's interpretation of blackness.

Rap interprets money in terms of a relation between "I" and "you." Specifically, money makes me *invisible* to you. If, in the examples quoted above, the desire to eliminate you is adjacent to the reference to my money, the figure of "bling-bling" conjoins the desire and the money in a single figure. The immense popularity of "bling-bling" in rap over the past seven years indicates its success in integrating both elements of the form. Popularized by the Hot Boys' 1999 hit of the same name, the term is onomatopoeia for the cartoon sound effect made by sparkles of light on a gem or precious metal. Bling is a visual form of money, a fact emphasized by such elements in the original song as the sample of the chimes of the cartoon convention in the chorus, and the references to "diamonds that'll bling-blind ya."[8] The literally thousands of other raps that take up the term also stress its visuality. From Nelly's "I like the way the light hit the ice and glare," to the Big Tymers', "when the light hit the ice, it twinkles and glistens," to B.G.'s "it's dark in the room, I hold up my watch / and it's light," "bling" always indicates light shining from the rapper's gold chain, platinum watch, diamonds ("ice"), or Bentley.[9] So complete is this identification that "shine" emerges as a synonym for "bling" almost at once.

Money-as-light shining from my wrist, neck, or car, bling-bling makes me invisible to you. The light reflecting off my money doesn't compel your recognition of my status, wealth, or fame. It doesn't force you to notice me. It *blinds* you, making such recognition impossible. "It's my turn to shine / Fifty karats or better on my wrist and they all blind."[10] "Folks say take that chain off boy ya blindin' me."[11] "You're blinded by the ice / While I release the confrontation."[12] "What kinda nigga / Got diamonds that'll bling-blind ya?" "The light projects off ice and flashes / Blinds your broke asses."[13] The speaker's shining money prevents the other from taking the subject as the object of her gaze. In case there should be any doubt as to the source of this power, rap insists that fake platinum, however shiny, won't blind. Fake bling produces not blindness, but questions: "Is that platinum, or is it only sterling?"[14] In order to blind you, the chain, watch, diamond, or Bentley has to be real, it has to be *money.* "Hundred thou' for the bracelet / Foolish, ain't I? / The chain'll strain your eye."[15] There are numerous variations on the power of money to render the subject invisible. "I'm still not a playa but you still a hater / Elevator to the top, bye, see you later, I'm gone."[16] "So much candy on the Chevy make a hater's eyes rotten. ... I'm a walking bank roll."[17]

If the antagonism between the first and second person defines the interpersonal relation in rap, my invisibility to you constitutes the master form of that relation. This theme reaches maximal condensation in the ubiquitous phrase, "you can't see me." "You can't see Snoop D O double G."[18] "Stares of a million pairs of eyes / And you'll never realize/ You can't see me."[19] "I'm invisible, invisible / Open your eyes vato, you can't see me."[20] "Get your binoculars on / And just try to see me."[21] Finally, such titles as 50 Cent's "You Are Not Like Me," Dr. Dre and Eminem's "What's The Difference Between Me and You?," and the Clipse's "I'm Not You," demonstrate at the most elementary level the formal *asymmetry* between the first and second person.[22] I can see you but you can't see me. I am a subject who takes you as an object, and not vice versa.

This asymmetry is absolute and general; it isn't contingent on any feature or attribute of the other. A line from Prodigy's 2000 hit "Y.B.E." pares this down to the essentials: "You couldn't understand my life if you lived it."[23] It doesn't matter who or what you are, we could even be substantively identical, but *you* are not like *me*. This opposition between me and you is more radical than a simple conflict between subject positions. The point is that there is a subject only in the "I" position: *you* are not a subject. This formal asymmetry, and the mechanism that produces it, suggests a *different* vision of human relations, rather than the empty "nihilism" projected onto rap by those critics who recognize its hostility towards the other.[24] After all, a basic mediator of human relationality is what establishes this asymmetry. "You're blinded by the ice." Money restricts subjectivity to me. What could this mean?

We can begin to approach this question by observing how different this dynamic is from what it looks like to most critics. Paul Gilroy, for example, reads rappers' reference to gold and platinum as part of the "complex symbolism of wealth and status in black popular culture."[25] Similarly, Kelefa Sanneh writes that Jay-Z, with "his big-money rhymes and real-life wealth," is "a man obsessed with status."[26] Adam Krims accounts for the popularity of the "crime-boss persona" in rap, which conjoins the display of money with an antagonistic stance towards the second person, by arguing this conjunction constitutes the "perfect nexus" of "conspicuous consumption."[27] Tricia Rose argues that the rap aesthetic is a model of "status formation."[28] And in his influential sociological study of the inner city, Elijah Anderson sees in rap the reflection of a street culture where expensive jewels are "status symbols," tools by which the individual "manag[es] his self-image, which is shaped by what he thinks others are thinking of him."[29] Whatever relevance these descriptions might have to "black culture," "real life wealth," or inner-city consumption, they fail to address the specific question posed by "big money rhymes." What kind of diamonds can "bling-blind ya"?

Nothing could be more foreign to the concept of the "status symbol," which depends on your recognition of me, than the fiction that money makes me invisible to you. In fact, one might usefully approach the social relation crystallized in bling by thinking of the rapper's Bentley or diamond as the *exact opposite* of the status symbol, the reverse of conspicuous consumption. "His self-image is shaped by what he thinks others are thinking of him." Does the speaker of the rap lyric think having money is good because it raises the self in the estimation of others? No. Money is good because it removes the other from the construction of subjectivity: "you can't see me." When I say that this is the *exact* opposite of conspicuous consumption, I mean to say something precise about the relation of money, subjectivity, and collectivity in rap.

But what exactly is "conspicuous consumption"? What model of self, society, and money does it reflect? Thorstein Veblen coined the term in the early twentieth century to describe his sense that social status in modern society is determined not only by wealth, but by its conspicuous display. People continually make relative "distinctions of superiority and inferiority" among themselves on the basis of their perceived wealth.[30] Individuals sort themselves in a shifting hierarchy through these "invidious distinction[s]," and are motivated to acquire and display wealth as a means of ascending this hierarchy.[31] Two features of Veblen's theory are particularly relevant in this context. First, conspicuous consumption stresses the importance attached to making money *legible*. As Veblen writes, "The signature of one's pecuniary strength must be written in characters which he who runs may read."[32] My money's value, its ability to establish an invidious comparison between me and you, depends on your seeing and acknowledging it. Second, the hierarchizing comparisons established through the display of money are always relative, contingent on the displays of other individuals. "The invidious comparison can never become so favorable to the individual making it that he would not gladly rate himself still higher relatively to his competitors in the struggle for pecuniary reputability."[33] There is no end to the game. One's status is always in play and at risk; who "I" am is never settled once and for all, but is always relative to "you."

The sociologist Colin Campbell puts a question to the idea of conspicuous consumption that helps elucidate the model of self and society that underlies its common sense. Who, Campbell asks, is the intended audience for the performance of one's "pecuniary strength"? Is it limited to those with whom the subject interacts on a regular basis, or "can it be said to embrace anonymous and unknown observers?"[34] Campbell finds implausible Veblen's idea that the subject will go to great pains and expense to impress "just anyone," indiscriminately lumping strangers in crowds whom she may never see again together with persons whose opinion matters deeply to her. This is at odds with the dominant model of the economic subject who carefully rations her resources to obtain the best advantage. Even if one were to imagine, as Veblen does not, that the subject selects vehicles and settings for her monetary display so as to maximize the effect on the specific target audience whose opinion most matters to her, a more fundamental problem remains. How would a conspicuous consumer know that others had been "suitably impressed?"[35]

Campbell misses Veblen's essential point. The primary motivation for conspicuous consumption lies in establishing the subject and the subject's relative position. The efficacy of money in establishing my relative status is that money expresses a value that is autonomous with respect to a given individual's interpretation. The specific reaction of the other is irrelevant to this crucial operation. I "know" how my money impresses you without getting inside your head. The fact that you may dislike the color of my Bentley does not at all detract from its efficacy in establishing my privileged status in relation to your much less expensive car. The knowledge of how much the display of a given value of money will impress an average social observer, someone who "knows the value of money," and not my success or failure at actually impressing an empirical observer, constitutes my subjectivity, and "places" me in the social world. George Herbert Mead, Veblen's colleague and contemporary, articulates the theory of subject formation that makes sense of conspicuous consumption.

The individual experiences himself as such, not directly, but only indirectly, from the particular standpoints of other individual members of the same social group, or from the generalized standpoint of the social group as a whole to which he belongs. For he enters his own experience as a self or individual, not directly or immediately, not by becoming a subject to himself, but only in so far as he first becomes an object to himself just as other individuals are objects to him or in his experience; and he becomes an object to himself only by taking the attitudes of other individuals toward himself.[36]

I become me insofar as I first become an object to you. Who are you? In conspicuous consumption, through the vivid legibility of money, I become an object not just to an empirical "you," but to "the generalized standpoint of the social group as a whole." There are thus three essential elements for subject formation in this model: me, you, and an index of social value. Money, the form of general social value, enables me to con-flate the empirical "you" with the "generalized standpoint of the social group as a whole." *My relation to "you" is at the same time a relation to society as a whole.* Thus the invidious comparison with the other, whether an anonymous stranger or a close friend, becomes the scene of subject for-mation, of my interpellation into the social world. The status established by such an invidious comparison is not subject either to my or to your idiosyncratic interpretation or revision, but receives, through money, a general social sanction. When I drive by you in my new car, the empiri-cal you "stands in" for the generalized social other to establish "me" and my place, and I function in the same way for you. If your car is more expensive than mine, my actual psychological reaction will be irrelevant to the role my recognition plays in "placing" you higher than me, just as your feelings and thoughts will be irrelevant to the role your recogni-tion plays in placing me lower. Although my subjectivity depends on your recognition of me, this recognition is not personal, but is standardized by the mediation of money. In order to become a subject, I identify with the object reflected in your eyes as you look at me. Insofar as my reflec-tion is mediated by money, the object I identify with is placed in a social hierarchy.

The idea of conspicuous consumption, or the "status symbol," depends on a strong sense of the mutuality of subject formation. "I" become a subject only by becoming an object to "you" and vice versa. "The general-ized standpoint of the social group as a whole" gazes out at me from your eyes. It gazes out at you from my eyes. It is ultimately *society itself* that, standing in "your" place, recognizes, judges, and places "me." This model of subject formation is hardly foreign to contemporary literary and cul-tural studies. Mead's discussion of subject formation derives from Hegel, who writes: "The self perceives itself at the same time that it is perceived by others ... self-consciousness exists in itself and for itself ... by the very fact that it exists for another self-consciousness; that is to say, it is only by being acknowledged or 'recognized.'"[37] This Hegelian notion that one becomes a subject by first becoming an object also reaches us through continental writers like Jacques Lacan and Louis Althusser, and the liter-ary and cultural theorists, from Stuart Hall to Judith Butler, influenced by them. The sense that I become a subject only through the recognition of the other takes on a strongly normative and ethical meaning in such otherwise different writers as Martha Nussbaum and Homi Bhabha. As I showed in Chapter 1, critics from Hannah Arendt to Susan Stewart have claimed that the primary function of aesthetics is to facilitate recognition. Charles Taylor, to recall another example, premises his influential study of the "Politics of Recognition" on the claim that "due recognition is not just a courtesy we owe people. It is a vital human need."[38] The political "demand for recognition" has "been made explicit … by the spread of the idea that we are formed by recognition."[39] Finally, this pervasive belief in the mutuality of subject formation underlies Elijah Anderson's reference to the role of conspicuous consumption in creating the rapper's "self-image, which is shaped by what he thinks others are thinking of him."[40] The first person is parasitic upon the second person, dependent upon the other's mirroring gaze.

We are now in a position to understand the alternative sense of self and society that underlies the display of money in rap. This display is not simply different from conspicuous consumption; it is its opposite. Through this inversion, a strategy of appropriation, of status played out between different subjects, becomes the fantasy of a radically transformed subjectivity. "What kinda nigga / Got diamonds that'll bling-blind ya?" Who am I? Blinded by my money, you can't see me, you can't recognize me, you can't make me an object. If by conspicuous consumption I become a subject by becoming an object to another subject, rap money makes me a subject by depriving the other of subjectivity. This disables the symmetrical me/you relation of conspicuous consumption. I don't see myself from your perspective. The light shining from my money blanks out your gaze. "I" don't depend on "you."

The rap form grounds its interpretation of economic value in this asymmetry. The second person, like the first person, is a social construct. By imagining a different way of constructing the first person, rap imagines the second person to be vestigial, disposable. If conspicuous consumption is like a stickup, compelling your recognition of my higher status, bling-bling is like murder. This identification of money and violence is not simply a metaphor; it is part of rap's formal structure. "My watch talks for me, my whip [car] talks for me / My gun talks for me / BLAM! What up homie?"[41] The money does the same thing the gun does: it closes your eyes. Whether the blinding light from the platinum watch or the bullet from the chrome gun hits "you" first, the function of the money/gun is to end "my" formal dependence on "you."

No mirror holds my image. Money frees me from the necessity of first becoming an object in order to become a subject. My subjectivity is not identified with an object, with a point or place in a status system. In rap, where the relation of the subject to collective value and power is *absolute and immediate* and not relative to any other, the very concept of status or social hierarchy loses its meaning. My position is not relative to yours; we are absolutely incommensurable. "How dare you try to compare us and say we're the same / The rose gold glows from my watch and my chain."[42]

To gauge the magnitude of the shift in subjectivity imagined by the rap form, remember who "you" are. "You," the Meadian/Hegelian generalized social other, is replaced by "me," as a generalized social subject. In conspicuous consumption, society stands in the place of the "you," assessing my money, judging and placing me as a subject. In rap the collective drops the form of "you" and takes the form of "me." Humanity stands in *my* place and you are nowhere. The access to collective power that money grants is not routed through the gaze of the other, but becomes directly available to me. Through the alchemy of rap money, the collective shines from the "I," the human world itself is experienced as an intense, amplified subjectivity.

We can describe the fictional money produced by rap performance according to the following formula: rap money is economic value minus social value. It is economic value in which the crucial element that renders it visible and makes it a technology of recognition has been removed. Rap money is economic value unbound from a social system, economic value that cannot play a role in social stratification, economic value that cannot establish a social relation between me and you.

Rap money is thus a purely economic form of value. Money becomes purely economic through the addition of an aesthetic interface to actual money. This interface works to remove economic value from intersubjectivity. We have seen how this works in the figure of "bling-bling." We find another, especially vivid instance of the use of aesthetic form to remove economic form from intersubjectivity in the widespread practice of putting tinted windows on expensive cars. This practice is associated with rap, and rap lyrics frequently reference it. "I represent homies with the money fly guys with gems / drive with the tints that be thirty five percent."[43] "5 percent tint so you can't see up in my window."[44] The value of the kinds of cars celebrated by rap is entirely a function of their *actual* monetary value. When in 2003 Mercedes' new car, the Maybach, became the most expensive production car in the world, it promptly became the most stylish car in rap, instantly proliferating in countless lyrics. The sense that value, in rap, just is economic value, is ubiquitous. Here is Jay-Z, one of the most successful and influential rappers of the past decade, discussing his major stylistic innovation. "When everybody else was doing gold, I was, like, 'I want something platinum.' And then seeing the whole [rap] world switch – the whole world, you know what I'm saying? For a kid from Marcy. No-one can take that away from me."[45] What is the relevant distinction between platinum and gold? Platinum costs more; it is worth more money. What is the relevant feature of a Maybach? Its economic value.

What counts about cars is their actual monetary value. So what is the aesthetic element? The aesthetic element consists of adding tinted windows to cars in order to prevent you from seeing the driver. When I'm driving my actual expensive car down the street, "you can't see me." The addition of aesthetic form removes actual money from intersubjectivity. The inventiveness of rap in creating such simple and elegant structures is what has enabled it to circulate economic fictions so widely and deeply.

In rap and its associated practices, the addition of aesthetic form to actual economic value creates pure economic value. Aesthetic form serves to block the element in actual economic value that renders it a technology of recognition, and entangles it with social value. Critics have been confused about this, typically arguing that rap, like all aesthetic form, turns economic value into social value. Tricia Rose reads the display of money in rap along the lines of Dick Hebdige's influential idea of subculture as a "struggle over the meaning(s) of popular expression" arguing that rap money is a *style*, "an alternative means of status formation," a form of cultural capital not to be confused with economic capital.[46] Here Rose's account of rap is analogous to Virginia Zelizer's sociological account of how the practice of "earmarking" money for particular uses creates what she calls "personalized currencies."[47] This popular aesthetic practice, people drawing or writing on money, serves to render money's entanglement in social networks more clearly visible, to make actual money a more efficient technology of intersubjective relations.

But of course, Rose's view of rap money as an alternate way of marking status, like Zelizer's view of earmarked money as marking money's social value, means that the difference between actual money and aesthetically altered money is just one of degree. Rap money and actual money both mark status, just in different ways. Thus Paul Gilroy and Elijah Anderson can offer identical accounts of money in rap as a "status symbol," despite the fact that Gilroy thinks rap's gold chains are aesthetic objects, while Anderson is thinking of actual greenbacks flashed on the street. Both money and style do the same thing, embody the same kind of social relation. A paradoxical feature of the criticism is that whether one thinks money in rap is an economic value or an aesthetic value, it will work the same way: as social value. But as we have seen, the whole point of the aesthetic in rap is to disable money's intersubjective function. Rap deploys aesthetic form to remove economic form from the social.

When we understand this basic operation of the rap form, this extraction of the economic from the social, we clear an approach to the question of blackness in rap. If the rap form interprets money, it also interprets blackness, and this latter interpretation constitutes the primary resource of the first. This resource explains why the most popular, widely disseminated form of the economic fiction necessarily developed as a *black* form. It tells us why black rappers and artists pioneered this form, and why the black performance of this form continues to elicit a special conviction. The meaning and value of blackness is transformed through rap and its associated aesthetic practices. The antagonism between rappers and the values of the civil rights generation that preceded them is rooted in this transformation. We can express this tension with a simple question: What can it mean for a black artist to proclaim "you can't see me," and to present invisibility not as a condition to be overcome through art, but as a project to be realized through art?

If an earlier generation of black writers and artists sought to defeat their social invisibility, rappers seek to defeat their social visibility. Blackness as invisibility, as a condition signifying the total absence of social recognition, a complete negation of the social world, was understood by writers of the early postwar period as a condition of total deprivation. In a world where whiteness enabled access to full intersubjectivity, black individuals didn't "show up." This was understood to be a structural feature, beyond any given individual's racist or antiracist beliefs. Thus in Ralph Ellison's *Invisible Man*, even the most "well meaning" white characters remain in crucial respects unable to see the protagonist, encountering instead a blank space onto which they project their expectations. If blackness is invisibility, and invisibility is exclusion from society, then the struggle is to make blackness recognizable, to transform it from a site of total social negativity to a positive site of identity.

Rap revalues black invisibility. This revaluation is made possible by the sense of a new form of value. If collective value can only be obtained through intersubjective recognition, then invisibility is pure deprivation. But if there is a route to collective value that does not pass through intersubjectivity, but that depends on evading intersubjectivity completely, then a position totally exterior to the social world becomes a unique resource.

Just as tinted windows on a Bentley remove it from intersubjective status games, blackness-as-invisibility removes money from the social world. Black invisibility plus money fictionalizes the economic. With the addition of money to invisibility, that invisibility ceases to mean deprivation, and becomes an impossibly dense concentration of collective value.

When one attends to the rap form, one notices how it endows invisibility with a new value. The new value of invisibility constitutes the essential horizon for understanding how black invisibility operates here. But most critics, popular and academic, ignore the dynamics of the form, and evaluate rap in terms of how well it facilitates the positive recognition of blackness, how it positions blackness as an identity within the social field. Thus for Timothy Brennan rap is an "aural museum" of African American culture erected to "codify, protect, and exalt the black traditions."[48] Houston Baker celebrates "positive sites of rap" as "raps designed to teach black children their own specific history."[49]

Since the goal of rap is to defeat recognition and to exit the social field, such an approach leads to inevitable distortions. This mistake underlies the tendency of many critics to conclude that rap has failed in its mission to create positive images of blacks. John McWhorter argues that the violence and materialism of rap show how "blacks have become the main agents in disseminating debilitating – dare I say racist – images of themselves."[50] And Greg Tate writes that rap has proved "structurally incapable of becoming what progressive black intellectuals ... want it to be."[51] But rap's "failure" is unrelated to the submerged patterns of cooptation writers like Tate and Paul Gilroy have in mind.[52] It is not as if an intention to create positive images of blacks has somehow been corrupted. This "structural incapacity" is right out in the open, in rap's rigorous formal opposition to the dynamics of recognition. The point of the blinding and negating of the "you" that defines the rap form is to nullify the relation to the other that objectifies the subject. Gilroy's error, thinking that money in rap is an instance of a status symbol, and the mistake made by Brennan, thinking that rap constructs a black identity, are two sides of the same basic problem. Both critics imagine that rap exists to mark the subject for display, to make the subject into a certain kind of object to be recognized by another subject. Both critics believe that rap is fundamentally concerned with facilitating recognition, facilitating intersubjectivity. And academic defenders of rap, such as Robin Kelley, only contribute to this confusion when they try to rescue a kind of social positivity from the form.[53] Instead of evading rap's profound social negativity we need to think about what this negativity means.

Let's try to think about a blackness that is not an identity in the social world. "I'm invisible, invisible / You can't see me." As I noted above, the equation of blackness and invisibility does not originate with rap. In early postwar writing blackness is not an identity, but an *absence*, a blank, an outside to the social world. The horror of Ellison's *Invisible Man* is that of a subject denied recognition in a social context where human subjectivity requires it. The black body does not mark a place in the social world: the gaze of recognition passes right through it. The racially coded invisibility of Ellison's protagonist enforces a formless, abyssal, empty subjectivity. "I ache with the need to convince myself that I do exist in the real world ... I curse and I swear to make them recognize me."[54] For me to exist to myself, you must see, recognize, acknowledge me. But my blackness renders me invisible to you, to the generalized social other of a racist nation. Race in this model is not a *place* in the social world; it determines *access* to the social world. If I am white, I gain access, I take a place, I get to have a social identity. If I am black, I remain outside; I have no place, no identity. And in a world where recognition is the ultimate horizon of human value, invisibility is an infinite loss.

If Ellison's novel is one locus classicus of black invisibility, Franz Fanon's *Black Skin, White Masks* is another. Fanon begins by saying that to be human is to be recognized. "Man is human only to the extent to which he tries to impose his existence on another man in order to be recognized by him."[55] And in nations defined by the history of racism and colonialism, blacks are outside recognition. Fanon's claim that blacks are denied recognition altogether marks a radical departure from the tradition of post-Hegelian philosophy he confronts. In Hegel's master-slave dialectic, the fact that the master requires recognition from the slave means that the dynamics of recognition hold the promise of the slave's social freedom. But for Fanon, in black-white relations there is no dialectic. Blackness places the person wholly outside of recognition, outside of the social world.

Fanon's decision in his later works to accept this asocial blackness and to pursue the possibilities of black liberation beyond recognition led him to what some critics have seen as a solipsistic position. And, so long as one equates collectivity with intersubjectivity, this would indeed seem to be the stark alternative: either blackness becomes a social identity, or it marks a pre-social solipsism. Black art and literature in America increasingly adopted the first strategy, creating artworks designed to facilitate recognition. Fanon, on some readings, adopted the second.[56] Rap invents a third option. Rap embraces blackness as invisibility, blackness as total exteriority to the social world, as complete resistance to recognition. As with Ellison and Fanon, blackness in rap is not an identity but the lack of access to the world of identities. But if for those earlier writers, this invisibility was pure loss, by fusing black invisibility with money, rap transforms it into pure plenitude. In rap, blackness is invisibility, and the color of money is black. This fusion transforms both of the terms. Money leaves the social world, and invisibility escapes deprivation. The black rapper in the Bentley with tinted windows is unrecognizable. Rap's black money defines a space outside the social world suffused with collective power.

The rap form's evolution of multiple strategies of invisibility, the definition of blackness in terms of social access rather than social identity, and the increasing numbers of white, Latino, and Asian rappers that successfully execute the rap form, means that black invisibility is no longer the form's sole resource. Yet since the history of black invisibility provided the conditions for the form's development, and since the performances of black rappers continue to inspire a special conviction, it would be a mistake to view blackness as having only a contingent relation to rap. The rap form is a black form. It is also a purely economic form. There is no contradiction here. In the development of this form, the interpretation of money and the interpretation of blackness evolved together. The historical experience of racially coded invisibility provided a powerful context for realizing a new relation to money. The black voice asking what kind of diamonds will "bling-blind you" on the radio constructs a purely economic form, a form of collective value outside the social world.

Rap fuses an asocial blackness with money. To understand black money in terms of blackness without money and money without blackness is to make a basic mistake. Consider this passage from Richard Price's 1992 novel *Clockers*. In it, Rodney, a middle-aged drug dealer from the seventies, confronts a young man. "'Charles, check this out man,' Rodney paused so the kid could get ready. 'How mutherfuckin' invisible do you think you are, that you got to have *all* this goddamn gold hangin' around your neck just so you could feel like you're bein' *seen,* man.' Charles blinked at him."[57] Charles doesn't understand what Rodney is talking about. Charles' blackness doesn't mean he has an obsessive need to be seen, and the gold he's wearing isn't a technique of recognition. The aesthetic that governs his dress code is driven by a desire for freedom from recognition, for a route of access to value that doesn't pass through recognition. But his performance, at least with Rodney, fails badly. Encountering Charles, Rodney doesn't hear "you can't see me," but "please look at me." Perhaps tomorrow Charles will change something, calibrate his performance differently. The inventiveness of one generation of black artists in evading invisibility is matched by the inventiveness of another generation in summoning it.

Charles' failure exposes a risk rap runs with every performance, and this constant risk spurs constant innovation. The radically free "I" of the rap lyric invites the audience to inhabit this nonrelative subjectivity. "I give niggas what they came to see / A reflection of oneself how they aim to be."[58] But by acknowledging this orientation towards an audience, by presenting the first person as a space the audience can occupy, rap risks reproducing at the level of the performance the very relation it cancels at the level of lyrical form. This contradicts the constitutive principle that gives the rap form its unique power. In other words, there is a basic tension between the rapper/audience relation of the performance and the formal I/you relation of the lyric. Rap excludes "you" qua generalized social other even as it solicits "you" qua audience.

The asocial rap "I" becomes a subject without first becoming an object, without entering intersubjectivity. The mutually constitutive relation between me and you is obviated by bling, which directly invests me with a collective subjectivity. The paradox is that the relation between the first and second person nullified by the rap lyric is reinstated by the rap performance. This paradox constantly threatens to undermine rap's project. Not infrequently, the hidden tension erupts and destroys the careers of rappers who fail to resolve it, and thus can no longer convincingly execute the rap form.[59] While the history of black invisibility constitutes an important resource for rap, this invisible blackness must itself ultimately be realized in performance, and this performance risks the possibility that, like Rodney, an audience will interpret "you can't see me" as "please look at me." This dilemma is not resolvable in principle, but it can be overcome, for a time, in practice. I take Michael Fried's analysis of the techniques employed by modern painters to establish the fiction of the beholder's absence before the canvas as a useful model for understanding the dynamics of the rap performance.[60] In rap, formal strategies for "keeping it real," for successfully sublimating the relation to the audience, are proposed and worn out in rapid succession, constituting the other side of the relatively stable features of the lyrical form examined above. Indeed, the flux and variation of these secondary formal features guarantees the integrity of the primary features, that is, of rap's interpretation of money.

The purpose of the rap performance is to hold the "I" open to the audience as a space of identification, but this very openness depends on the "I"'s theatrical repression of its relation to its audience. Presenting it as an object of identification for an audience wastes the radical integrity of an "I" that becomes a subject without becoming an object. In the course of its propagation, bling risks becoming its opposite: a status symbol. The very relation destroyed by rap's formal reversal of conspicuous consumption continually threatens to reappear in the performance. One particularly seductive way of resolving this tension between rap's orientation to the two referents of "you," the generalized social "you" and the empirical "you" of the audience, is for the rapper to treat them identically. The animus directed towards the formal second person thus overlaps with a theatrical hostility to the audience. In such cases, the audience becomes a virtual stand-in for the formal, lyrical "you." Much of the gestural repertoire of the rap performance of the mid-nineties, especially the tendency of the rapper to point threateningly at the audience when referring to "you," reflects this approach.

But this strategy has very clearly defined limits, and constantly risks highlighting the very solicitation of the audience that it seeks to efface. The invisibility accomplished in the lyric by the "blinding" of the second person, for example, can obviously not be effected in relation to the audience. Notorious B.I.G.'s contemptuous dismissal of other rappers, "niggas is actors, niggas deserve oscars," refers to the risk run by the rapper who issues threats to the audience he can never fulfill.[61] "I see you in your videos … holding a gun, [but you] ain't gonna bust [shoot]."[62] The rapper who presents a theatrically aggressive stance towards the audience simply highlights his ultimate dependence on the audience, his status as performer. Such a status effectively disables his ability to convincingly execute the rap form's total and uncompromising hostility to the other.

Rappers' appreciation of the dimensions of this tension has led to the current pervasive sense that the rap form can only be successfully executed by someone who is *not* a rapper. Thus the ascendant performance conceit is that there is no performance going on. This strategy is explicitly thematized in lyrics, instantiated by the physical stance of the rapper in videos, and by the rapper's verbal delivery, or "flow." The stance presents an alternative to that of the rapper who treats the audience in the same way as the formal "you," and ends up manifesting a debilitating *awareness* of the audience through her theatrical and implausible aggression. Now everything tends to establish the fiction that the rapper standing before the audience is unaware of its presence. The audience observes the rapper obliquely, overhearing him as he talks to himself. This oblique, unacknowledged relation minimizes the tension between the performance and the projection of rap's fundamental fiction, the nonrelative social subject constructed by the rap lyric.

Numerous factors contribute to the success and popularity of this, at first sight quite dubious, strategy. For example, rap's defiant allegiance to the simple elements of its lyrical form, the interpretation of money in the context of an intense hostility to the other, itself strenuously resists the performance values of variety and innovation constantly pushed on it by its critics. The widespread adoption of this strategy also enables the form to mark a vivid and decisive break with earlier forms of rap. Consider the following verses by Rakim, one of the most influential rappers of the mid-eighties. "I just put your mind on pause / and I beat you when you compare my rhyme with yours"; "The scene of a crime every night at the show / The rhyme fiend on the mic that you know."[63] Rakim's lyrics foreground his talents as a rapper, brag about his power over an audience, and challenge other rappers. This stance, characteristic of early rap from Grandmaster Flash to Run DMC, is taken by many critics to characterize rap generally. Thus Timothy Brennan writes that rap's fundamental metaphor is that "words and minds are guns, and winning the talent clash [with a rival rapper] is 'killing the other.' "[64] This sense that the violence directed at the other is a *metaphor* for the rap *performance* pervades most rap through the late eighties.

By the mid-nineties, this dynamic has been reversed. Now the performance, if referenced at all, becomes a metaphor for the violence directed at the other. Jay-Z warns "you" that he's not trying to overcome you with his rap skills: "Here's the shock of your life / The gun not the mic."[65] Consider the chorus of a popular rap by Big Pun. "Whatcha gonna do when Pun comes / Knocking at your front door / and wants war / Holy shit! He ain't a rapper he'll kill you."[66] The frame of a performance cannot contain the hostility towards the second person, and Pun underlines this conceit by the abrupt abandonment of the rhyme in the last line. By the mid-nineties rap has acquired a new focus and new formal priorities in interpreting money in terms of an antagonistic relation to the other. Nothing presents a greater threat to the requirements of this form than the idea that the lyrical antagonism to "you" is bounded by the context of a performance for an audience. My desire to kill, blind, and cancel "you" is absolutely not a metaphor for rapping, and the strongest way of putting this is to declare, "I'm not a rapper."[67] "Thought I told y'all / I'm not a rapper."[68] "I'll kill you ants with a sledgehammer, I overdo it / So you won't confuse it with just rap music."[69] "If you think I'm just a rapper / You got me fucked up."[70] "You're just a rapper."[71] The attempt to resolve the tension between the formal "you" of the rap lyric and the "you" of the audience thus has the unexpected effect of turning the once-celebrated figure of the rapper into rap's ritualized object of scorn.

One of the most effective ways for a rapper to show that he isn't a rapper is to demonstrate that he isn't very good at rapping. Kelefa Sanneh, in his article on Jay-Z, writes that in his later records, Jay-Z "has simplified his intricate rhyme style: his lyrics have become less tightly constructed, and less descriptive."[72] In an interview, Jay-Z provides the following extraordinary metaphor for his choice to move away from the verbal virtuosity displayed in his early raps. "In his early days, [Michael] Jordan was rocking a cradle, cranking it, all crazy, but he wasn't winning championships ... And then, later in his career, he just had a fadeaway jumpshot, and they won six titles. Which was the better Jordan?"[73] Sanneh, while admitting that Jay-Z's change in style has contributed to his immense popularity, argues that the rapper has forsaken the "artistic ambition" of his earlier career. "No one wants to watch a man make jump shots forever."[74]

But verbal virtuosity doesn't correspond to "artistic ambition" here. Like most critics, Sanneh projects alien aesthetic values onto rap. Jay-Z's decision to simplify his rap style is produced by the immanent contradiction between the performer/audience relation and the me/you relation. By drawing attention to his spectacular style Jay-Z, like the early Jordan, wasn't "winning championships." His technical skill came at the expense of his success in executing the rap form. Sanneh betrays a fundamental confusion about rap. The essence of nineties rap is its interpretation of money. The persistence of the rap "formula" is only an enigma if one imagines that something else, like an "intricate rhyme style," is essential. Not only is verbal virtuosity essentially irrelevant to rap's core values, in certain cases, as with Jay-Z, it can even be opposed to it. Rap's primary formal feature, the conjunction of the reference to money with an antagonism to the second person, is threatened by Jay-Z's conspicuous status as a performer.

Thus the fiction that Jay-Z is *not* a performer proves essential to making his raps believable. This fiction is facilitated by predictable, simple language. If Jay-Z's early rap foregrounds its status as a special, artistic form of language, his later work masquerades as plain speech. A number of critics have noted this tendency of rap to approximate everyday speech. The new "spoken" style, muting the stresses and rhymes, de-emphasizing line breaks, provides a vivid contrast to the heavily stressed, "singsong" style of such early rappers as Too Short and Run DMC. As Krims writes, rap's "enunciation and delivery [is now] closer to those of spoken language, with little sense often projected of any underlying metric pulse."[75] I'm not a rapper, I'm just talking, and you're just overhearing me.

Jay-Z's style exemplifies the fiction that rap is not a performance. A variation on this strategy is for the rapper to acknowledge the performance, but to suggest that he is such a bad performer that he is incapable of the performative self-objectification that threatens rap. He's *trying* to perform, but his basic stance towards the world, codified by the conjunction of the display of money with hostility to "you," constantly undermines the performance. Thus the performance fails, and in failing, the rap succeeds. Noreaga and Lil' Flip provide perhaps the best individual examples of this strategy, but it can also be seen in the general rise in the incidence of redundancy in rap. The minimal sign of performative competence in early rap, coming up with new and inventive rhymes, is replaced by the null repetition of the same. "I'll be forever thugged out / Because I'm thugged out."[76] "Diamonds in my fuckin' teeth – when I talk, I spark / Don't fuck around with beef – when it start, I spark/ Me and my Hot Boy creeps – when it's dark, I spark."[77] The numbing repetitiveness of elements of the rap form also contributes to this effect. "Hoppin' out the platinum Hummer with the platinum grill / With the platinum pieces, and the platinum chains / With the platinum watches, and the platinum rings."[78] Since, as Sanneh suggests, no one wants to see a performer doing the same thing over and over again, there must be something else going on. Maybe the performance isn't the point.

The "I'm not a rapper" theme and its variations have had a major impact on the visual performance of rap, the primary vehicle of which is the music video. Anything so obvious as *dancing* in a video became taboo relatively early, and this taboo was often expressed in the ridicule directed at such infamous dancing rappers as MC Hammer. But the problem of how to perform nonperformance in a video has seemed intractable, and a wide variety of solutions were tried and rejected throughout the late nineties. One idea was to present the rapper as a criminal, shooting at police and crowds. Thus the video took the form of a miniature narrative film, which evaded the appearance of rap performance at the cost of leaving the rapper more literally vulnerable to the charge of being an actor.[79] Another approach, which shows the rapper driving in an expensive car or yacht mouthing the lyrics as if to himself, runs the risk of reproducing the scenario of conspicuous consumption, particularly since, despite abortive experiments with lighting effects,[80] there is no way to reproduce the "blinding" caused by money in the video.

The first years of the millennium saw an extraordinary development in relation to this difficult problem. The solution adopted by rappers like Fam-Lay, Cam'ron, Juvenile, and Lil' Flip has simply been to face the camera directly, but to convey, through their gestures and expressions, a kind of catatonic unawareness of being observed. Each rapper brings his own idiosyncratic techniques to the task of appearing to be unable to recognize the camera, unable to respond to an audience, unable to return the other's gaze. At certain moments Juvenile, in the video for "In My Life," stares listlessly into the camera with his mouth open, not forming any words, a dull, vacant look in his eyes.[81] Lil' Flip stands absolutely still with his feet planted wide apart, a grin frozen on his face.[82] Fam-Lay alternately looks at the camera, up at the sky, and down at the ground while walking aimlessly and making obscure private gestures with his hands.[83]

These examples all imply slightly different forms of non-relation to the audience. Juvenile appears to be completely unaware that anyone is looking at him. Lil' Flip appears to be aware, but that awareness appears to make no *difference* to his maximally vacant persona. His intention may in fact be to smile for the audience, but if this is the case, he has failed so badly that the effect is more extreme than if he was ignoring it. Rather than pretending to be oblivious to the presence of an audience, he represents himself as aware, but totally incapable of responding to that presence with the modulated recognition it requires. To take one more example, B.G.'s broad smile at the camera in "Y.B.E.," combined with his ultraviolent, almost entirely bleeped-out lyrics, produces the effect of someone unsuccessfully attempting to conceal his real intentions from the audience. This is a *fake* performance: B.G. is attempting to perform the role of a performer, and failing. With these recent innovations, the video has become a supple instrument capable of realizing the fiction that there is no performance going on, as with Juvenile, or, as with B.G. and Lil' Flip, the fiction that the performer, though trying, is actually incapable of the self-objectifying performance that threatens the rap form.

I want to end by noting a final paradox. The more rap effaces the difference between performance and life, the more rigorously closed, formalized, and artificial the lyric becomes. As rap approaches ever closer to speech, as its definition of the social relation is disseminated more widely and successfully, as more drivers turn up the rap on their stereos and disappear from your view, its movement into the open reaches another margin, another border, that pushes it back into the status of art. It encounters competition. The farther rap pushes into social space, the more its interpretation of money comes up against rival interpretations, enclosed and protected by their own forms, with their own strategies for convincing. From the critical interpretation of bling as status symbol, to advertising campaigns that show my money's value reflected in the envious eye of the other, to the social networks in which money is made and spent, the overwhelming strength of the social value of money presents a final barrier. The rap form rests at the equilibrium between two rival forces. If on the one hand rap is driven to erase the aesthetic frame by declaring "This isn't performance," on the other hand it embraces aesthetic formalization in order to protect antisocial money from absorption by the social world.

At such moments the rap form retreats from its position as a mobile interface with actual economic forms, and takes refuge behind sharply delineated frames, in autonomous aesthetic spaces. The precariousness of the first position can be seen in the ways rap's emblematic interface – the tinted car window – can be seamlessly refunctioned as a technique of recognition. The moment when one is recognized stepping out of the car assumes priority over the time one is not recognized while driving. The tinted windows then simply signal a level of restricted access, like the velvet ropes separating those who walk right into the club from those who wait on the sidewalk. Ultimately, money can only be assured of its status as a pure economic form when it is sheltered by aesthetic form. Money as invisibility, society as subject, community without identity, the first person without the second: rap's propositions remain frozen, not believed but not unbelievable, in the stasis of aesthetic form. The price money pays for its absolute freedom from the social world is to be bound to the artwork's paradoxical relation to the social world. It is now time to take up the question of that relation.

The invisible world

In the preceding chapters I have attempted to show how, in a set of postwar literary works, the aesthetic disembeds the economic from social relations grounded in recognition. Using a variety of techniques, these works remove the economic from what Hannah Arendt calls the "public world," the social space where visibility confers reality. This removal transforms the market in basic ways. Instead of a social structure facilitating the mutual recognition of individuals, or mediating between the different desires of individuals, the economic becomes a means of shaping and organizing individuals' experience of the world. The economic relations at work in the aesthetic spaces I study present an alternative to the regime of recognition, the regime of the social, the regime of the visible. The fiction of this invisible economy opens the fascinating prospect of a new mode of experience.

In discussing these works, I have been primarily concerned with delineating the internal dynamics of the aesthetic spaces they set up. Sometimes an attention to the cultural and political contexts in which the writers worked has helped to clarify the distinctive shape of these dynamics. But while describing the features of this phenomenon, I have largely bracketed the question of the relation of the economic fiction to existing social and economic conditions. Having completed the description, my conclusion now takes up this question. I address it in two parts. First, I will investigate the hypothesis that economic fictions perform the ideological function of concealing actual economic inequality. Second, I will argue that a surprising result of this investigation is to demonstrate the inadequacy of existing ways of understanding the category of the aesthetic. I will then suggest a new way.

I.

Throughout my description of the economic fiction, I have been concerned to foreground the collective dimension of the economic experience set up by these works. Some readers might feel that a certain irony attaches to my use of the word "collective" in this context. One might well think that invisibility is necessary for the idea of any market-based collective to become fascinating. Specifically, one might think that the economic fiction creates a fascination with the market by making economic inequality invisible. And so it does. Isn't this ideological? Doesn't the economic fiction ultimately have an ideological function?

One might be tempted to answer this question quickly: of course it is ideological. This fictional economy fascinates by blinding us to actual economic inequality. The economic fiction relies on the market system. The market system produces an extremely unequal distribution of resources among individuals. The works I consider are unconcerned with this inequality, and fail to invent or to imagine a mechanism that might address it. They ignore economic inequality; they sweep it under the rug. And yet this inequality is precisely that feature of the market that cannot be ignored. It explains why the free market can never serve as the basis of a desirable collective life. The persistent inequality of market distribution explains why the free market remains the natural enemy of progressive thought. To cover up this inequality is to perform the most base and basic ideological function.

But it requires only a moment's reflection to realize the inadequacy of this kind of response. The economic fiction does not cover up actual economic inequality. This fiction is not a mimesis of actual economic conditions. It does not present an image of economic reality, but a space in which the economic undergoes a change. These works foreground the transformative, rather than the mimetic, quality of the aesthetic. They transform economic inequality. In what does this transformation consist? In this: the economic fiction makes economic inequality invisible. So now we must ask: What happens when inequality ceases to be visible?

When economic inequality ceases to be visible it ceases to be social. The aesthetic supplement deletes from the economic those features that make economic value recognizable, that allow economic value to function in the regime of recognition. In the economic fiction, money loses the feature that renders it capable of making what Bourdieu calls "distinctions." What can this mean? If the economic cannot be used to draw intersubjective distinctions, how then does economic inequality work? Doesn't the fascination elicited by the vision of a collective that preserves economic inequality still do some suspect ideological work?

By raising these questions – of the collective, the ideological, the unequal – I mean to signal that now a sustained engagement with Marx can no longer be postponed. I mean to address the questions raised by the fiction of a new mode of collective, economic experience by way of a reckoning with Marx's legacy. For Marx, a beautiful new mode of collective life develops out of the immanent principles of the market system. The market contains the seed of a change so basic as to make all existing history look like the prehistory of this new world.

The status of Marx's thought is an urgent and immediate question for us because what happens to inequality in the economic fiction is the same thing that happens to inequality in Marx's vision of communism. Inequality, for Marx, is not eliminated but transformed. I will show how Marx's understanding of what supports this transformation of inequality differs from the genre I have described in one important respect. But before inquiring into the significance of the difference, I wish to establish the extent of the identity.

2.

My text is Marx's "Critique of the Gotha Program," a work which contains the fullest expression of the mature Marx's understanding of the transition between capitalism and communism.[1] He develops his view by way of an attack on the program advanced by a faction of the German Social Democratic movement in 1875. The key section of Marx's argument responds to the following sentence of the proposed program: "The proceeds of labor belong undiminished with equal right to all members of society" (CG 525).

Marx attacks this sentence's reliance on the concept of equality. "*Equal right* is still constantly stigmatized by a bourgeois limitation," he writes (CG 530). Equality is "*a right of inequality, in its content, like every right*" (CG 530). Some people, through health or motivation or talent or age, can contribute more than other people. There are two ways equality can be applied in this situation. One can give to each person a share equivalent to his contribution, thus ratifying natural inequality. Or one can give an identical share to each, thus unjustly punishing the more productive people. In either case, "this *equal* right is an unequal right" (CG 530).

Equality fails because it involves "the application of an equal standard" to "unequal individuals (they would not be different if they were not unequal)" (CG 530). Marx calls upon the framers of the Gotha program to reject this "ideological nonsense about right" (CG 531). Their obsession with equality, he argues, results from the mistake of thinking of the question of socialism "as turning principally on distribution" (CG 532). So far from being its central feature, Marx thinks that in socialism the question of distribution will simply cease to be a question. This will happen without the application of a principle of equality. The collective will simply take "from each according to his ability," and it will give "to each according to his needs" (CG 531). Individuals will not be equal in what they give or in what they take, or in the ratio between the two. But no one will care.

Who or what will determine how much each individual should give or take? Who or what will determine an individual's "needs" or "abilities"? These are complex questions. They are also part of the question of distribution, and therefore Marx doesn't care about them. Who does care? When does the question of distribution become an important question? When the different abilities and desires of different individuals are seen as potentially conflicting. For the Gotha framers, looking at things from the perspective of prevailing social conditions, the question of distribution is so important they address it in the very first point of their socialist program. They think that in order for socialism to exist, the subjective desire of the individual to work, and the subjective desire of the individual to consume, must be regulated by an objective principle. Different individuals must be coordinated, must be brought into line with each other, and this requires a principle like equality.

The Gotha position seems intuitively correct. Let us imagine, as Marx does, that the great productive powers of capitalism will eliminate all forms of basic want. Let's go much further and imagine that this productive power is strong enough not simply to eliminate biologically defined want, but also to satisfy current desires, and to apply its vast power to the satisfaction of new desires as fast as they arise. But this economy of superabundance will still be an economy of scarcity. Even if we imagine an economy so powerful that it will enable every individual to get everything they want, there is still a problem with allowing each individual to decide on their own how much to consume.

This is because, as the Gotha framers recognize, individuals' desires are not developed in isolation, but are calculated relative to what other individuals have. Even if we can each have everything we want, there will still be a very good reason for me to want *more* than you. This is because seeing how much you have relative to how much I have is a very good way to determine my status. This fact, the principle that links consumption to social position, the principle that links what I have to what you have, ensures that intersubjective conflict is not simply an effect of limited productive capacities. If I am hungry, I want to eat. Then I might want a car. And then I want more than you have.

Intersubjective conflict appears to be built into individual desire.[2] This tendency of an individual's desire to conflict with that of another makes the question of distribution pressing and complicated. So long as the collective functions according to a regime of recognition, and so long as economic goods and values are technologies of recognition, individuals cannot be allowed to decide what and how much they want on their own. Insofar as the economy is oriented towards social recognition, the economy will be an economy of scarcity, and distribution will be an urgent and difficult question.

And yet Marx says that this concern with distribution is a mistake. He takes the Gotha framers to task for approaching the question of socialism as the problem of regulating the kind of individuals one finds in capitalist society. He admits their program makes perfect sense on this basis. The individual subjects who make up capitalist society cannot be left to do what they want. Intersubjective conflict is coded into their desires. To produce collective harmony under these conditions, subjective desire must be regulated by an objective principle.

But Marx thinks people in socialism will not be like people in capitalism. In socialism, Marx argues, people can be left to do what they want. "From each according to his ability; to each according to his needs" (CG 531). The absence of any need to regulate what people want to do and to consume implies a change in what and how people want. This transformation of desire, and not the regulation of an existing mode of desire, is the key question for socialism. Marx believes that the economic transformation that separates capitalism from communism involves a transformation of subjectivity. This new, socialist subjectivity will lack the inherent tendency to conflict with the desires of others manifest by the subjects of capitalist society. Socialist desire will not require regulation by a principle like equality.

What is this transformed subjectivity like? The two most perceptive analysts of this dimension of Marx's thought have described it as a "radical subjectivity." This term designates a mode of human experience that is not constituted or maintained by recognition. It is invisible, nonsocial experience. And it is this experience, for Marx, that frees itself from within the capitalist economy.

3.

Two writers, Michel Henry and Hannah Arendt, have argued that Marx is the philosopher of a radical, nonrecognizable subjectivity. Arendt describes Marx's vision of socialism as entailing the liquidation of the space of recognition. She argues that the assault on what she calls "the visibility and audibility of the public realm" "received its most coherent and greatest expression in Marx's work" (*HC* 112, 88–89). The "common realm," for Arendt, is a space illuminated by the gaze of recognition. "The presence of others who see what we see and hear what we hear assures us of the reality of the world and ourselves" (*HC* 50). This intersubjective play of recognizing gazes is anchored by "the intermediary, stabilizing, and solidifying influence of things" (*HC* 182). Human action and experience must be "transformed, reified as it were, into things," objectified, so as to ground this between-space (*HC* 95). These "worldly" things preserve the identity of subjects by preserving the space between them. "To live together in the world means essentially that a world of things is between those who have it in common, as a table is located between those who sit around it; the world, like every in-between, relates and separates men at the same time" (*HC* 52).

Marx undertakes a sustained assault on the reification of human life. The "communistic fiction" he advances involves the destruction of the "common world" supported by the objectification of human labor (*HC* 44). Marx's critique of reification foresees that in socialism, the things of the world will cease to maintain a distance from their human makers. In Marx's communistic fiction, "all things would be understood, not in their worldly, objective quality, but as results of living labor power and functions of the life process" (*HC* 89).

What is this "life process?" Arendt understands it as "the most radical subjectivity, in which I am no longer 'recognizable'" (*HC* 51). Marx's communistic fiction shows the reified things and separate, delimited subjects of the common world being gathered into this radical subjectivity. Marx advances radical subjectivity as the goal of progressive politics, and the end point of the development of market society. In socialism the objective, public world that relates us by separating us disappears. This liquidation of what separates us abruptly solves the problem of inequality in a way that looks to Arendt like a catastrophe.

Marx's "radical subjectivity," his "life" is material; it is the life of human bodies. Yet this materialism of the "life process" lacks a certain reality for Arendt. The "forces of intimate life ... lead an uncertain, shadowy kind of existence unless and until they are transformed, deprivatized and deindividualized, as it were, into a shape to fit them for public appearance" (*HC* 50). The recognition of others is required to give the body a delimited shape, to turn the "life process" into an object. Marx, in seeking to interrupt this reification, prevents human life from assuming a definite form. This "life" cannot be identified with any object. It is a kind of non-objective material. From Arendt's perspective, a perspective that endows recognition with an ontological quality, this life appears unreal. Radical subjectivity looks fictional.

The radical subject emerges with the collapse of the reified, public "between-space." Thus this subjectivity is not pre- but post-social, a "communistic fiction." This post-social subjectivity is unable to sustain a distinction between itself and others. "The 'who' [of an individual], which appears so clearly and unmistakably to others, remains hidden from the person himself" (*HC* 179). This "who," the assignment of subjectivity to a singular, objective, and differentiated body, is lost with the visibility of that body. Who speaks when it speaks, who acts when it acts? Its namelessness conceals a multitude.[3] The unrecognizable post-social subject is not an individual, but a collective.

Arendt clearly grasps what Marx berates the Gotha framers for missing. The "radical subjectivity" that emerges after the communistic transformation is not the same as the individual subjectivities that exist prior to that transformation. When the visibility of the between world is eradicated, "society ... must be conceived as a single subject" (*HC* 44). The specter of this collective subject frightens Arendt. Instead of assaulting the visibility of the public world in the name of a radical, material "life," we should "sacrifice" part of our lives to sustain it (*HC* 95). "World alienation, and not self-alienation as Marx thought," is the real threat (*HC* 254).

Marx's "communistic fiction" seeks to reverse the objectification of human life. The market in capitalist society is a process of objectification. The economy is tied, as Arendt suggests, to the production of the objects that facilitate recognition. Within the market system, Marx sees the possibility of a counter-process. This counter-process can be realized through the development of that system. If the capitalist market is a process of objectification, the counter-process seen by Marx is a process of subjectification. Reification will be reversed, and a new mode of collective life will arise with the collapse of the space between subjects. Arendt calls this collective life "radical subjectivity." In the "communistic fiction," life and experience continue to be the material activity of different human bodies. But the "I" that emerges in those unrecognizable human bodies does not take account of their differences.

I will have more to say about this objectless subjectivity in relation to embodiment. But for now I want to emphasize that, in a situation where subjectivity is not oriented to recognition, equality ceases to be a question worth caring about. The desire that arises in a human body is not keyed to what the other has. The essentially conflictual nature of human desire, which makes the Gotha program's concern with equality seem so intuitively correct, disappears.

Michel Henry's 1981 book *Marx* constitutes the most sustained meditation on Marx as a philosopher of "radical subjectivity." For Henry, the crucial question in interpreting Marx concerns the nature of Marx's critique of Hegel. What does Marx mean by "materialism"? How precisely is this distinguished from idealism? The key text for Henry is the "Theses on Feuerbach," the work where Marx establishes the philosophical underpinning of his mature program. These are the first and last theses:

The chief defect of all hitherto existing materialism – that of Feuerbach included – is that the thing, reality, sensuousness, is conceived only in the form of the object or of *contemplation*, but not as *human sensuous activity, practice*, not subjectively.

The philosophers have only *interpreted* the world, in various ways; the point, however, is to *change* it.[4]

Here Marx distinguishes his revision of Hegel from that of Feuerbach. Both Marx and Feuerbach think Hegel errs by giving mental and spiritual phenomena a privileged ontological status relative to material reality. Both writers, in Marx's celebrated formula, want to take Hegel, who has been standing on his head, and place his feet back on the ground.

But whereas Feuerbach sees material reality as an "object," Marx sees it as an "activity." For Marx, Henry writes, "reality is not objective reality … it is practice" (*M* 139–40). From the perspective of this ontology of "practice," Feuerbach's materialism and Hegel's idealism are identical. In both philosophies, Henry argues, "reigns sight, the primordial theoria which presents being as what is seen, as an object" (*M* 141). Hegel is the great philosopher of recognition, for whom reality is visibility. The subject becomes real, becomes universal, by becoming visible, being seen as an object. "It has always been the case, from the time of ancient Greece, that the subjectivity of the subject is but the objectivity of the object" (*M* 144).

The subject of philosophy is a visible object. Before becoming visible, recognized in the mirror or by the other, the subject lives an empty, shadow existence. In Hegel's philosophy, human experience, activity, practice are imprisoned in the stasis of an object. There is no room in this world for an activity other than vision. No account is taken of the creative power of bodies: it is enough to be seen. This philosophy "substitutes for living reality a universe petrified by the gaze" (*M* 153). Feuerbach, who thinks he overturns Hegel by presenting the world as "matter," as an object posing before the gaze of the thinker, does nothing of the kind. Feuerbach's materialism, like Hegel's idealism, is a philosophy of the object, which locates the ontological principle of the world in vision. "This structure of being is what is ultimately rejected in the 'Theses on Feuerbach'" (*M* 141).

Marx does not deny or reject sight. But he deprives sight of its ontological significance, and replaces it with "practice." "Action, considered in itself, has nothing to do with this gaze ... with the discovery of a spectacle, with the appearing of an object" (*M* 143). Again: Feuerbach thought he could "grasp being as an object," whereas Marx sees being only in practice (*M* 142). And in practice "there is no object" (*M* 143). Marx abandons the philosophy of the visible. Henry uses the same term as Arendt to describe the significance of Marx's break with Hegel. Marx's breakthrough consists of the movement from "a subjectivity establishing and receiving the object, an 'objective' subjectivity ... to a radical subjectivity from which all objectivity is excluded" (*M* 145).

The abstraction of Henry's formulations risks making Marx's concept of practice seem stranger than it is. It will be useful to consider this argument more slowly. On Henry's account, there are two distinct levels of Marx's understanding of practice. (1) Practice, as radical subjectivity, constitutes the basic level of human reality. (2) Communism consists of freeing this radical subjectivity from its alienation in a regime of recognition.

Let's begin with the first step, Marx's assertion of the invisibility or nonobjectivity of practice. This is not a fiction, but a dimension of lived reality. Arendt also describes embodied experience as invisible. "Nothing, in fact, is less common and less communicable, and therefore more securely shielded against the visibility and audibility of the public realm, than what goes on in the confines of the body" (*HC* 112). Mark Hansen's recent work interpreting and extending Merleau-Ponty's phenomenology enables us to grasp the extent to which "invisible" straightforwardly describes embodied activity.

Hansen develops an account of human action that privileges the "*operational* perspective of the organism over any observational perspective."[5] He distinguishes between "body schema" and "body image." The body schema refers to embodiment as a process, a movement, a grip on the world. The body schema is the "operational perspective" of human action. From this "operational" perspective, my body endows a space with up-down directionality, with ways, routes, and lines of force. My body inhabits a space as a set of possible and actual postures and movements. The "observational perspective," on the other hand, shows my body as fixed to a certain delimited point in space.

There is an unbridgeable gap between the way I experience my body and the way an observer sees it. Body schema cannot be reduced to an image of the body. Hansen describes the "disconnection of the (fundamentally motile) body schema from the (fundamentally visual) body image."[6] The image produced by the mirror or the eye of another presents my body as a self-identical, static object. But "movement always displaces the self, thus preventing it from coinciding with itself."[7] My embodied experience is characterized by actual and potential movements, lines of force, directionality. The body schema is not available to "any observational perspective," it is not visible.

Henry writes, "in action there is no object" (*M* 143). Hansen writes that "the body as object ... belongs to a derivative ontological plane."[8] The nonobjective subjectivity of the body schema should be understood as the primary dimension of human existence. This account of embodiment helps us to recover the "subjective" materialism of the "Theses on Feuerbach." What Marx calls "human sensuous activity" is this invisible subject of embodiment, an "operational perspective" nonidentical with any recognizable object. This is the "radical subject" Arendt identifies both with the body and with the "communistic fiction."

How might this immediate, pre-objective embodiment extend past the skin of an individual body to constitute what Arendt calls a collective subject? My description of the dynamics of the economic fiction in the preceding chapters suggests one answer to this question. The market and price system, interfacing with individual bodies, coordinates the actions, perceptions, and movements of those bodies.[9] This coordination does not include a moment of recognition; it does not involve an objective principle regulating distinct individual subjectivities. Rather, it works from within, by shaping and organizing the body schema, the perception of an environment, the perception of what movements, choices, or actions are possible. In the economic fiction, an invisible economy unlocks and extends an invisible body. The negativity of the economic settles in the negativity of the body. In the economic fiction, the market is a structure of radical subjectivity.

I will soon turn to the basic difference between the ways Marx and the works I explore in this book approach the economic. But now I want to stress that the economic fiction, like Marx's texts, delineates a basic transformation of human subjectivity that alters the question of inequality.

The communism Marx describes in the "Critique of the Gotha Program" is understood from the perspective of this transformed, "radical" subjectivity. In actually existing capitalism, where the economy is oriented to the accumulation of resources in the hands of individual subjects, the people demand equality. In the regime of visibility, where what individual subjects want is pegged to what they see other subjects have, fair distribution is a complex and crucial question.

From the perspective of the transformed subjectivity elucidated in the "Critique of the Gotha Program" and in the economic fiction, it is impossible to care about the question of distribution. There is no equality. No one suffers from its absence.

4.

The economic fiction gives us the opportunity to see what is vital, capable of inspiring conviction and desire in the great modern dream: that the strange connections of the market economy shelter the possibility of a beautiful new world. The obvious way to do this is to compare the economic fiction with Marx, the great modern exponent of this dream.

The preceding investigation suggests three areas of contact between Marx and the economic fiction. In both: (1) A new collective life develops through the operation of principles immanent to the market economy. (2) This collective life is conceived as a radical, objectless, invisible subjectivity, contrasted by Marx with the visible subject of recognition (theorized by Hegel), and by economic fictions with the visible subject of recognition (realized in society). (3) This new collective life is brought about not by the establishment of economic equality, but by the transformation of economic relations such that economic inequality becomes irrelevant.

The crucial difference between Marx's modern vision and its successor concerns the first point. The immanent principles of the market economy are understood differently in these two sets of texts. We can sketch this difference by way of three related propositions advanced by Marx and conspicuously absent in the economic fiction. (1) Labor is the source of all value. (2) Money represents the mystification of labor. (3) The labor process involves the development of conflicting classes.

These three differences reduce to a single difference: Marx believes in the labor theory of value. He identifies the contradictions produced by the alienation of labor in price as the immanent movement that liberates the collective. The collective subject of the economic fiction, on the other hand, is liberated when the market gets disembedded from objectifying social relations. There is no trace of the labor theory of value in the texts I consider. What does this difference mean? Does it suggest that the economic fiction is ideological after all?

I think there are two principal ways of attributing an ideological function to the works I study. To describe these works as ideological is to say that the fascination elicited by these texts serves to produce an interest in an oppressive social system. The first way to do this is to say that the economic fiction makes economic inequality invisible. As we have seen, it does do this, but in such a way as to make economic inequality irrelevant. The radical transformation that makes inequality irrelevant in these works has the same structure as the radical transformation that inaugurates communism in Marx.

The second way to say that economic fictions are ideological is from the standpoint of the labor theory of value. From this perspective, it is easy to show that the reliance of the economic fiction on the market and on circulation is ideological on its face.[10] From the perspective of the labor theory of value, money and circulation add nothing but a malevolent illusion to the value placed in things at their birth by the production process. By setting money to work organizing experience, these works perform the ideological work of concealing the source of all value: the worker's productive labor. The economic fiction envisions a radical collective subject, but money is the poison in its bloodstream.

The idea that economic fictions conceal or justify actual economic inequality is a serious and plausible one, to which I devoted serious consideration in the pages above. But there is no reason why we should credit the idea that these works conceal the source of all value in labor, or that they obscure the nature of class identity as a relation to the means of production, or that they blind us to the real basis of money. I don't think we need worry about any description of the relation between the economic fiction and actual conditions that relies on the validity of the labor theory of value. That theory has been discredited for well over a century. The arguments advanced against it are strong, and I know of no place where they have been refuted. I believe the labor theory of value to be indefensible. The absence of any reference to the labor theory in the economic fiction does not show us what is ideological in these works, but what is dead in Marx. Marx's particular route between actually existing capitalism and a beautiful collective life has been closed.

But we still don't understand the opening of a new route in postwar aesthetic works. The easiest way of accounting for the economic fiction would be to identify an ideological function. Such an identification would enable us to understand what happens to the economic in these works in terms of a relation to social interests, structures, logics, or discourses linked to the actual economy. In investigating the idea that these works conceal economic inequality, I have investigated and rejected what I feel to be the most likely source of such a function.

I want to emphasize that in addressing the question of inequality, we have addressed a broad range of potential analyses of the work performed by economic fictions. One might understand economic inequality, differences in the distribution of resources among individuals, either as a basic feature of the market, or as reflecting a wide variety of noneconomic factors. Such factors might include institutional racism, the historical effects of racism, the legacy of colonial underdevelopment, or gender discrimination. These are all different sources of actual economic inequality. The benefit of considering inequality as such is that it enables us to be agnostic about these sources. We can be abstract. The economic effect of all the noneconomic social powers listed above is to produce economic inequality. If the economic fiction does not cover up or justify inequality, it does not perform an ideological function on behalf of any of these oppressive social forces.[11]

There remain many ways one might disagree with the values expressed by the works I describe. One might not feel their fascination. One might have an ethical commitment to the dynamics of recognition. One might be uninterested in this transformation of the economic. But I do not think there are other ways of describing this relation of the aesthetic to the economic as ideological, as distorting the image of the economy on behalf of actual interests. This is a significant finding. Wherever we locate the oppressive social forces organizing actually existing capitalism – in individuals, groups, discourses, logics, institutions, or histories – the economic fiction is somewhere outside. So where is it?

5.

We have seen that the economic fiction does not cover up or justify actual economic inequality. These works transform economic relations in such a way that inequality ceases to be of conceivable interest to anyone. The economic fiction consists of this aesthetic transformation of the economic.

It is important to be clear about the narrow scope of this claim. This relation between art and the economic pertains to some works and not to others. It is possible, as in Bret Easton Ellis' fiction or Elizabeth Bishop's poetry, to create artworks that do not transform the economic in this way, or that do not transform the economic at all.

Yet the very narrowness and modesty of my claim leads me to make a rather immodest critical intervention. For by identifying a relation between art and the economy that applies only to some works, I am suggesting that there is no essential relation between the economic and the aesthetic, no way to decide this relation in advance. And yet the effort to understand artworks on the basis of just such an essential relation has marked most criticism concerned with the economic. We will see that there is a good reason for why this should be so, and that something basic about our understanding of art must change to make room for the kind of modest claim I am making.

Adorno's *Aesthetic Theory* is an influential example of the effort to articulate a single relation between the aesthetic and the economic. Adorno approaches this relation by way of the Marxist account of the commodity. The capitalist commodity, Marx argues, presents itself in the guise of an illusory autonomy by distancing itself from its conditions of production. Artworks, Adorno writes, gain a distance from society, a way of looking at it from outside, by imitating the structure of the commodity fetish. "The truth content of artworks, which is indeed their social truth, is predicated on their fetish character."[12] Artworks become social by distancing themselves from social concerns, by virtue of their apparent disconnection from society. Thus the commodity form provides the template for aesthetic production.

For Adorno, the structure of the commodity fetish arises in the context of capitalist society, a "total exchange society" organized by a singular "principle of exchange."[13] There is no sense that the economic itself might be susceptible of transformation, that it is anything other than a rigid and totalizing social structure relentlessly co-opting everything in its path. In fact, Adorno sees works that reflect upon or thematize the economic as compromising what is truly aesthetic in them. "The thematic," Adorno declares, "the open or covert treatment of social matters, is the most superficial and deceptive" feature of artworks.[14] Artworks become social by distancing themselves from social or economic questions, concerns, and relations. If works begin to take up social and economic questions, they lose their social and economic quality, and they also cease to be art. What can this astonishing claim mean?

Adorno's theory is predicated on the labor theory of value, and involves a distinction between the subjective character of the evaluations of things produced by a market process, and the objective value placed in things by labor at the scene of production. The "thematic" qualities of artworks address themselves to "reception," they seek to change or to modify subjective perceptions of the world.[15] But "the relation of art to society is not to be sought primarily in the sphere of reception. This relation is anterior to reception, in production."[16] Aesthetic form carries an "objective social content" by virtue of its "conditions of production," conditions that impart to the artwork its fetish character. This "objective content" is only obscured and diminished by the "manifest opinions," the spurious "thematics" oriented to "reception."[17] A hierarchy of aesthetic value unfolds from this distinction between subjective thematics and the objective social content encoded in the fetish character of the work at its birth. "Kafka, in whose work monopoly capitalism appears only distantly, codifies ... what becomes of people under the total social spell more faithfully and powerfully than do any novels about corrupt industrial trusts."[18]

Thus Adorno claims there is one essential relation between the economic and the aesthetic. The persuasiveness of this analysis depends on the idea that the artwork's "manifest" capacity to think about the economic can amount to nothing more than uninteresting "opinions." Of course, nothing is more natural in reading than to ignore what we take to be uninteresting. This is simply the work of interpretation. But Adorno claims to distinguish mere opinion from what is aesthetically interesting categorically and in advance. What is mere opinion? Any presence of the economic in the artwork other than the formal structure imposed by the work's imitation of the commodity fetish. This strong rejection of what Adorno calls a work's "manifest" thought amounts to a hobbling of the aesthetic, and a limiting of its possibilities.

Instead of many possible relations between art and the economy, in Adorno's aesthetics there can be only one "objective" relation. It is as if the aesthetic can only relate authentically to the economic by not thinking about it. Why is this? One might think that the problem lies in the particular view of the economy that underlies *Aesthetic Theory*. Perhaps Adorno's commitment to the labor theory of value accounts for his resistance to other modes of relation between art and economic form. Perhaps *Aesthetic Theory* shows how subtle a form "crude" economic determinism can take.

But – as I showed in my introduction – we see an analogous resistance to the possibility of the aesthetic in critics with quite different accounts of the relation between art and the economy. Some say that a single logic imposes an identical form on the economic and the aesthetic (New Historicism); some think the economic and the aesthetic are distinct forms of social value (Bourdieu); some think the aesthetic offers a rival theory of the actual economy (New Economic Criticism). All of these approaches were advanced and defended as improvements over the crude determinism of the old Marxist accounts. And yet none of them has conceptual space for the kind of difference the aesthetic makes to economic form in the works I consider. None of them has room for the simple idea that the economic might work differently in an artwork than it does in the world. None of them can accept the idea that money might spend differently in a book than on Wall Street.

At the opening of the postwar era, Karl Polanyi and Hannah Arendt identified the detachability of the economic from the social. They argued that this detachment happens in aesthetic space. Through a hybrid of aesthetic and economic form, a purely economic mode of experience arises. The economic works one way in the world; it is embedded in social relations, entangled with government agencies. But in the economic fiction the market works differently; it becomes the organizing principle of a nonsocial collective.

In the postwar era, the logic of disembedded economic forms challenges an embedded economic logic. But criticism has room for only one economic logic. This economic logic might be identical with the aesthetic, it might determine the aesthetic, or the aesthetic might be autonomous with respect to it. But the economic remains singular. Polanyi and Arendt see two economies, two kinds of money, two markets, two price systems. They understand this splitting of the economic, and the conflict it inaugurates, as a major social and historical event. Yet it is an event the disciplines of cultural and literary criticism have been unable to describe.

This inability is due to the role of a third term in the criticism: the social. Criticism has been unable to identify the artwork's capacity to transform the economic because it has been unable to see the aesthetic as a category outside of the social. The possibility of an aesthetic transformation of economic form becomes a test of our ability to conceive the asocial qualities of the aesthetic. And this is precisely because the economic is taken to be so thoroughly embedded in the social. From Adorno to Deleuze to Jameson to the New Economic Critics to Agamben, to refer to the economic is to refer to capitalist society. To refer to money is to refer to a set of social relations.

The invisibility of the economic fiction to the critics isn't hard to understand. The idea that a nonsocial economy might emerge in an artwork is to suggest, in the most implausibly strong fashion, that the very fabric of the social might come apart in the fragile textures of artworks.

Yet this is precisely what I have argued in this book. I might have argued that these works pretend to open a space outside society, while actually working according to a social logic. But this argument is what was rejected in my rejection of a possible ideological relation between these works and social forces. The economic doesn't work here the way it works in society, and this discrepancy is not determined by a social logic. The economic fiction simply isn't in the social world. It's somewhere else. This is an important social fact, with important social consequences. This fact just can't be found in the places where criticism has been looking.

My account of the economic fiction offers no radical new theory about how aesthetic works operate. Heidegger's aesthetic theory – on which I have relied – shows us how artworks set certain principles to work organizing experience. I just notice a change in the principles. In some works, money replaces social norms, racial types, historical conventions, gender roles. This is the only difference, but it is not a modest one. The postwar discovery of the market as a nonsocial principle for organizing experience changes everything for aesthetic form. In the conditions of postwar America, whatever political or social attitude we end up taking towards this phenomenon, we need to begin by taking it seriously. And to take it seriously we need to become less comfortable with modest claims about what art can do.

6.

What art can do is to make things disappear. The vast body of critical work on utopia is linked by the common argument that utopia is hard to see. Most writers understand this negatively, and read this feature as a sign of the difficulty or impossibility of seeing a world unlike our own. In the economic fiction, invisibility is not a sign of the impossibility of another world, but its guarantee. Here invisibility is a practice. The theory of fictional economics revolves around the claim that art disembeds economic form from the social. Its practical aesthetics are concerned with disappearance.

Consider the practice of putting tinted windows on cars, discussed in Chapter 5. Think of this as a very early popular technology for removing the economic from the visible. The tinted windows remove the practice of driving a new car from its place in an embedded economy, a social economy, an economy of recognition, a visible economy.

The literal quality of this kind of technique, while fascinating, does not exhaust the possibilities. What is set to work in the aesthetic spaces I have described is a nonsocial principle of association and coordination. Thus the oldest aesthetic power, the power to absorb the attention, becomes a technique of the invisible. Absorbed in one of these works, we attain a virtual experience of the invisible economy. The woman reading *Neuromancer* on the subway, the man driving to work with B.G. on his stereo: little sections of the market wink in and out of visibility. With the first experiences of such works, a fault line appears down the center of every actual exchange. An invisible economy detaches from the visible economy.

What will be the social effects?

Notes

INTRODUCTION

1. Frederic Jameson, *Postmodernism, or, the Cultural Logic of Late Capitalism* (Durham: Duke University Press, 1991), p. 274.
2. Ibid.
3. Ibid., p. 275.
4. See David Harvey, *A Brief History of Neoliberalism* (Oxford: Oxford University Press, 2005). He argues that the appeal of conservative free-market rhetoric rests on an ideology of individual freedom, which he sees as masking the determining influence of social forces.
5. For influential examples see Milton Friedman, *Capitalism and Freedom* (Chicago: University of Chicago Press, 1962); and Robert Nozick, *Anarchy, State, and Utopia* (New York: Basic Books, 1974).
6. Practitioners of the "New Economic Criticism," for example, argue that literary texts reveal the social embeddedness of economic relations, thus critiquing the individualism of neoclassical economics. See especially *The New Economic Criticism: Studies at the Intersection of Literature and Economics*, ed. Martha Woodmansee and Mark Osteen (London: Routledge, 1999); and Regenia Gagnier, *The Insatiability of Human Wants: Economics and Aesthetics in Market Society* (Chicago: University of Chicago Press, 2000). Michael Tratner, in *Deficits and Desires: Economics and Sexuality in Twentieth Century Literature* (Stanford: Stanford University Press, 2001), argues that modern literature and economics register the way individual desires become embedded within social systems under the logic of "consumerism." Accounts that have privileged individual sovereignty have been less common in literary studies. (But see Barbara Herrnstein Smith's argument in *Contingencies of Value: Alternative Perspectives for Critical Theory* [Cambridge: Harvard University Press, 1988] for a neoclassical, individualist account of aesthetic value.) For a recent study that traces the genealogy of neoclassical individualism to the "romantic individualism" of Dickens' and Gaskell's images of the market, see Gordon Bigelow, *Fiction, Famine, and the Rise of Economics* (Cambridge: Cambridge University Press, 2003). Catherine Gallagher's *The Body Economic* (Princeton: Princeton University Press, 2005) presents an interesting twist to this kind of argument. She claims that the

individual's desiring body, rather than their calculating mind, serves as the site of economic agency in both neoclassical thought and nineteenth-century fiction. A basic question for all these critics, as well as for writers like John Guillory, Alan Liu, and Robert Kaufman, is the relation of literary images of the market to actual social and economic conditions. A related question is the relation of literary criticism to social scientific discourse. I examine the range of responses to these questions, and defend my own approach to them, below.

7. See the account of preference in practically any microeconomics textbook, for example, "Rational choice theory begins with the assumption that consumers enter the marketplace with well-defined preferences" (Robert H. Frank, *Microeconomics and Behavior* [Columbus: McGraw-Hill, 2006], p. 62).

8. The "New Economic Sociology" has been especially vigorous in promoting this view. The classic essay is Mark Granovetter's "Economic Action and Social Structure: The Problem of Embeddedness" (*American Journal of Sociology* 91 [November 1985], pp. 489–515). For a sense of the range of projects inspired by the idea that economic agency is embedded in social networks, see Michel Callon's *The Laws of the Markets* (London: Blackwell, 1998).

9. Interestingly, a group of economists and psychologists at M.I.T. have completed a study that suggests that real-world preferences are in fact sensitive to price ("Price Sensitive Preferences," working paper by D. Ariely, B. Koszegi, N. Mazar, and K. Shampan'er). Working in the wake of Kahneman and Tversky's work on context-dependent preference, they take price to be part of what constitutes a consumer's context. (See Daniel Kahneman and Amos Tversky, "The Framing of Decisions and the Psychology of Choice," *Science* 211:4481 [January 30, 1981].) Given the extent to which the idea of context-dependent preference has penetrated economics, and the extent to which it seems reasonable to think that prices are a particularly relevant part of a consumer's context, it is somewhat surprising that little work appears to have been done in this area. Ariely and his collaborators' experiments find evidence of price sensitivity, and are designed to eliminate the kind of sensitivity that would be compatible with neoclassical assumptions (i.e. that consumers use price as information about how well a given good would satisfy their preformed preference). However, the conclusions the authors draw from this phenomenon are quite different from the dynamics that animate the economic fiction as I present it here. While admitting that the kind of experiment they perform has limited ability to ascertain the source of preference, they argue that the findings do not reveal true price-sensitive preferences so much as the fact that individuals consistently make mistakes in articulating their price-independent preferences (ibid., p. 1).

10. Retrospective discussions of New Historicism have proliferated in recent years. (See, for example, Vincent Leitch, *Theory Matters* (London: Routledge, 2003); and John Xiros Cooper, *Modernism and the Culture of Market Society* (Cambridge: Cambridge University Press, 2004).) For an influential early

example, see George Levine's introduction to his *Aesthetics and Ideology* (New Brunswick: Rutgers University Press, 1994).

11. See for example Richard Godden's *Fictions of Capital: The American Novel from James to Mailer* (Cambridge: Cambridge University Press, 1990); and Richard Halpern's *The Poetics of Primitive Accumulation* (Ithaca: Cornell University Press, 1991).

12. See Robert Kaufman's description of Jameson's utopianism in "Red Kant," *Critical Inquiry* 26:4 (Summer, 2000), pp. 682–724.

13. Pierre Bourdieu, *Distinction: A Social Critique of the Judgment of Taste* (Cambridge: Harvard University Press, 1984).

14. My discussion of Bourdieu is indebted to the emphases in Craig Calhoun's account in "Habitus, Field, and Capital," in *Bourdieu: Critical Perspectives*, ed. Craig Calhoun, Edward Lipuma, and Moishe Postone (Chicago: Chicago University Press, 1993). Calhoun foregrounds the extent to which Bourdieu, by declaring the ubiquity of intersubjective status competition in all human spheres, "*assumes*, rather than empirically demonstrates, a high level of homology among fields" (ibid., p. 82). Hubert Dreyfus and Paul Rabinow make much the same point, criticizing Bourdieu's "metaphysical" assumption that all human endeavor is oriented towards "the competition for a social life that will be known and recognized" ("Can There Be a Science of Existential Structure and Social Meaning?," in Calhoun, Lipuma, and Postone, *Bourdieu: Critical Perspectives*, p. 39). Scott Lash offers a way of responding to criticisms that Bourdieu makes different fields look the same by arguing that, with the new importance of niche advertising, flexible production, and design, "real economic production comes increasingly to resemble symbolic production" ("Pierre Bourdieu: Cultural Economy and Social Change," in Calhoun, Lipuma, and Postone, *Bourdieu: Critical Perspectives*, p. 207).

15. John Guillory, *Cultural Capital* (Chicago: University of Chicago Press, 1993), p. 270.

16. Alan Liu, *The Laws of Cool: Knowledge Work and the Culture of Information* (Chicago: University of Chicago Press, 2004). Mark McGurl, "The Program Era," *Critical Inquiry* 32:1 (Fall 2005), pp. 102–29.

17. Liu, *The Laws of Cool*, p. 192.

18. See Woodmansee and Osteen, *The New Economic Criticism*, and Gagnier, *The Insatiability of Human Wants*.

19. Robert Kaufman, "Adorno's Social Lyric and Literary Criticism Today," in *The Cambridge Companion to Adorno*, ed. Tom Huhn (Cambridge: Cambridge University Press, 2004), p. 360.

20. Ibid., p. 359.

21. Ibid., p. 368.

22. Kaufman, "Red Kant," p. 721.

23. Ibid., p. 709.

24. Gunter Leypoldt ("Aesthetic Specialists and Public Intellectuals," *Modern Language Quarterly* 68:3 [September 2007]) makes this point, arguing that

the belief in the autonomy of the aesthetic has historically led to an anxiety on the part of literary intellectuals about their marginalization. Critics then respond to this anxiety by trying to make their claims about aesthetic artifacts refer back to a social world. But Leypoldt thinks the attempt to discover a genuine social relevance in the aesthetic is undermined by this "post-Kantian" way of understanding the artwork. He argues for a view of art as "world-making" which, when examined in the contexts in which it is produced, will lead to an understanding of art's social embeddedness that evades the "post-Kantian" problem. "I take the trope of world making to imply that while form is always political, its political content depends on the propositions with which it is connected in specific social practices: it cannot be abstracted from its readerly and writerly contexts" (Ibid., p. 435). Below, I pursue the possibility of "world-making" as an alternative to post-Kantian aesthetics along rather different lines.

25. In using this term – which is absent from Heidegger's text – I follow Hubert Dreyfus' use of the word "exemplar" to describe the relation of artwork to the world in his lucid discussion of Heidegger's philosophy of art in "Nihilism, Art, Technology, and Politics," in *The Cambridge Companion to Heidegger*, ed. Charles Guignon (Cambridge: Cambridge University Press, 1993).

26. Ibid., p. 298.

27. A Heideggerian approach has indeed proved richly successful in the analysis of American literature. For example, Sharon Cameron writes in her classic study *Lyric Time* (Baltimore: Johns Hopkins University Press, 1979) that "a specific fiction is predicated on the unique organization of temporal-spatial reality … a novel organizes experience" (p. 22). The works with which I am here concerned confront Heidegger's model with a special problem: accounting for a mode of organizing experience that does not originate in the social world.

28. There is a model for describing literature's exteriority with respect to the social that may appear closer to the subject of my study than Heidegger's aesthetics: Richard Poirier's *A World Elsewhere: The Place of Style in American Literature* (1966; Madison: University of Wisconsin Press, 1985) argues that the attempt to create a literary space outside of society is at the heart of American literature from Emerson through Fitzgerald. While Poirier is indispensable to any attempt to situate the specific features of the postwar writing I examine in relation to the total development of American literature, his model is inappropriate for analyzing those specific features for two related reasons. In the first place, the "world elsewhere" is on his account impossible; the works he takes up ultimately exemplify the struggle rather than the achievement. Thus we find in Poirier a prototype of the critical story of literature as the failure of resistance to social power that will proliferate in the New Historicism. In the second place, Poirer locates the energy mobilized by literature to effect its break from society in "style." But it is hard to see how style – understood in terms of linguistic pattern,

stress, and emphasis – can structure a world (as opposed to a text) in any robust fashion without being parasitic on structural concepts (nature, individualism), which turn out to be socially and culturally embedded. Thus to describe the dynamics of the *successful* creation of a literary world elsewhere, a somewhat different model seems necessary. None of this is to deny the importance of Poirier's book – and the interestingly-related later work of Leo Bersani – to the broad themes of this study, and I will have occasion to return to both later.

29. The classic account is H. Leibenstein's 1950 article "Bandwagon, Snob, and Veblen Effects in the Theory of Consumers' Demand," *Quarterly Journal of Economics* 64 (May 1950), pp. 183–207. The problem that Veblen effects present for the neoclassical view of the independence of preference from price can be neutralized if you accept the following argument: A consumer's preference in such cases is not determined by price itself, but by prestige. Price simply gives consumers information about how much social prestige a given good has. (For an example of this argument, see Donald Lichtenstein, Nancy Ridgway, and Richard Netemeyer, "Price Perceptions and Consumer Shopping Behavior," *Journal of Marketing Research* 30 [May 1993], pp. 234–45.) Of course, one might still think that there is rather more to price here than information about prestige, especially when one thinks of the preference for a Veblen good in terms of a desire to project the price of the good one owns. (And doesn't the prestige of a Rolls simply depend on its price?)

30. Thorstein Veblen, *The Theory of the Leisure Class* (1899; New York: Penguin, 1994), p. 87.

31. These poles define the desire for money in modernist fiction. For example, Theodore Dreiser, in *The Financier* (1912; New York: Meridian, 1995), distinguishes between the financier's desire for money, and that of ordinary people: "They want it [money] for what it will buy in the way of simple comforts, whereas the financier wants it for what it will control – for what it will represent in the way of dignity, force, power" (p. 182).

32. See Tim Conley's account of Gaddis' fiction as a "telephonic novel; the novel of multiplying, sometimes unrecognizable voices, and the ironic interplay between the proximity of voices and the distance of the speakers" ("William Gaddis Calling: Telephonic Satire and the Disconnection of Authority," *Studies in the Novel* 35:4 [Winter 2003], p. 528).

33. Joseph Schumpeter, *Capitalism, Socialism, and Democracy* (1942; New York: Harper, 1976).

34. Dreiser, *The Financier*, pp. 438–44.

35. For early and influential examples of this critical tradition see George Simmel's discussion of money as the "objectification" of desire in *Philosophy of Money* (London: Routledge, 2004), and Gyorgy Lukacs' discussion of reification in *History and Class Consciousness* (Cambridge: M.I.T. Press, 1971). I will argue in my conclusion that an important strain of Marx's own writings counters this equation of the economic with objectification.

36. John Johnson, *Carnival of Repetition: Gaddis's "The Recognitions" and Postmodern Theory* (Philadelphia: University of Pennsylvania Press, 1990), pp. 198, 185. In Johnson this deconstructive approach turns out to be compatible with reading the novel in relation to cybernetic theory, insofar as he takes the novel's fractured dialogues to demonstrate the entropy of information in the "run-away system" of capitalist communication. See Joseph Tabbi's "The Cybernetic Metaphor in William Gaddis's *JR*", *American Notes & Queries* (1989), pp. 147–51; and Christopher Knight's *Hints and Guesses: William Gaddis' Fiction of Longing* (Madison: University of Wisconsin Press, 1997) for broadly similar accounts of Gaddis.

37. See Chapter 3 for a full consideration of the relation between Hayek and the economic fiction.

38. The extent to which market agency for Hayek depends on simply looking has been vividly brought out by his critics within the Austrian tradition, who have attacked his tendency to replace entrepreneurial interpretation of market signals by a simple "awareness." (See especially Ludwig Lachmann, *The Market as Economic Process* [Oxford: Blackwell, 1986]; and Issac Kirzner, "The Subjectivism of Austrian Economics," in *New Perspectives on Austrian Economics*, ed. Gerrit Meijer [London: Routledge, 1995]). I will confine myself here to pointing out that the structure of this awareness in Hayek, and the role price plays in structuring that awareness, makes the things awareness can do in his work less baffling. For an extended discussion of Hayek's price theory, see my Chapter 3.

39. Johnson notes that the accumulation of "fragmented speech" produces "an almost seamless montage effect" (*Carnival of Repetition*, p. 198).

40. Thomas Sowell expresses this most basic economic assumption when he writes of "the limitations of nature and the unlimited desires of man" (*Knowledge and Decisions* [New York: Basic Books, 1978], p. 45).

41. The non-formalist understanding of genre adopted here is also indebted to the example of M. M. Bakhtin's theory of the novel (*The Dialogic Imagination*, ed. Michael Holquist [Austin: University of Texas Press, 1981]). Bakhtin analyzes the "novelistic" as an artistic mode of organizing voices, and rejects the traditional understanding of genre in terms of stylistic features (see especially pp. 262–67).

CHAPTER I. FREEDOM FROM YOU

1. Nancy Fraser, "Rethinking Recognition," *New Left Review* 3 (May/June 2000), p. 109.

2. Hegel quoted in Dimitri Shalin, "George Herbert Mead," in *The Blackwell Companion to Major Social Theorists,* ed. George Ritzer (Oxford: Blackwell, 2000), p. 310.

3. Charles Taylor, "The Politics of Recognition," in *Multiculturalism*, ed. Amy Gutmann (Princeton: Princeton University Press, 1994), p. 26.

4. Susan Stewart, *Poetry and the Fate of the Senses* (Chicago: University of Chicago Press, 2002), pp. 10–12.

5. Irving Howe, "The Plath Celebration: A Partial Dissent," in *Modern Critical Views: Sylvia Plath*, ed. Harold Bloom (New York: Chelsea House, 1989), p. 13.

6. For a contemporary poetic representation of the suffering of intersubjectivity, see Elizabeth Bishop's "In the Waiting Room": "But I felt: you are an *I* / you are an *Elizabeth*, / you are one of *them*. / *Why* should you be one, too?" "It was sliding / beneath a big black wave, / another, and another" (*The Complete Poems* [New York: Farrar, Straus, and Giroux, 1984], pp. 160–61). The "awful" perception (ibid., p. 161), the fall from innocence in Bishop's poem, is the moment of consciousness that one's subjectivity is that of the subject-in-relation, that one is subject to intersubjectivity.

7. Craig Owens, *Beyond Recognition: Representation, Power, and Culture* (Berkeley: University of California Press, 1994), p. 193.

8. See Slavoi Zizek on the failure of interpellation (*The Sublime Object of Ideology* [London: Verso, 1989], pp. 85–131). His account, like so many other versions of the necessary failure of recognition, draws on Jacques Lacan's celebrated essay "The Mirror Stage as Formative of the 'I' Function," in *Ecrits* (New York: W. W. Norton, 2002). Lacan locates the possibility of subjectivity, as well as the necessarily split nature of the subject, in the gap between the I and the specular other in the mirror. For an influential variation on this theme, see Judith Butler's argument that the individual's "susceptibility to the call of recognition" is qualified by the performative dimension of the language in which that call is delivered (*Excitable Speech: A Politics of the Performative* [London: Routledge, 1997], p. 26). The iterability of the call across contexts ensures that recognition never quite hits its target.

9. As Gayatri Chakravorty Spivak writes, "In every possible sense, translation is necessary but impossible" ("Translation as Culture," *Parallax*. 6:1 [2000], p. 13). Emmanuel Levinas' profound influence on contemporary secular thought is, as Alain Badiou has noted, something of a mystery (*Ethics: An Essay on the Understanding of Evil* [London: Verso, 2001], pp. 18–23). Levinas' idea that the attempt to cross the space between the self and the other constitutes the fundamental ethical wrong, and his sense of the absolute otherness of the other, is grounded, as Colin Davis writes, in Levinas' belief that "god is the other" (*Levinas: An Introduction* [Cambridge: Polity Press, 1996], p. 40). Badiou argues that this sense of *absolute* otherness requires reference to the divine, and that the secular appropriation of Levinas inevitably rewrites his ethics of the other as another version of the appreciation of the same. (I respect your inviolable otherness insofar as you, like me, respect inviolable otherness.) The argument I elaborate in this chapter will suggest, in contrast, that the gap between Levinas' god and self, like the gap between the mirror and self in Lacan, becomes important because it provides a figure for the postwar sense of the impassable intersubjective space. *This* sense of the impossibility of intersubjectivity is grounded not in god but in the prospect of a relation of another kind. From this perspective, Levinas' god–self relation is just another way of describing the impossibility of the relation between subjects.

10. Unlike Levinas, god for Plath is in the "I" position, not in the "you" position. Plath's subject is not an asocial loner but the source of universal value.
One might dismiss this as a delusion, but, as I will argue, it is in the valor-
izing sense of anti-psychiatry an *insane* delusion.

11. Jacqueline Rose, *The Haunting of Sylvia Plath* (Cambridge: Harvard
University Press, 1992), p. 5.

12. Christina Britzolakis, *Sylvia Plath and the Theatre of Mourning*
(Oxford: Oxford University Press, 2000), p. 110.

13. Ibid., p. 118.

14. Amy Hungerford notices the fraught relation to the audience figured in
this poem, which she analyzes as a problem with a particular kind of audience. The audience in "Lady Lazarus" lacks the "knowledge of suffering"
that would render it sufficiently empathetic to the speaker. "The exceptional poet and the one exceptional at dying require an equally exceptional
audience" (*The Holocaust of Texts: Genocide, Literature, and Personification*
[Chicago: University of Chicago Press, 2003], p. 38). I am suggesting here
that Plath's problem is with the audience as such, beyond any particular
feature that can be ascribed to it. Deborah Nelson (*Pursuing Privacy in Cold
War America* [Columbia University Press, 2002]) offers an interesting historical reading of Plath's basic problem with being seen. Nelson reads the
poet's "extraordinary hostility to surveillance" in the context of the early
postwar fears about the erosion of privacy (p. 81).

15. This is not to elide the role of gender here. Heterosexual relations in Plath
present a particularly intense mode of otherness. See Leo Bersani's *Homos*
(Cambridge: Harvard University Press, 1995) for a discussion of the hetero
eminently applicable to Plath's representations in her poetry and prose.

16. Kelly Oliver's *Witnessing: Beyond Recognition* (Minneapolis: University of
Minnesota Press, 2001), provides a cogent critique of the "pathology of recognition" (pp. 23–50). Oliver's response to the impasses of recognition – to
develop an ethics of a "witnessing gaze" – is quite different from Plath's
more radical solution.

17. The relation between Plath's work and anti-psychiatry has received some
attention in the criticism. I think all of these accounts tend to soften the
radical nature of anti-psychiatry's rejection of intersubjectivity. Maria
Farland, for example, reads anti-psychiatry and the *Bell Jar* as symptoms of
the "dismantling of the welfare state," in their assault on the mental institution. Institutions are to be replaced by privatized relations epitomized by the
"consensual doctor-patient relations that were the utopian ideal of the anti-
psychiatry movement" ("Sylvia Plath's Anti-Psychiatry," *Minnesota Review*
Ns. 55–57 [2002], p. 248). But, as I will argue, in this literature intimate
interpersonal relations are not opposed to institutional power, but continuous with it. See also Susan Lanzoni's recent account of the roots of anti-
psychiatry in German phenomenological psychiatry. She (again, I believe,
mistakenly) finds a belief in the "possibility of direct, intersubjective understanding" at the heart of anti-psychiatry's project ("An Epistemology of the

Clinic." *Critical Inquiry* 30: 1 [Fall 2004], p. 171). Marjorie Perloff, in a 1972 article, also sees Laing as an illuminating parallel to *The Bell Jar*'s representation of insanity as "an index to the human inability to cope with an unlivable situation" ("A Ritual for Being Born Twice: Sylvia Plath's *The Bell Jar*," *Contemporary Literature* 13: 4 [Autumn 1972]). She reads this inability not as an inevitable feature of intersubjectivity as such, but a call to reject masks and "simply to be oneself" in order to reach a healthy intersubjectivity (p. 521). Similarly, Paul Breslin's argument about the relation of Laing to postwar poetry in *The Psycho-Political Muse* (Chicago: University of Chicago Press, 1987) assimilates Laing's assault on social relations to the New Left critique of conformity, where the problem is not relations with the other as such, but with sameness or, in Marcuse's term, "one-dimensionality" (p. 5).

18. Michel Foucault, *Madness and Civilization* (New York: Vintage, 1988). Felix Guatarri, "Divided Laing," in *A Guatarri Reader* ed. Gary Genosko (Oxford: Blackwell, 1996).

19. Gregory Bateson, *A Sacred Unity: Further Steps to an Ecology of Mind* (1958; New York: Harper Collins, 1991), p. 113.

20. Ibid., p. 117.

21. For an important account influenced by Bateson, see Niklas Luhmann's study of interpersonal intimacy as a "code of communication" that requires people to "directly" "internalize another person's subjectively systematized view of the world," so as to maintain the fiction of "interpersonal interpenetration" by a correct and "intuitive" interpretation of the other's desire (*Love as Passion: The Codification of Intimacy* [Stanford: Stanford University Press, 1982], p. 26). Obviously, under such conditions "successful communication becomes increasingly improbable" (p. 22).

22. R. D. Laing, *Interpersonal Perception: A Theory and Method of Research* (New York: Springer Publications, 1966), p. 21.

23. Laing's work, like much of the postwar discourse of recognition, is heavily indebted to Jean-Paul Sartre's *Being and Nothingness* (1943; New York: Washington Square Press, 1993). For Sartre, the other is "the radical negation of my experience, since he is the one for whom I am not subject but object" (p. 310). "Between the Other and myself there is a nothingness of separation … as a primary absence of relation, it is originally the foundation of all relation between the Other and me" (pp. 312–13). We see a first "knot" in such formulations as the following: "Therefore as the subject of knowledge I strive to determine as object the subject who denies my character as subject and who himself determines me as object" (p. 310). Sartre is the crucial philosopher in the prehistory of the dynamic I am sketching. His enormously influential formulations led him to the brink of dismissing intersubjectivity as such, but he could not bring himself to do this, partly because he continued to see the only alternative to intersubjectivity as solipsistic individuality. For Laing and Plath, the dawning possibility of a non-solipsistic alternative to intersubjectivity as a social relation forms the horizon that enables the swift, guiltless cutting of the knot.

24. R.D. Laing, *Knots* (New York: Vintage, 1970), p. iii.
25. Ibid., p. 26.
26. Ibid., p. 2.
27. Ibid., p. 24.
28. Jameson, *Postmodernism*, pp. 154, and 26–28.
29. Juliet Mitchell, in *Psychoanalysis and Feminism* (New York: Pantheon, 1974), mounted an influential attack on Laing as committed to a quasi-mystical individualism.
30. Paul Thomas Anderson, dir. *There Will Be Blood*. Perfs. Daniel Day Lewis, Paul Dano, Kevin J. O'Connor. Paramount, 2007.
31. My thinking about this aspect of the film has been shaped by discussions with Jason Gladstone.
32. The key text for this view of lyric is J. S. Mill's "Thoughts on Poetry and its Varieties," in *Autobiography and Literary Essays, Vol. 1 of The Collected Works of John Stuart Mill* (Toronto: University of Toronto Press, 1981). The Plathian image of lyric consciousness as a *space of relation* – and the way the first person is projected in the works considered throughout this study – offers an "insane" lyrical countertradition to that analyzed by Victoria Jackson in *Dickinson's Misery* (Princeton: Princeton University Press, 2005).
33. It is against this failure of the two kinds of fictional blood that the literal blood of the final scene appears to shocking effect.
34. My reference here to the problem of the objecthood of the image – and the possibility of defeating it – is indebted to the work of Michael Fried, especially his *Art and Objecthood* (Chicago: University of Chicago Press, 1998). I pursue this problem more fully in Chapter 5.
35. Amiri Baraka, "Das Kapital," *Transbluesency: The Selected Poetry of Amiri Baraka* (New York: Marsilio Publishers, 1995), p. 154.
36. Karl Marx, "Preface to the First German Edition of *Capital*" (1867), in *The Marx-Engels Reader,* ed. Robert C. Tucker (New York: W. W. Norton, 1978), p. 297.
37. Ibid.
38. Marx's critique of Pierre-Joseph Proudhon, from which the sentences cited here derive, is the classic nineteenth-century analysis of the tendency to personify the economy. Walter Benn Michaels analyzes this tendency in the American context in his influential study of nineteenth-century naturalist fiction, arguing that the personification of the economy is the logical consequence of the belief in individual subjectivity: "The desire to personify the economy is the desire to bridge the gap between our actions and the consequences of our actions" (*The Gold Standard and the Logic of Naturalism* [Berkeley: University of California Press, 1987], p. 179). Personification of the economy for Michaels is a mistake, but one that reveals the logic that makes it possible to imagine individuals as autonomous intentional agents. More generally, poststructuralist literary studies and its successors have focused on the representation of individual subjects as a species of the personification of a system. Paul de Man, for whom personification is the

"master trope" of literature, argues that what "seemed at first sight to celebrate the self-willed and autonomous inventiveness of a subject," is in fact
the effect of the "impersonal precision of grammar" (*Allegories of Reading*
[New Haven: Yale University Press, 1979], p. 16). As Hungerford points out,
the New Historicism that succeeds deconstruction also takes personification
as its master trope, in its characteristic argument that "what we think of as
persons are the products of particular signifying systems" (*The Holocaust of
Texts*, p. 153). The economic fiction, even when it employs personification,
does not make the "mistake" denounced by New Historicism. The collective
subjectivity set up in the fiction is not reducible to personification. Rather,
each instance of what Arendt calls the "communistic fiction" is founded on
one of several more or less coherent relations between agency and market
structure. In Chapter 3, I discuss the incompatibility of this mode of agency
with critical conceptions of the "systematic" at some length.

39. Marx, "Preface," p. 295.
40. Ibid.
41. Baraka, "Das Kapital," pp. 153–54.
42. Ibid., p. 153.
43. Marx, "The Communist Manifesto" (1845), in *The Marx-Engels Reader*,
     p. 475.
44. Karl Polanyi, *The Great Transformation*.(1944; Boston: Beacon Press, 2001),
     p. 3.
45. Ibid., pp. 60, 71.
46. Ibid., p. 257.
47. Ibid., p. 171.
48. Marx, *Capital Vol. 1* (1867; New York: Penguin, 1992ª), p. 209. For Marx,
     market relations are a form of social relations, dialectically related to earlier
     and later (communist) forms. Meghnad Desai points out that while Marx
     thinks the transformation of all relations into market relations is the defin-
     ing feature of actual capitalism, Polanyi thinks it is the defining feature of
     an economic utopia (Desai, *Marx's Revenge: The Resurgence of Capitalism
     and the Death of Statist Socialism* [London: Verso, 2002], pp. 211–12).
49. Polanyi, *The Great Transformation*, p. 266.
50. John Gray reads "utopia" in Polanyi as synonymous with "delusion" (Gray,
     False Dawn: The Delusions of Global Capitalism [New York: New Press,
     2000]). David Harvey also interprets Polanyi's analysis of the "utopia" of
     disembedded relations as the exposure of a mistaken view (*A Brief History of
     Neoliberalism*, p. 37). What these writers neglect is the question of how and
     where (in what kind of space) the idea of disembedded relations begins to
     look plausible and begins to fascinate.
51. Callon takes Polanyi as equating disembedded relations with neoclassical
     individualism and arguing that this individualism is always supported by
     a subterranean network of social connections. For Callon, the neoclassical
     description of the sovereign, calculating individual is substantially correct.
     However, he argues that this individual is "framed, formatted and equipped

with prostheses that help him in his calculations" (*The Laws of the Markets*, p. 51). His innovation is to focus on the role of nonhuman actors (calculators, economic textbooks), in helping to constitute the networks in which economic action is embedded. Price does not figure in his account of economic action.

52. Hanna Pitkin, *The Attack of the Blob: Hannah Arendt's Concept of the Social* (Chicago: University of Chicago Press, 2000), p. 196.

53. Margaret Canovon, "Hannah Arendt as a Conservative Thinker", in *Hannah Arendt: Twenty Years Later*, ed. Larry May (Cambridge: M.I.T Press, 1997), p. 23. This is perhaps a good place to clear up a potential terminological confusion. While many writers use the term "social" in referring to this intersubjective space, Arendt never does. She reserves it exclusively for the "collective subject" that threatens the between-world. In *Attack of the Blob*, Pitkin analyzes the phantasmatic quality the word "social" takes on in Arendt. In this study I adopt a more conventional usage, applying it not to the collective subject of the "communistic fiction," but to the intersubjective.

54. Bruno Latour has recently developed this notion that intersubjectivity is constructed with objects, although his account lacks the normative dimension of Arendt's. The illusion of an unmediated intersubjectivity is, he suggests, "obtained by removing all traces of inter-objectivity" (*Reassembling the Social* [Oxford: Oxford University Press, 2005], p. 195). The opposite view is held by Donald Davidson, who argues that the perception of objectivity is logically dependent on an intersubjective relation ("The Second Person," in *Subjective, Intersubjective, Objective* [Oxford: Oxford University Press, 2001]. pp. 107–23).

55. There has been insufficient attention to the centrality of aesthetics in Arendt's philosophy, but this may be changing. Deborah Nelson, for example, has recently argued that for Arendt, ordinary objects must pass through an aesthetic lens in order to be sharable, in order to take up a place in the between-world. She points to Arendt's "aesthetic of the fact" as "a discipline of perception as well as a practice of representation" ("The Virtues of Heartlessness: Mary McCarthy, Hannah Arendt, and the Anesthetics of Empathy," *American Literary History* 18: 1 [2006], p. 92). Nelson argues, convincingly, that McCarthy is the supreme practitioner of this aesthetics of the between-world.

CHAPTER 2. FRANK O'HARA AND FREE CHOICE

1. Helen Vendler, *Part of Nature Part of Us: Modern American Poets* (Cambridge: Harvard University Press, 1980), p. 183; Charles Molesworth, *The Fierce Embrace: A Study of Contemporary American Poetry* (Columbia: University of Missouri Press, 1979), p. 85. In my discussion of the first generation of O'Hara's critics, I am more interested in their formulation of the problem his poetry poses as a representation of the personal

that seems to block the representation of the person, than in their various conclusions. Framing the problem in this way is typically the prelude to reading the "personal" as a late variety of modernist formal experimentation. (See, for example, Charles Altieri, *Enlarging the Temple: New Directions in American Poetry in the 1960's* [(Lewisburg: Bucknell University Press, 1979), pp. 108–22] on the influence of Dada on O'Hara's "poetics of the surface.") I think this approach is most successful with early poems like "Second Avenue," while I share Hazel Smith's criticism of their readings of the mature personal poetry as blunting its transgressive edge (*Hyperscapes in the Poetry of Frank O'Hara: Difference, Homosexuality, Topography* [Liverpool: Liverpool University Press, 2000], pp. 17–20).

2. Molesworth, *The Fierce Embrace*, 19.
3. Marjorie Perloff, *Frank O'Hara, Poet Among Painters* (Chicago: University of Chicago Press, 1997), p. 131.
4. The more interesting of the second generation of essays on O'Hara develop the approach taken by Andrew Ross in "The Death of Lady Day," *Poetics Journal* 8 (1989), pp. 68–77. Where earlier critics tend to focus on how the contingent personal detail blocks the presence of the person, Ross sees personal poetry as carving out a space where a threatened individual agency might survive. He reads the personal details of O'Hara's poems as instantiating a postmodern "micro-politics," in which an oppressive, multiform power is contested with a local, pragmatic "personal code" rather than a broad "totalizing" political program (ibid., p. 70). For recent studies along broadly similar lines, see John Lowney's reading of personal detail as a Foucauldian "local knowledge," in "The Post-Anti-Aesthetic Poetics of Frank O'Hara," *Contemporary Literature* 31 (1991), p. 248. See also Caleb Crain on the poems as dramatizing "the process by which O'Hara's fragmented self integrates" around a "resistant" homosexual identity ("Frank O'Hara's 'Fired' Self," *American Literary History* 9:2 [Spring 1997], p. 290); and Mutlu Blasing's sense of personal poetry as an attempt "to save an intimate bodily language from the violence of politicization – of being reduced to representing a group" (*Politics and Form in Postmodern Poetry* [Cambridge: Cambridge University Press, 1995], p. 65).
5. Ludwig Mises, quoted in David Riesman, *Conservative Capitalism: The Social Economy* (Basingstoke: Palgrave Macmillan, 1999), p. 17. Neoclassical economics is a relatively broad term that covers the mainstream of economic thought after 1945, and is distinguished from other brands of economic thought (Institutional, Austrian, Marxist, Keynesian) by its model of the rational economic agent and a mathematical and scientistic rhetoric. The origins of the discipline date to the 1870s and the work of William Stanley Jevons and Carl Menger. It suffered an eclipse during the Great Depression, and triumphantly reemerged in the context of postwar prosperity and Cold War ideology, where its model of individual and society began to circulate beyond the confines of economics. For the pivotal figure in the exportation of neoclassical models to political theory, see my discussion of Kenneth

Arrow below. For an influential discussion of the discourse of neoclassicism, see Donald McClosky, *The Rhetoric of Economics* (Madison: University of Wisconsin Press, 1985). For critical accounts of the history of neoclassical economics, see Phillip Mirowski's *More Heat Than Light: Economics as Social Physics, Physics as Nature's Economics* (Cambridge: Cambridge University Press, 1989); and his *Machine Dreams: Economics Becomes a Cyborg Science* (Cambridge: Cambridge University Press, 2002). For a sociological perspective on the centrality of the concept of choice in postwar culture, see Zygmunt Bauman's discussion of consumerism as "firstly about falling in love with choice," and "secondly, and by no means indispensably, about consuming more goods" (*Work, Consumerism, and the New Poor* [London: Open University Press, 1998], p. 138).

6. Perloff, *Frank O'Hara*, 123.

7. Jacobs' principal goal in eliminating zoning laws is to allow commercial enterprises to spring up on every block. Healthy cities, she writes, "are the natural economic homes of immense numbers and ranges of small enterprises" (*DL* 145). The chief crime of planning lies in its "subtraction of commerce, and of culture too," from cities (*DL* 4).

8. Michael Warner ("Zones of Privacy," in *What's Left of Theory?*, ed. John Guillory and Judith Butler [London: Routledge, 2000]) has drawn on Jacobs in his attack on New York City's late-nineties attempt to use zoning to limit adult businesses. Warner's account of queer desire emphasizes the free play of desire unmoored from identity, sited in a commercial space free from "community," "privacy," and the state (p. 106).

9. The biological metaphor is evident throughout Jacobs' book. But it is in the final chapter, "The Kind of Problem a City Is," that she mounts a sustained argument for using the terms and methods of the life sciences to describe cities, rather than the statistical methods of the social sciences. The basic unit of this pseudo-organic, self-organizing order, the "cell" of this "body," is the free choice. Jacobs is most radical, and most revealing of her commitments, in her suggestion that the city constitutes a subject. These moments are fragmentary and allusive, but represent some of her most compelling writing. For example, at one point she argues that it is impossible to create an adequate map of a city, and compares a healthy city to a fire on a dark field (*DL* 376–77). The fire illuminates and gives form to a space. The processes of the healthy city constitute a kind of vision. Such moments might be compared with the lyrical ending of a work like "Personal Poem."

10. Matthew Rabin, "Daniel Kahneman and Amos Tversky," in *American Economists of the Late Twentieth Century*, ed. Warren Samuels (Cheltenham: Edward Elgar, 1996), p. 112.

11. Ibid., p. 123.

12. Ibid., p. 122.

13. Ibid., p. 124.

14. Such an approach would be broadly compatible with the "New Economic Criticism" discussed in the Introduction.

15. William Watkin, in claiming that in O'Hara "the artist judges beyond the realm of rationality," mistakes this absence of rational self-interest for the absence of rationality as such (*In the Process of Poetry: The New York School and the Avant-Garde* [Lewisburg: Bucknell University Press, 2001], p. 31). For O'Hara, the point of the abstract choice is not some radical loss of or, in Watkin's terms, "liberation" from rationality, generality, totality, but the separation of economic rationality from individual rationality, interest from self-interest. The radical message here is not that one doesn't have any grounds for choosing between options; it's that these grounds can't, or shouldn't, be articulated in terms of individual self-interest. This is a basic distinction.

16. O'Hara's lover Vincent Warren is the most popular candidate. See Perloff, *Frank O'Hara*, and Terrel Herring, "Frank O'Hara's Open Closet," *PMLA* 117 (2002), p. 416.

17. See also Ross' discussion of O'Hara's "feminine obsession with trivia" ("The Death of Lady Day," p. 73); and Smith's study of O'Hara's performance of a "nonessentialist gay identity" (*Hyperscapes in the Poetry of Frank O'Hara*, p. 106).

18. Herring, "Frank O'Hara's Open Closet," p. 422.

19. Bersani, *Homos*, 1995, p. 123.

20. Cf. Warner's account of how unregulated, unzoned, and commercial city space facilitates a queer desire shaped neither by social norms nor by individual identities ("Zones of Privacy"). The distinctiveness of O'Hara's vision with respect to this account lies above all in his interest in the "who" of this kind of desire. The space of Warner's Christopher Street bears no trace of the aggregated fictional subjects of a poem like "Ode to Joy" or a book like *DL*.

21. Frank O'Hara, *Art Chronicles 1954–1966* (New York: George Braziller, 1975), p. 112.

22. Brad Gooch, *City Poet: The Life and Times of Frank O'Hara* (New York: Harper Perennial, 1993), p. 302.

23. Friedman, *Capitalism and Freedom*, 1962, p. 200.

24. Ibid., p. 23.

25. Ibid., p. 15. Kenneth Arrow gives a mathematical explanation for Friedman's and O'Hara's sense of conformity through coercion, of the tendency of American political democracy to become a "hunter." In his celebrated "Impossibility Theorem" of 1951, for which he later won the Nobel Prize, Arrow demonstrates that the general interest produced by majority voting is actually contrary to the individual interests of a majority of the voters. He develops a mathematical proof that, given certain assumptions, that people express their individual preference when voting for a candidate and that there be at least three candidates, the result of the ballot box will most often fail to produce the result actually favored by the majority. "The political procedure of majority ballot will generally produce social rankings of alternatives that violate the preferences of a majority of the voters" (Arrow, quoted in Mirowski, *Machine Dreams*, p. 302). The "general will," which

the nominal democracy of the political process provides with an alibi, is not derived from what most people actually want, but from an institutional malfunction. For Arrow, the political structures mediating between individual choice and social result introduce radical distortions. He concludes that "voting is strangled communication through a degraded channel," and given the far more accurate and flexible register of individual choice available through the market mechanism, is intolerable in a society with claims to democracy (ibid., p. 304). From Arrow's perspective, the market and the voting booth aren't different kinds of institutions oriented towards separate spheres of social life, but competing means of adjusting social action to individual choice.

26. M. Friedman, *Capitalism and Freedom*, p. 15.
27. Ibid.
28. John Kenneth Galbraith, *The Essential Galbraith* (New York: Mariner Books, 2001), p. 31.
29. Ibid., p. 33.
30. Theodor Adorno and Max Horkheimer, *The Dialectic of Enlightenment* (1947; Stanford: Stanford University Press, 2002), p. 115.
31. Ibid., p. 117.
32. Galbraith, *The Essential Galbraith*, p. 37.
33. Clement Greenberg, "The Case for Abstract Art," in *Affirmation and Refusal: The Collected Essays and Criticism of Clement Greenberg 1950–1956*, ed. John O'Brian (Chicago: University of Chicago Press, 1995), p. 80.
34. Ibid., p. 81.
35. Ibid., p. 83.
36. Ibid.
37. Barbara Herrnstein Smith, *Contingencies of Value*, 1988, p. 33.
38. Ibid., p. 42.
39. Ibid.
40. Ibid., p. 43.
41. Ibid., p. 31.
42. Larry Rivers quoted in O'Hara, *Art Chronicles*, 118.
43. Ibid.
44. Ibid.
45. David Reisman, *The Lonely Crowd: A Study of the Changing American Character* (1950; New Haven: Yale University Press, 1967), p. 339.
46. Ibid.
47. Ibid.
48. Ibid., p. 340.
49. Ibid.
50. See O'Hara's "Answer to Voznesensky and Evtushenko" (*CPO'H* 468) and "Mayakovsky" (*CPO'H* 201), for two striking examples of poems invoking the Russian poet.
51. Vladimir Mayakovsky, "A Most Extraordinary Adventure," *For the Voice* (Cambridge: M.I.T. Press, 2000), p. 58.

CHAPTER 3. WILLIAM BURROUGHS' VIRTUAL MIND

1. William S. Burroughs, "Origin and Theory of the Tape Cut-Ups," on the audio compact disc *Break Through in Grey Room* (Sub Rosa 3HH2, 2001).
2. William S. Burroughs, *The Word Virus: The William S. Burroughs Reader,* ed. James Gauerholz and Ira Silverberg (New York: Grove Press, 1998), p. 272.
3. For accounts of the cut-ups as random, see N. Katherine Hayles, *How We Became Posthuman: Virtual Bodies in Cybernetics, Literature, and Informatics* (Chicago: University of Chicago Press, 1999); Robin Lydenberg, *Word Cultures: Radical Theory and Practice in William S. Burroughs* (Urbana: University of Illinois Press, 1987); and Oliver Harris, *William S. Burroughs and the Secret of Fascination* (Carbondale: Southern Illinois University Press, 2003). For the classic account of postmodern indeterminacy, see Marjorie Perloff, *The Poetics of Indeterminacy* (Princeton: Princeton University Press, 1981). Harris, in seeing Burroughs as opposing the random to allegory as literary forms, expresses the exact opposite of the view I argue here, in which randomness is itself the allegory of a different kind of order (*Burroughs and the Secret of Fascination*, p. 232). Most accounts of Burroughs' supposed interest in randomness celebrate it as a postmodern liberation from rigorous and constraining modernist forms of order. David Lodge, in an early review, comes at this from the other side in rejecting Burroughs' work as the product of "mere chance," and unworthy of comparison to figures like Eliot or Joyce ("Objections to William Burroughs" [1966], in *William S. Burroughs at the Front*, ed. Jennie Skerl and Robin Lydenberg [Carbondale: Southern Illinois University Press, 1991], pp. 80–81).
4. William S. Burroughs, *The Third Mind* (New York: Grove Press, 1978), p. 29.
5. Burroughs quoted in Barry Miles, *William S. Burroughs: El Hombre Invisible* (New York: Virgin, 2002), p. 110.
6. Ibid., p. 99. Lydenberg has a rather good formulation of this. "Burroughs' aim is to cut predetermined lines of association or contiguity. In the cut-up text, the only contiguity is that created in the text itself by random juxtaposition – an infinite rather than a limited set of associations" ("Notes from the Orifice: Language and the Body in William Burroughs," *Contemporary Literature* 26:1 [Spring, 1985], p. 71). I agree that Burroughs represents a shift away from associations governed by norms to the juxtapositions in one's immediate context. I disagree with Lydenberg's sense that this is a shift towards the infinite and random; as I will show, the contiguity represented by the context manifests a coherent, integrated, and integrating structure for Burroughs.
7. William S. Burroughs, *Burroughs Live: The Collected Interviews of William S. Burroughs,* ed. Sylvere Lotringer (Los Angeles: Semiotext(e), 2001), pp. 67–68.
8. Cary Nelson, "The End of the Body: Radical Space in Burroughs" (1973), in Skerl and Lydenberg, *Burroughs at the Front,* p. 120.
9. William S. Burroughs, *Naked Lunch: The Restored Text* (1959; New York: Grove Press, 2001), p. 184.

10. Burroughs, *The Third Mind*, p. 113.
11. Marshall McLuhan, "Notes on Burroughs" (1964), in Skerl and Lydenberg, *Burroughs at the Front*, p. 71.
12. Hayles, *How We Became Posthuman*, p. 2.
13. Ibid., p. 42.
14. Ibid., p. 4.
15. Ibid., p. 34.
16. Ibid., p. 35.
17. Ibid., p. 218.
18. Ibid., p. 18.
19. Mark Hansen has attacked posthuman criticism for "[its] perpetuation of a misguided notion concerning the autonomy of information" (*New Philosophy for New Media* [Cambridge: M.I.T. Press, 2004], p. 76). His point is that the information we use is always "framed" by the body. Hansen argues that digital technologies, by exploding the conventional "frame" around works, highlight the basic role the body plays in organizing information. Thus, contra posthuman critics, the development of information technology hardly renders the body dispensable. In his representation of an informational stream in his cut-ups, Burroughs constantly stresses this "framing" role of the body, and it strongly distinguishes his vision from the models of distributed cognition it otherwise resembles. Hansen's work on new media thus illuminates crucial aspects of Burroughs' writing.
20. Charles Taylor, "Engaged Agency and Background in Heidegger," in *The Cambridge Companion to Heidegger*, ed. Charles Guignon (Cambridge: Cambridge University Press, 1993), p. 325.
21. Ibid., p. 327.
22. Ibid., p. 328.
23. Hubert Dreyfus, *What Computers Still Can't Do: A Critique of Artificial Reason* (Cambridge: M.I.T. Press, 1999), pp. 265–66.
24. Ibid., p. 261.
25. Ibid.
26. Merleau-Ponty quoted in Hubert Dreyfus, "Merleau-Ponty and Recent Cognitive Science," in *The Cambridge Companion to Merleau-Ponty*, ed. Taylor Carman and Mark Hansen (Cambridge: Cambridge University Press, 2005), p. 136.
27. *The Third Mind* contains Burroughs' most developed theoretical writing on the cut-up method. For an extended discussion of this term, and of its derivation from Burroughs' reading of "The Waste Land," see the final section of this chapter.
28. Hubert Dreyfus, *Being-in-the-World: A Commentary on Heidegger's Being and Time Division 1* (Cambridge: M.I.T. Press, 1991), p. 158.
29. Ibid., p. 159.
30. Ibid.
31. Ibid., p. 153.

32. T. S. Eliot, "The Waste Land," in *The Norton Anthology of Poetry*, ed. Margaret Ferguson, Mary Jo Salter, and Jon Stallworthy (New York: W. W. Norton, 1996), p. 1248.

33. Dreyfus, *Being-in-the-World*, p. 161.

34. Hubert Dreyfus, Fernando Flores, and Charles Spinosa, *Disclosing New Worlds: Entrepreneurship, Democratic Action, and the Cultivation of Solidarity* (Cambridge: M.I.T. Press, 1999), p. 14.

35. In this analysis of how Burroughs intends language to stand for a different kind of communication, I am indebted to Allen Grossman's description of an analogous feature in Hart Crane's work ("Hart Crane and Poetry: A Consideration of Crane's Intense Poetics with Reference to 'The Return,'" in *The Long Schoolroom* [Ann Arbor: University of Michigan Press, 1997]).

36. In addition to examining the difference between Burroughs' symbols and code, one might usefully contrast his symbols with Heidegger's language. Heidegger deemphasizes the systematic, code-like structure of language and renders it compatible with his account of context. But for Heidegger, in a move that will become familiar in many postmodern thinkers, language seems to instantiate what is essential about culture. In the late essays, language replaces cultural norms while conserving many of their crucial features, features utterly alien to Burroughs' symbols. (See, for example, Heidegger, "Language" [1950], in *Poetry, Language, Thought* [New York: Harper, 2001].) Heidegger constantly emphasizes the specificity of particular languages, the etymology of particular words, the historicity and groundedness of ways of speaking.

37. This association is most understandable in Hayek's often immoderate attacks on state socialism, especially in popular works like *The Road to Serfdom* (Chicago: University of Chicago Press, 1944). But, as I will show, that attack is itself grounded in values and analyses that could not be more distinct from the rights-based, individualist free-market ethos for which Hayek is often either rejected or praised.

38. Mirowski, *Machine Dreams*, p. 241.

39. Ibid., pp. 240–41.

40. Hayek's relation to the word "utopia" strongly distinguishes him from Arendt and Polanyi – to say nothing of thinkers like Milton Friedman with whom he is frequently associated. While Hayek, like Arendt and Polanyi, refers frequently to the total functioning of the price system as a "utopia," he calls for the "courage to consider utopia" ("Why I Am Not a Conservative" [1960], in *The Essence of Hayek*, ed. Chiaki Nishiyama and Kurt R. Leube [Stanford: Stanford University Press, 1984], pp. 281–99).

41. Hayek drew his understanding of embodied knowledge from Michael Polanyi's account of "tacit knowing." (See Polanyi, *The Tacit Dimension* [New York: Doubleday, 1966]; see also John Gray on Hayek's reading of Polanyi in *Hayek on Liberty* [London: Routledge, 1998], pp. 4, 14–16. Dreyfus points out the similarity of Polanyi's view with Heidegger's in *Being-in-the-World*, pp. 45–46.)

42. Hayek quoted in Emiel Wubben, "Austrian Economics and Uncertainty," in *New Perspectives on Austrian Economics*, ed. Gerrit Meijer (London: Routledge, 1995), p. 122.

43. Here this economic fiction differs from a neoclassical description of substitution effects only in what it leaves out. The price of gas goes up, so I ride a bike to work. The neoclassical economist will assume, in addition to the facts, the existence of a calculus in the individual's head such that I know, independent of price, how much I want to drive and how much I want to walk. He or she will assume that I like to drive more than bike, but that the benefit of driving to me is lower than the benefits I must forgo to continue paying for gas at the new price. I know, in all price environments, that I prefer driving to biking. But only in some will I decide to drive rather than bike. In the Hayekian model, by contrast, as I look around this particular price environment, and wonder how to get over there, I ride a bike. One cannot say: but I would really rather drive. Preference here, as in the studies conducted by Kahneman and Tversky, is determined by the immediate context. In Hayek's economic fiction, price structures this immediate context. Price is imagined as shaping the environment in which preferences and perceptions are formed. What in neoclassical theory happens in the dark, in the individual's head, happens here in the open, in the operation of the price system in an environment. This is not to say that individual consciousness is somehow displaced by the price system. It is rather to say that price makes a crucial contribution to individual consciousness. Price can't tell me how to ride a bike or what color the grass is, but it is part of what organizes my awareness of these concrete and specific features of my situation.

44. Hayek, *The Road to Serfdom*, pp. 86, 85, 55.

45. Murray N. Rothbard's influential critique of Hayek draws on Hayek's teacher Ludwig von Mises in making exactly the opposite point (*The Logic of Action I: Method, Money, and the Austrian School* [Cheltenham: Edward Elgar, 1997]). Rothbard attacks Hayek's view of the market agent as "a passive, if alert, recipient of 'knowledge' provided by the price system," claiming that Hayek cannot account for the way the individual interpretations of market signals by the creative entrepreneur drives the market order (ibid., p. 129). Similarly, Mirowski notes that Hayek's model "leaves little room for the conscious [individual] subject to intentionally alter her own cognition ... the entrepreneur is banished here" (*Machine Dreams*, p. 239). Hayek's student, G. L. S. Shackle, broke with his teacher in emphasizing the creative power of entrepreneurs as driving the spontaneous order of the market. But the critics' implicit division of agency into (passive) perception of external facts and (active) internal interpretation of those facts misses the point. Hayek's nuanced account of perception shows how the dynamic structuring of agents' perceptual fields is accomplished not exclusively in individual skulls but also "out there," by the coordinating price system. The price system interfaces with individuals' perception of their surroundings in such a way as to map out an individual's environment in lines of action, or what Hayek calls "means-ends" chains. The quality of Hayekian

perception, insofar as that perception involves the continual shaping and reshaping of the individual's immediate environment by price, needs no additional "entrepreneurial" element to yield flexible and creative market agency. Discussions like Rothbard's rest on the assumption that perception is transformed into action by an alchemy that can only occur in a private internal space. This kind of attack on Hayek's account of engaged agency thus resembles the charge leveled by some philosophers of mind against phenomenology: that it constitutes a kind of crypto-behaviorism. To pursue this critique, and the defenses of engaged agency that might be marshaled against it, would be to distract from my aim in this book, which is not to probe the feasibility of fictional exchange as a plausible account of some real-world state of affairs, but to describe the features that make it a source of cultural fascination.

46. Daniel Dennet's influential account of individual subjectivity offers a useful contrast with the structure of collective subjectivity in Hayek and Burroughs: "In an organism with genuine intentionality – such as your-self – there are, right now, many parts, and some of these parts exhibit a sort of semi-intentionality, or *as if* intentionality … and your own genuine, fully fledged intentionality is in fact the product … of the activities of all the semi-minded and mindless bits that make you up … each playing its own role in the 'economy of the soul'" (*Darwin's Dangerous Idea: Evolution and the Meanings of Life* [New York: Simon and Schuster, 1995], p. 206). The relevant difference is between a model of subjectivity as a system composed of various semiautonomous individual parts and the unified context of embodiment as the ontological basis of subjectivity. Dennet's view of intention as the aggregate of individual parts has much in common with the traditional conception of the market as the aggregate of the actions of discrete individuals. For the implications of the abandonment of this traditional model in the postwar market imaginary, see my discussion of Habermas' concept of market coordination below.

47. Eliot, "The Waste Land," p. 1246.

48. Burroughs, *The Third Mind*, p. 19.

49. Cf. this with Heidegger's treatment of objections to his own discussion of the "who" of everyday Dasein. The criticism that Heidegger neglects the "inner life" of Dasein, and makes the subject of everyday existence a kind of phantom is founded on "the perverse assumption that the entity in question has at bottom the kind of being which belongs to something occurrent, even if one is far from attributing to it the solidity of an occurrent corporeal thing" (Heidegger quoted in Dreyfus, *Being-in-the-World*, p. 148).

50. William S. Burroughs, *Nova Express* (New York: Grove Press, 1964), p. 90.

51. I would remind the reader that, as I showed in Chapter 2, the postwar free-market imaginary identifies the logic of advertising as profoundly antithetical to the market order. For a writer like David Riesman, advertising amounts, in effect, to a superimposition of an alien governmental logic over what he sees as the possibilities of free choice. Burroughs locates the alien element in the intersubjective form of address of the advertisement.

52. Burroughs quoted in Miles, *Burroughs: El Hombre Invisible*, p. 117. Timothy Murphy sees Burroughs' representation of control as an "allegorization of the contemporary social order" (*Wising Up the Marks: The Amodern William S. Burroughs* [Berkeley: University of California Press, 1997], p. 145). This is right, but he curiously adds that Burroughs' problem is he can't see a way outside this order. I think this allegorization of reality is in fact made possible by the perspective of a rather different kind of space. See also Elizabeth Wheeler on Burroughs as a gritty "realist" whose problem is that he can't find a way beyond the violent, oppressive reality he helplessly mirrors (*Uncontained: Urban Fiction in Postwar America* [New Brunswick: Rutgers University Press, 2001], p. 213).

53. Lydenberg is quite right that in Burroughs "the lyricism of person-to-person communication is replaced by a vibrating network" (*Word Cultures*, p. 50). But she wrongly associates this network with language, arguing that the cut-up "implies that it is always language that speaks within a network of infinite and anonymous citations" (ibid., p. 45). The "network" is not language, but Burroughs' vowel-colors, which, as I have shown, demonstrate a unique and thoroughly nonlinguistic character.

54. Adam Smith, *The Wealth of Nations* (1776; Indianapolis: Hackett, 1993), p. 130.

55. Jameson, *Postmodernism*, pp. 273, 278.

56. Habermas quoted in Stephen D. Parsons, *Money, Time, and Rationality in Max Weber: Austrian Connections* (London: Routledge, 2003), p. 100. My description of Habermas' position relies upon Parsons' sensitive and nuanced account. Parsons finds a predecessor for Hayek in Max Weber, who argues, against objectivist theories of money, that "the use of money is highly context dependant" (ibid., p. 11). "For Weber, individuals do not even relate to prices as something 'objective'" (ibid.). But the point of this reference, and the point of Parsons' emphasis on the opposition between cooperation and coordination in Habermas, is to argue that money is actually a form of intersubjectivity. Thus money, like language, is a form of communication between subjects in the setting of a particular lifeworld, governed by particular norms, etc. This view of money is obviously quite different than Hayek's conception of the strange symbol.

57. Parsons, *Money, Time and Rationality in Max Weber*, p. 100.

58. Ibid., p. 106.

59. Ibid., pp. 98–99.

60. Ibid., p. 109.

61. As time goes on, Burroughs becomes increasingly obsessed with identifying those aspects of contemporary America that from his perspective appear to block the real human context, and is correspondingly less concerned with finding forms to represent this virtual reality. One impulse is a consequence of the other, and one might argue that Burroughs simply lost the creative ability to hold these two aspects of his vision in vital suspension. But one might also, more charitably, believe that over time the experimental space

became the background, the context of Burroughs' vision, and he gradually lost his ability to give it the high degree of explicitness one finds in the first two books of the trilogy. On the other hand, one might reject Lodge's judgment, and take this complete absorption in the perspective developed by the trilogy, this speech that issues from a fictional condition, as the heart of Burroughs' achievement. The terms of Kathy Acker's engagement with him suggest this last position. This writer, who considered herself to be Burroughs' successor, is at her most consistent and creative when working with the tone established by novels such as *Nova Express*.

CHAPTER 4. BLOOD MONEY

1. Kathy Acker, "A Few Notes on Two of My Books" (1989), in *Bodies of Work* (New York: Grove Press, 1997), p. 11.
2. Michael Hardt and Antonio Negri, *Empire* (Cambridge: Harvard University Press, 2001), pp. 146–47.
3. Kathy Acker, *Pussy, King of the Pirates* (New York: Grove Press, 1996), p. 10.
4. Ibid., p. 112.
5. Acker, "A Few Notes," p. 12.
6. Ibid.
7. Cf. Acker's treatment of pirates with that of Burroughs, an often-cited influence on her work. In the introduction to his late novel *Cities of the Red Night*, Burroughs writes that the pirate communes of the seventeenth century represent "an example of utopia as it actually could have happened" ([New York: Grove Press 1981], p. xiv).
8. F. A. Hayek, "The Denationalization of Money" (1976), in *The Collected Works of F. A. Hayek*, Volume 6, ed. Stephen Kresge (Chicago: University of Chicago Press, 1999), p. 128. Hayek's article is written partly in response to Milton Friedman's criticism of an earlier version of his call for private money. Hayek provides a concise statement of the distinction between his position and that of the monetarists: "monetary management cannot aim at a particular predetermined volume of circulation," since "no authority can beforehand ascertain, and only the market can discover, the 'optimal quantity of money'" (Ibid., p. 183). To this criticism of the possibility of establishing the necessary quantity of money, Hayek adds his doubt that there is a necessary quality, or form, of money: "Although we usually assume there is a sharp line of distinction between what is money and what is not – and the law generally tries to make such a distinction – so far as the causal effects of monetary events are concerned, there is no such clear difference" (ibid., p. 161). Friedman's reply argues that Hayek monetary theory is inconsistent with Hayek's own anti-interventionist bias, in that the proposal to free money from the government is itself a "constructionist" attempt to destroy the "natural" and "evolved" association of money and state (Milton Friedman and Anna Schwartz, "Has the Government Any Role in Money?," *Journal of Monetary Economics* 17 [1986], pp. 37–62). Friedman appears unwilling even to contemplate the

immense political and social dislocations entailed by Hayek's proposal (ibid., p. 46), and situates the latter's demand for private money in "an unexplored terrain" suffused with "an air of unreality and paradox" (ibid., p. 59). Acker's myth occupies this same terrain, rendering in vivid detail the radical, brutal, and liberatory dislocation Friedman responds to, and recoils from, in Hayek's modest proposal.

9. John Gray, *Hayek on Liberty* (London: Routledge, 1998), p. 90.
10. Ibid., pp. 35–36.
11. Hardt and Negri, *Empire*, p. 346. The authors' analysis of "capitalist sovereignty" is partly derived from Gilles Deleuze and Felix Guattari's account of capitalism in *Anti-Oedipus: Capitalism and Schizophrenia* (1972; Minneapolis: University of Minnesota Press, 1993), which also has exerted an important influence on Acker. Market circulation, in this text, is a "decoded flow" the "revolutionary potential" of which is continually "recoded," managed, and administered by various "state controls and regulations" (ibid., p. 253). Thus a progressive "revolutionary potential" is located in market circulation, while the countertendency belongs to the "state controls" extrinsic to a system of exchange that now appears as "pure flow." This is as far from Marxism as it is close to Hayek's position. (See especially his implicit celebration of the radical and destabilizing character of market exchange versus the retarding and preservative tendencies of state action in "Why I Am Not a Conservative".) For Deleuze and Guattari, writing in 1972 while Keynesian policy remained ascendant, the identification of monetary controls as the paradigmatic instance of the "recoding" of circulation would naturally have been somewhat obscure. *Empire* rectifies this.
12. In declaring the classical use-value/exchange-value dyad obsolete Hardt and Negri are in good post-Marxist company, despite their insistence to the contrary. The sense that there is no longer a "real" value that is obscured by market price disables an analysis of exploitation by making the mystified difference between two forms of value, Marx's "surplus value," vanish. Erik Olin Wright (*Classes* [London: Verso, 1985]), argues that this shift from an analytic centered on exploitation to one centered on domination makes any opposition to the capitalist market as such problematic. The issue for the postmodern left, exemplified here by Hardt and Negri, is the domination of market processes by sovereign power. (For the classic post-Marxist argument, see Ernesto Laclau and Chantal Mouffe, *Hegemony and Socialist Strategy: Towards a Radical Democratic Politics* [London: Routledge, 1985]. For a critical account of this position see Daniel McGee, "Post-Marxism: The Opiate of the Intellectuals," *Modern Language Quarterly* 22 [1998], pp. 201–25.)
13. Hardt and Negri, *Empire*, p. 346.
14. Ibid., p. 349.
15. Michael Shapiro, *Reading "Adam Smith": Desire, History, and Value* (Newberry Park: Rowland and Littlefield, 1993), p. 9.
16. Ibid., p. 18.

17. Ibid., p. 17. For Shapiro the alienation of interpersonal exchange is relative, dependent on the form of the mediation. Thus he thinks that if the mediation takes a form that minimizes abstraction, such as bodily fluids, alienation can be banished. Shapiro's (mis)appropriation of Goux's analysis of exchange is instructive here. For Goux, exchange-value is absolutely alienating, regardless of the concrete form it takes; it "alienates subjects as it dominates relations" (Jean-Joseph Goux, *Symbolic Economies: After Marx and Freud* [Ithaca: Cornell University Press, 1990], p. 163). In a familiar poststructuralist move, Goux argues that the coherence of the universal value form is governed by an "excluded other," a controlling trope that is able to guarantee the consistency of the system only by remaining outside its substitutive logic. The commitment underlying Shapiro's claim that alienation is a local and relative effect of a particular form of exchange-value – legal tender – rather than a property of exchange itself, is articulated by Hayek. Goux's structural "third entity" governing exchange corresponds, in Hayek, to an actual governor: the Federal Reserve Bank.

18. Shapiro, *Reading "Adam Smith,"* p. 17.

19. Ibid.

20. Gray, *Hayek on Liberty*, p. 123.

21. Ibid., p. 94.

22. Ibid., p. 36.

23. Larry McCaffery, "The Artists of Hell: Kathy Acker and Punk Aesthetics," in *Breaking the Sequence*, ed. Ellen Friedman and Miriam Fuchs (Princeton: Princeton University Press, 1994), p. 218.

24. Acker quoted in Ellen Friedman, "A Conversation with Kathy Acker," *Review of Contemporary Fiction* 9:3 (1989), p. 18.

25. Frederic Jameson, *The Seeds of Time* (New York: Columbia University Press, 1994), p. 57.

26. Gray, *Hayek on Liberty*, p. 125.

27. Acker, "A Few Notes," p. 12.

28. Claude Levi-Strauss, *The Elementary Structures of Kinship* (Boston: Beacon Press, 1969), p. 24.

29. Ibid., p. 42.

30. Ibid., p. 51.

31. Ibid., p. 62.

32. Ibid., p. 479.

33. SAMOIS, a lesbian S/M collective, originated in San Francisco in the late seventies. The group took its name from the estate of Anne-Marie, the lesbian dominatrix in *The Story of O*. (See SAMOIS, *Coming to Power* [Boston: Alyson Books, 1987], pp. 245–80.)

34. Gayle Rubin, "The Traffic in Women: Notes on the Political Economy of Sex," in *Toward an Anthropology of Women,* ed. Rayna Reiter (New York: Monthly Review Press, 1975), p. 176.

35. Ibid., p. 203.

36. Acker, *Pussy*, p. 68.

37. Kathy Acker, "Writing, Identity, and Copyright in the Net Age," (1995) in *Bodies of Work*, p. 104.
38. Gray, *Hayek on Liberty*, p. 35.
39. Kathy Acker, "Reading the Lack of the Body: The Writing of the Marquis De Sade" (1996), in *Bodies of Work*, p. 71.
40. Arthur Redding, "Bruises, Roses: Masochism and the Writing of Kathy Acker," *Contemporary Literature* 35: 2 (1994), p. 284.
41. SAMOIS, *Coming to Power*, p. 224.
42. Ibid., p. 223.
43. Gray, *Hayek on Liberty*, p. 25.
44. William Gibson, *Neuromancer* (1984; New York: Ace Books, 2000), p. 78.
45. Ibid., p. 51.
46. Hansen, *New Philosophy for New Media*.
47. Gibson, *Neuromancer*, p. 232.
48. Ibid., p. 17.
49. Ibid.
50. Ibid., p. 11. Importantly, for Gibson as for Acker the efficient market is a *black* market; as Gibson writes, the black market is "a deliberately unsupervised playground for technology itself" (ibid.).
51. Redding, "Bruises, Roses," pp. 287, 284. In this paragraph I simply reproduce the sense of the cut-ups shared by Acker's critics. As detailed in Chapter 3, I disagree with the view that the cut-ups constitute a kind of ultimate objectification of language. As will become clear, I also disagree with the critics' account of Burroughs' influence on Acker. Especially in her late novels, Burroughs' techniques are less important than his thematizing of those techniques. Acker's oddly compelling prose style is oriented not towards the stunning juxtapositions of *The Soft Machine*, but the curious didacticism of *Nova Express*.
52. Sciolino quoted in Redding, "Bruises, Roses," p. 287.
53. Kathryn Hume, "Voice in Kathy Acker's Fiction," *Contemporary Literature* 42: 3 (Summer 2001), p. 489.
54. Acker, "A Few Notes," p. 11.
55. Cathy Caruth, *Unclaimed Experience: Trauma, Narrative, and History* (Baltimore: Johns Hopkins University Press, 1996), p. 9.
56. Ibid., p. 74.
57. Ibid., p. 82.
58. Ibid., p. 89.
59. I am indebted to Frances Ferguson for this formulation.
60. Acker, *Pussy*, p. 31.
61. Hayek, The "Denationalization of Money," p. 145.

CHAPTER 5. "YOU CAN'T SEE ME"

1. Black Rob, "Whoa," *Life Story* (Bad Boy 73026, 2000).
2. Mobb Deep, "Eye for an Eye," *The Infamous* (Loud 66480, 1995).

3. B.G., "I Know," *Checkmate* (Cash Money 860909, 2000).

4. Notorious B.I.G., "I Love the Dough," *Life After Death* (Bad Boy 73011, 1997).

5. G-Unit, "Poppin' Them Thangs," *Beg For Mercy* (Interscope 159142, 2003).

6. I will use "he" and "she" interchangeably in this chapter. This practice reflects the gender symmetry that characterizes the rap form. While male rappers are disproportionately represented in my examples, as they continue to be in rap generally, the elements of the rap form I examine here are also available to the increasing number of female artists such as Lil' Kim and Foxy Brown. Gender symmetry doesn't take the form of an acknowledgment of gender "equality," since, as I will show, in rap *no* other can be equal to the first person. Rather, the terms by which "I" overcome "you" are identical for both men and women.

7. This is true of *popular* rap as of early 2008. Critics have been predicting the imminent exhaustion of rap's lyrical focus on money and violence since the mid-nineties, during which time it has only become more pervasive. (See especially Timothy Brennan, "Off the Gangsta Tip," *Critical Inquiry* 20 [Summer 1994], pp. 663–93; and Robin Kelley, "Kickin' Reality, Kickin' Ballistics: Gangsta Rap and Postindustrial Los Angeles," in *Droppin' Science,* ed. William Eric Perkins [Philadelphia: Temple University Press, 1996].) By 2001 Kelefa Sanneh can write, regretfully, "'gangsta rap' is no longer a useful term; over the past ten years, it has come to denote any rapper who talks about gunplay in the first person, and this includes almost every one" ("Gettin Paid," *The New Yorker* [August 20, 2001], p. 68). By 2006 there were definite signs that the form had begun to weaken, although, given its past resilience, I hesitate to choose an end-date for the form that first crystallizes in the early nineties.

8. B.G., "Bling Bling," *Chopper City in the Ghetto* (Cash Money 53265, 1999).

9. Nelly, "Ride With Me," *Country Grammar* (Uptown 1577413, 2000); Big Tymers, "Number 1 Stunna," *I Got That Work* (Cash Money 157673, 2000); Lil' Wayne, "Loud Pipes," *Tha Block Is Hot* (Cash Money 153919, 1999).

10. B.G., "Bling Bling."

11. Ibid.

12. Raekwon, "Ice Water," *Only Built For Cuban Linx* (Loud 66663, 1995).

13. Notorious B.I.G., "I Love the Dough."

14. Missy Elliott, "Slide," *Under Construction* (Elektra 62813, 2002).

15. Jay-Z, "Money Ain't a Thing," *Vol. 2: Hard Knock Life* (Roc-A-Fella 558902, 1998).

16. Big Pun, "Still Not A Player," *Capital Punishment* (Loud 57883, 1998).

17. Project Pat, "Rubberband Me," *Walkin' Bank Roll* (Koch VBIE5G, 2007). "Candy" refers to expensive custom paint.

18. Snoop Dogg, "Tha Shiznit," *Doggystyle* (Death Row 50605, 1993).

19. Lil' Rob, "Peek-A-Boo," *Can't Keep a Good Man Down* (Lideres 950226, 2001).

20. Ibid.

21. Lil' Wayne, "Hey DJ," *The Carter* (Cash Money 27JYPI, 2004). Lil' Wayne is perhaps the most consistent of rappers in this respect. In a recent interview, he is asked the usual question about how his success has changed him. "Q: 'Do you ever wonder how the perception of you has changed?' A: 'If I thought about that, I'd be the craziest dude in the world. 'Cause perception is from somebody else's eyes. I can't get in your head and see what you see, so why would I even care about what you see? Fuck what you see. I wish all you bitches was blind'" (Clover Hope, "Lil Wayne, Last Time I Checked," *XXL* 99 [January 2008], p. 76).

22. 50 Cent, "You Are Not Like Me," *Get Rich or Die Tryin'* (Interscope 493544, 2003); Dr. Dre, "What's the Difference?," *The Chronic 2001* (Aftermath 490486, 1999); Clipse, "I'm Not You," *Lord Willin'* (Star Trak 4735, 2002).

23. Prodigy, "Y.B.E.," *HNIC* (Relativity 1873, 2000).

24. Critics influenced by Cornel West's account of black "nihilism" (*Race Matters*, Boston: Beacon Press, 1993) have seen rap as an expression of negative, antisocial attitudes plaguing the black inner city. Various groups within society at large condemn rap in similar terms. As Greg Wahl writes, "Rap has become, for many parents, politicians, and church leaders, a destructive influence, a site of practically pure anti-social values, of 'negativity'" ("I Fought the Law and I Cold Won: Hip Hop in the Mainstream," *College Literature* 26:1 [1999], p. 98). Ronin Ro argues that rap "casts its shadow, its self-hate over this generation" of black youth (*Gangsta: Merchandizing the Rhymes of Violence* [New York: St. Martin's Press, 1996], pp. 2–3).

25. Paul Gilroy, *Against Race* (Cambridge: Harvard University Press, 2002), p. 199.

26. Sanneh, "Gettin' Paid," p. 74.

27. Adam Krims, *Rap Music and the Poetics of Identity* (Cambridge: Cambridge University Press, 2001), p. 83.

28. Tricia Rose, "A Style Nobody Can Deal With," in *Microphone Fiends*, ed. Andrew Ross and Tricia Rose (London: Routledge, 1994), p. 80.

29. Elijah Anderson, *Code of the Street* (New York: W. W. Norton, 1999), p. 73.

30. Thorstein Veblen, *The Theory of the Leisure Class* (1899; New York: Penguin, 1994), p. 8.

31. Ibid., pp. 12–15.

32. Ibid., p. 87.

33. Ibid., pp. 31–32.

34. Colin Campbell, "Conspicuous Confusion? A Critique of Veblen's Theory," *Sociological Theory* 13:1 (March 1995), p. 43.

35. Ibid., p. 44.

36. George Herbert Mead, *Mind, Self, and Society* (Chicago: University of Chicago Press, 1967), p. 138.

37. Hegel quoted in Shalin, "George Herbert Mead," Ritzer, 2000, p. 310.

38. Charles Taylor, "The Politics of Recognition," in *Multiculturalism,* ed. Amy Gutmann (Princeton: Princeton University Press, 1994), p. 26.

39. Ibid., p. 64.

40. Anderson, *Code of the Street*, p. 73.
41. 50 Cent, "Life's on the Line," *Get Rich or Die Tryin'* (Interscope 493544, 2003).
42. T.I., "Be Easy," *Trap Muzik* (Atlantic 83650, 2003).
43. Puff Daddy feat. Mase, "Been Around the World," *No Way Out* (Bad Boy 39QD, 1997).
44. Mike Jones feat. Slim Thug, "Still Tippin'," *Who Is Mike Jones?* (Warner Brothers 7YMV1K, 2005).
45. Sanneh, "Gettin Paid," p. 70.
46. Rose, "A Style Nobody Can Deal With," p. 85.
47. Viviana Zelizer, *The Social Meaning of Money* (Princeton: Princeton University Press, 1997), p. 129.
48. Brennan, "Off the Gangsta Tip," p. 681.
49. Houston Baker, *Black Studies, Rap, and the Academy* (Chicago: University of Chicago Press, 1993), pp. 74–75.
50. John McWhorter, "How Hip Hop Holds Blacks Back," *City Journal* (Summer 2003), p. 6.
51. Greg Tate quoted in Andrew Ross, "Introduction," in Ross and Rose, *Microphone Fiends*, p. 2.
52. Gilroy sees rap as falling victim to a process of co-option whereby "oppositional imaginings [are] first colonized and then vanquished by the leveling values of the market" (*Against Race*, p. 272).
53. Robin Kelley, for example, argues that "rap is a window into, and a critique of, the criminalization of black youth" ("Kickin' Reality, Kickin' Ballistics," p. 118). On this account, rap grants visibility to an unrecognized social problem. The disproportionate levels of imprisonment among young black men is indeed a serious and pressing social problem, and an underrecognized one. But I would hesitate to equate the social negativity of the rap form ("you can't see me"), with the very different modes of negativity Kelley has in mind.
54. Ralph Ellison, *Invisible Man* (1952; New York: Random House, 2002), p. 3. (I have adjusted the pronouns. In the text, the Invisible Man refers to himself in the second person.) For an account of Ellison's depiction of invisibility as a "refusal of recognition" which produces "an effacement of humanity," see Martha Nussbaum, "Invisibility and Recognition: Sophocles Philoctetes and Ellison's Invisible Man," *Philosophy and Literature* 23:2 (1999), p. 259. Kenneth Warren (*So Black and Blue: Ralph Ellison and the Occasion of Criticism* [Chicago: University of Chicago Press, 2003]) argues that *Invisible Man* is, or rather should be, dated by its representation of a world defined by the racial dynamics of a segregated society. In that world, recognition by the racial other, respect for one's identity, is the crucial struggle. I read rap's radical inversion of the invisibility trope as enacting what Warren calls the utopian work of "making Ellison's novel more a story of the world that was, and less an account of the world that still is" (ibid., p. 108). For a striking fictional effort along broadly similar lines, see Colson Whitehead's novel

The Intuitionist (New York: Anchor Books, 2000). This fantasy revisits civil-rights era racial relations, an era in which blackness is defined not as a posi-tive social identity but in terms of a lack of access to the social. Unlike in Ellison, value in this novel is not located in visible social space. Whitehead sharply distinguishes the heroism of his protagonist from the efforts of a black "first" (the character Pompey) to make a place for blacks in society. Rather, the novel presents blackness as a space outside the "pernicious vis-ible" (ibid., p. 124), and this exteriority is to be prized rather than escaped. Blackness – from the "black box" of a utopian invention to the black skin of the heroine – is suffused with value as a site of technical and relational possibility. Insofar as we are persuaded by Richard Poirier's identification of a longing for invisibility at the heart of American literature, this revaluation was perhaps inevitable once black invisibility became an aesthetic question (*A World Elsewhere*, pp. 48–49).

55. Franz Fanon, *Black Skin, White Masks* (1967; New York: Grove Press, 1994), p. 216.
56. But for an alternative reading, see Kelly Oliver's account of love in Fanon as an "affect-based alternative to the Hegelian-Lacanian economy of desire" (*Witnessing*, p. 42).
57. Richard Price, *Clockers* (New York: Picador, 1992), p. 299.
58. T.I., "Be Easy."
59. Examples of rappers who have "fallen off" include Smith and Ja Rule. Smith's primary identity as an *actor*, and Ja Rule's inability to defend him-self from 50 Cent's charge that Rule is (just) a *rapper*, contributed to their respective downfalls.
60. My discussion of various strategies for overcoming the audience/performer relation in rap, and for establishing what I follow Michael Fried in call-ing the "fiction" of the audience's absence, is particularly indebted to his *Absorption and Theatricality* (Chicago: University of Chicago Press, 1988).
61. Notorious B.I.G., "I Love the Dough."
62. Westside Connection, "Gangsta Nation," *Terrorist Threats* (Priority 24030, 2003).
63. Eric B. and Rakim, "I Ain't No Joke," *Paid in Full* (6th and Broadway 444005, 1987); and their "Lyrics of Fury," *Follow the Leader* (Uni UNID3, 1988).
64. Brennan, "Off the Gangsta Tip," p. 692.
65. Jay-Z, "Come and Get Me," *Vol. 3: The Life and Times of Sean Carter* (Roc-A-Fella 558906, 2000).
66. Big Pun, "Whatcha Gonna Do," *Endangered Species* (Relativity 1963, 2001).
67. Clipse, "I'm Not You."
68. Jay-Z, "Heart of the City," *The Blueprint* (Roc-A-Fella 586396, 2001).
69. Ibid., "The Takeover," *The Blueprint*.
70. Scarface feat. W.C., "I Ain't the One," *The Fix* (Def Jam 986909, 2002).
71. B.G., "Niggas in Trouble," *Chopper City* (Cash Money 9690, 1996).
72. Sanneh, "Gettin Paid," p. 73.

73. Ibid.
74. Ibid.
75. Krims, *Rap Music and the Poetics of Identity*, p. 51.
76. B.G., "Thugged Out," *Baller Blockin'* (Cash Money 153291, 2000).
77. Big Tymers, "Number 1 Stunna."
78. Ibid.
79. See the music video for DMX's "Party Up," *And Then There Was X* (Def Jam 3IE26, 1999).
80. See, for example, the video for "It's In Me" by Turk, *Young and Thuggin'* (Cash Money 5K9R8, 2001).
81. Juvenile, "In My Life," *Juve the Great* (Cash Money 12FXCW, 2003). For a different version of this strategy, see Kanye West's video for "When It All Falls Down", *College Dropout* (Roc-A-Fella 20300, 2004). The visual conceit is that the camera's view is his view; thus he never addresses the camera, and is only seen periodically through his reflection on a car window and on a mirror in a bathroom.
82. Lil' Flip, video for "The Way We Ball," *Undaground Legend* (Sony 6GOAo, 2002).
83. Fam-Lay, video for "Rock and Roll," *The Neptunes Present … Clones* (Startrack AKOMH, 2003).

CONCLUSION

1. My discussion of this text is indebted to that of Michel Henry in *Marx* (Bloomington: University of Indiana Press, 1983); I engage his argument at length below.
2. The sociology of desire, from Veblen through Bourdieu, has given exhaustive elaboration to the intuition Marx detects in the Gotha framers' insistence on the priority of the question of distribution. (See the discussion of the new literary sociology in my introduction.)
3. Giorgio Agamben (*Homo Sacer: Sovereign Power and Bare Life* [Stanford: Stanford University Press, 1998]), has drawn attention to this theme of Arendt's thought, which he describes as a concern with the "improper" (pp. 126–34).
4. Karl Marx, "Theses on Feuerbach" (1845), in *The Marx-Engles Reader*, pp. 143, 145.
5. Mark Hansen, *Bodies in Code* (London: Routledge, 2006), p. 12.
6. Ibid., p. 20.
7. Ibid., p. 17.
8. Ibid., p. 41. The opposition between body image and schema sketched here is the prelude for Hansen's development of a more productive view of the relation between specularity and embodiment. Hansen sees specularity as an extension of the body schema, one's body "fills the space" between the eye and the image in the mirror. The relation between body and image is not one of identification but of extension. Thus specularity is a primal version

of the technicity Hansen sees in human embodiment, and that allows it to extend beyond the skin. The direction of Hansen's argument has been important to my attempt to think the distributed embodiment of the economic fiction.

9. Henry would be hostile to this view of embodiment as interpenetrated and extended by the market. Henry is strongly committed to the integrity of individual experience and the individual human body, a commitment that emerges even more strongly in his later work. The idea that embodiment extends past the skin through a network like the one elaborated here is profoundly alien to the values of Henry's work, which demonstrates a continuity with an older, humanistic phenomenology. In some ways these values are in tension with his most provocative claims about radical subjectivity. What is to guarantee the integrity of the human-body image without the look of recognition that affixes each subject to an object, to a human image?

10. See, for example, Jameson's treatment of market circulation as ideological (*Postmodernism*, pp. 260–79). Henry is also strongly committed to the labor theory of value, though with a twist. The labor theory is usually associated with the propensity of classical economics to discover "objective" or "natural" values beneath the oscillations of "subjective" market valuations. The "marginal revolution" which overturned the labor theory at the turn of the last century is thus often called the "subjectivist revolution." Henry, however, understands the value produced by labor in terms of the objectless radical subjectivity he finds in human action.

11. At least it does not perform any ideological function in terms of its image of the economy. Here I am bracketing the wide range of relations the works I study take up towards race, gender, sexuality, and religion, and which my individual chapters have examined in the context of particular works and writers. No general formula about these relations applies to all the examples I consider. Sometimes recognition is identified as the central mechanism of oppression, and freedom from recognition is identified with liberation from gender or race regimes (as in Acker, for example); but there are other cases (Burroughs, notoriously) where extremely and negatively gendered bodies move unimpeded through fictional space.

12. Theodor Adorno, *Aesthetic Theory* (1970; Minneapolis: University of Minneapolis Press, 1997), p. 227.

13. Ibid., pp. 226–27.

14. Ibid., p. 229.

15. Ibid., p. 228.

16. Ibid.

17. Ibid.

18. Ibid., p. 230.

Bibliography

50 Cent, "Life's on the Line," *Get Rich or Die Tryin'* (Interscope 493544, 2003).
"You Are Not Like Me," *Get Rich or Die Tryin'* (Interscope 493544, 2003).
Acker, Kathy, *Empire of the Senseless* (New York: Grove Press, 1988).
—, "A Few Notes on Two of My Books" (1989), in *Bodies of Work* (New York: Grove Press, 1997).
—, *In Memoriam to Identity* (New York: Grove Press, 1991).
—, "Writing, Identity, and Copyright in the Net Age" (1995), in *Bodies of Work*.
—, *Pussy, King of the Pirates* (New York: Grove Press, 1996).
—, "Reading the Lack of the Body: The Writing of the Marquis De Sade" (1996), in *Bodies of Work*.
Adorno, Theodor, *Aesthetic Theory* (1970; Minneapolis: University of Minneapolis Press, 1997).
—, and Max Horkheimer, *The Dialectic of Enlightenment* (1947; Stanford: Stanford University Press, 2002).
Agamben, Giorgio, *Homo Sacer: Sovereign Power and Bare Life* (Stanford: Stanford University Press, 1998).
Altieri, Charles, *Enlarging the Temple: New Directions in American Poetry in the 1960's* (Lewisburg: Bucknell University Press, 1979).
Anderson, Elijah, *Code of the Street* (New York: W. W. Norton, 1999).
Anderson, Paul Thomas, dir. *There Will Be Blood*. Perfs. Daniel Day Lewis, Paul Dano, Kevin J. O'Connor (Paramount, 2007).
Arendt, Hannah, *The Human Condition* (1958; Chicago: University of Chicago Press, 1998).
Ariely, D., B. Koszegi, N. Mazar, and K. Shampan'er, "Price Sensitive Preferences" (Working Paper, 2007).
B.G. "Niggas in Trouble," *Chopper City* (Cash Money 9690, 1996).
—, "Bling Bling," *Chopper City in the Ghetto* (Cash Money 53265, 1999).
—, "Thugged Out," *Baller Blockin'* (Cash Money 153291, 2000).
—, "I Know," *Checkmate* (Cash Money 860909, 2000).
Badiou, Alain, *Ethics: An Essay on the Understanding of Evil* (London: Verso, 2001).
Baker, Houston, *Black Studies, Rap, and the Academy* (Chicago: University of Chicago Press, 1993).

Bakhtin, M.M., *The Dialogic Imagination*, ed. Michael Holquist (Austin: University of Texas Press, 1981).

Baraka, Amiri, *Transbluesency: The Selected Poetry of Amiri Baraka* (New York: Marsilio Publishers, 1995).

Bateson, Gregory, *A Sacred Unity: Further Steps to an Ecology of Mind* (1958; New York: Harper Collins, 1991).

Bauman, Zygmunt, *Work, Consumerism, and the New Poor* (London: Open University Press, 1998).

Bersani, Leo, *Homos* (Cambridge: Harvard University Press, 1995).

Big Pun, "Still Not A Player," *Capital Punishment* (Loud 57883, 1998).

"Whatcha Gonna Do," *Endangered Species* (Relativity 1963, 2001).

Big Tymers, "Number 1 Stunna," *I Got That Work* (Cash Money 157673, 2000).

Bigelow, Gordon, *Fiction, Famine, and the Rise of Economics* (Cambridge: Cambridge University Press, 2003).

Bishop, Elizabeth, *The Complete Poems* (New York: Farrar, Straus, and Giroux, 1984).

Black Rob, "Whoa," *Life Story* (Bad Boy 73026, 2000).

Blasing, Mutlu, *Politics and Form in Postmodern Poetry* (Cambridge: Cambridge University Press, 1995).

Bourdieu, Pierre, *Distinction: A Social Critique of the Judgment of Taste* (Cambridge: Harvard University Press, 1984).

Brennan, Timothy, "Off the Gangsta Tip," *Critical Inquiry* 20 (Summer 1994), pp. 663–93.

Breslin, Paul, *The Psycho-Political Muse* (Chicago: University of Chicago Press, 1987).

Britzolakis, Christina, *Sylvia Plath and the Theatre of Mourning* (Oxford: Oxford University Press, 2000).

Burroughs, William S. *Naked Lunch: The Restored Text* (1959; New York: Grove Press, 2001).

—, *The Soft Machine* (New York: Grove Press, 1961).

—, *The Ticket That Exploded* (New York: Grove Press, 1962).

—, *Nova Express* (New York: Grove Press, 1964).

—, *The Third Mind* (New York: Grove Press, 1978).

—, *Cities of the Red Night* (New York: Grove Press, 1981).

—, *Word Virus: The William S. Burroughs Reader*, ed. James Gauerholz and Ira Silverberg (New York: Grove Press, 1998).

—, *Burroughs Live: The Collected Interviews of William S.Burroughs*, ed. Sylvere Lotringer (Los Angeles: Semiotext(e), 2001).

—, "Origin and Theory of the Tape Cut-Ups," in *Break Through in Grey Room* (Sub Rosa 3HH2, 2001).

Butler, Judith, *Excitable Speech: A Politics of the Performative* (London: Routledge, 1997).

Calhoun, Craig, "Habitus, Field, and Capital," in Calhoun, Lipuma, and Postone, *Bourdieu: Critical Perspectives*.

—, Edward Lipuma, and Moishe Postone (eds.), *Bourdieu: Critical Perspectives* (Chicago: Chicago University Press, 1993).

Callon, Michel, *The Laws of the Markets* (London: Blackwell, 1998).

Cameron, Sharon, *Lyric Time* (Baltimore: Johns Hopkins University Press, 1979).

Campbell, Colin, "Conspicuous Confusion? A Critique of Veblen's Theory," *Sociological Theory* 13:1 (March 1995), pp. 37–47.

Canovon, Margaret, "Hannah Arendt as a Conservative Thinker," in *Hannah Arendt: 20 Years Later*, ed. Larry May (Cambridge: M.I.T Press, 1997).

Caruth, Cathy, *Unclaimed Experience: Trauma, Narrative, and History* (Baltimore: Johns Hopkins University Press, 1996).

Clipse, "I'm Not You," *Lord Willin'* (Star Trak 4735, 2002).

Conley, Tim, "William Gaddis Calling: Telephonic Satire and the Disconnection of Authority," *Studies in the Novel* 35:4 (Winter 2003), pp. 526–42.

Cooper, John Xiros, *Modernism and the Culture of Market Society* (Cambridge: Cambridge University Press, 2004).

Crain, Caleb, "Frank O'Hara's 'Fired' Self," *American Literary History* 9:2 (Spring 1997), pp. 287–308.

Davidson, Donald, "The Second Person," in *Subjective, Intersubjective, Objective* (Oxford: Oxford University Press, 2001).

Davis, Colin, *Levinas: An Introduction* (Cambridge: Polity Press, 1996).

Deleuze, Gilles, and Felix Guatarri, *Anti-Oedipus: Capitalism and Schizophrenia* (1972; Minneapolis: University of Minnesota Press, 1993).

de Man, Paul, *Allegories of Reading* (New Haven: Yale University Press, 1979).

Dennet, Daniel, *Darwin's Dangerous Idea: Evolution and the Meanings of Life* (New York: Simon and Schuster, 1995).

Desai, Meghnad, *Marx's Revenge: The Resurgence of Capitalism and the Death of Statist Socialism* (London: Verso, 2002).

DMX, "Party Up," *And Then There Was X* (Def Jam 3IE26, 1999).

Dr. Dre, "What's the Difference?," *The Chronic 2001* (Aftermath 490486, 1999).

Dreiser, Theodore, *The Financier* (1912; New York: Meridian, 1995).

Dreyfus, Hubert, *Being-in-the-World: A Commentary on Heidegger's Being and Time Division 1* (Cambridge: M.I.T. Press, 1991).

—, "Nihilism, Art, Technology, and Politics," in *The Cambridge Companion to Heidegger*, ed. Charles Guignon (Cambridge: Cambridge University Press, 1993).

—, *What Computers Still Can't Do: A Critique of Artificial Reason* (Cambridge: M.I.T. Press, 1999).

—, "Merleau-Ponty and Recent Cognitive Science," in *The Cambridge Companion to Merleau-Ponty*, ed. Taylor Carman and Mark Hansen (Cambridge: Cambridge University Press, 2005).

—, and Paul Rabinow, "Can There Be a Science of Existential Structure and Social Meaning?," in Calhoun, Lipuma, and Postone, *Bourdieu: Critical Perspectives*.

—, Fernando Flores, and Charles Spinosa, *Disclosing New Worlds: Entrepreneurship, Democratic Action, and the Cultivation of Solidarity* (Cambridge: M.I.T. Press, 1999).

Eliot, T. S., "The Waste Land," in *The Norton Anthology of Poetry*, ed. Margaret Ferguson, Mary Jo Salter, and Jon Stallworthy (New York: W. W. Norton, 1996).

Ellison, Ralph, *Invisible Man* (1952; New York: Random House, 2002).

Eric B. and Rakim, "I Ain't No Joke," *Paid in Full* (6th and Broadway 444005, 1987).

—, "Lyrics of Fury," *Follow the Leader* (Uni UNID3, 1988).

Fam-Lay, "Rock N' Roll," *The Neptunes Present … Clones* (Startrack AKOMH, 2003).

Fanon, Franz, *Black Skin, White Masks* (1967; New York: Grove Press, 1994).

Farland, Maria, "Sylvia Plath's Anti-Psychiatry," *Minnesota Review* 55–57 (2002), pp. 245–57.

Foucault, Michel, *Madness and Civilization* (New York: Vintage, 1988).

Frank, Robert H., *Microeconomics and Behavior* (Columbus: McGraw-Hill, 2006).

Fraser, Nancy, "Rethinking Recognition," *New Left Review* 3 (May/June 2000), pp. 107–20.

Fried, Michael, *Absorption and Theatricality* (Chicago: University of Chicago Press, 1988).

—, *Art and Objecthood* (Chicago: University of Chicago Press, 1998).

Friedman, Ellen, "A Conversation with Kathy Acker," *Review of Contemporary Fiction* 9:3 (1989), pp. 12–22.

Friedman, Milton, *Capitalism and Freedom* (Chicago: University of Chicago Press, 1962).

—, and Anna Schwartz, "Has the Government Any Role in Money?," *Journal of Monetary Economics* 17 (1986), pp. 37–62.

Gaddis, William, *JR* (New York: Penguin, 1975).

Gagnier, Regenia, *The Insatiability of Human Wants: Economics and Aesthetics in Market Society* (Chicago: University of Chicago Press, 2000).

Galbraith, John Kenneth, *The Essential Galbraith* (New York: Mariner Books, 2001).

Gallagher, Catherine, *The Body Economic* (Princeton: Princeton University Press, 2005).

Gibson, William, *Neuromancer* (1984; New York: Ace Books, 2000).

Gilroy, Paul, *Against Race* (Cambridge: Harvard University Press, 2002).

Godden, Richard, *Fictions of Capital: The American Novel from James to Mailer* (Cambridge: Cambridge University Press, 1990).

Gooch, Brad, *City Poet: The Life and Times of Frank O'Hara* (New York: Harper Perennial, 1993).

Goux, Jean-Joseph, *Symbolic Economies: After Marx and Freud* (Ithaca: Cornell University Press, 1990).

Granovetter, Mark, "Economic Action and Social Structure: The Problem of Embeddedness," *American Journal of Sociology* 91 (November 1985), pp. 489–515.

Gray, John, *Hayek on Liberty* (London: Routledge, 1998).

—, *False Dawn: The Delusions of Global Capitalism* (New York: New Press, 2000).

Greenberg, Clement, "The Case for Abstract Art," in *Affirmation and Refusal: The Collected Essays and Criticism of Clement Greenberg 1950–1956*, ed. John O'Brian (Chicago: University of Chicago Press, 1995).

Grossman, Allen, "Hart Crane and Poetry: A Consideration of Crane's Intense Poetics with Reference to 'The Return,'" in *The Long Schoolroom* (Ann Arbor: University of Michigan Press, 1997).

Guatarri, Felix, "The Divided Laing," in *A Guatarri Reader*, ed. Gary Genosko (Oxford: Blackwell, 1996).

Guillory, John, *Cultural Capital* (Chicago: University of Chicago Press, 1993).

G-Unit, "Poppin' Them Thangs," *Beg For Mercy* (Interscope 159142, 2003).

Halpern, Richard, *The Poetics of Primitive Accumulation* (Ithaca: Cornell University Press, 1991).

Hansen, Mark, *New Philosophy for New Media* (Cambridge: M.I.T. Press, 2004).

—, *Bodies in Code* (London: Routledge, 2006).

Hardt, Michael, and Antonio Negri, *Empire* (Cambridge: Harvard University Press, 2001).

Harris, Oliver, *William S. Burroughs and the Secret of Fascination* (Carbondale: Southern Illinois University Press, 2003).

Harvey, David, *A Brief History of Neoliberalism* (Oxford: Oxford University Press, 2005).

Hayek, F. A., *The Road to Serfdom* (Chicago: University of Chicago Press, 1944).

—, "The Use of Knowledge in Society" (1949), in *Individualism and Economic Order* (Chicago: University of Chicago Press, 1958).

—, "Why I Am Not a Conservative" (1960), in *The Essence of Hayek*, ed. Chiaki Nishiyama and Kurt R. Leube (Stanford: Stanford University Press, 1984).

—, "The Denationalization of Money" (1976), in *The Collected Works of F. A. Hayek*, Volume 6 ed Stephen Kresge (Chicago: University of Chicago Press, 1999).

Hayles, N. Katherine, *How We Became Posthuman: Virtual Bodies in Cybernetics, Literature, and Informatics* (Chicago: University of Chicago Press, 1999).

Heidegger, Martin, "The Origin of the Work of Art" (1935), in *Off the Beaten Path* (Cambridge: Cambridge University Press, 2002).

—, "Language" (1950), in *Poetry, Language, Thought* (New York: Harper, 2001).

Henry, Michel, *Marx: A Philosophy of Human Reality* (Bloomington: University of Indiana Press, 1983).

Herring, Terrell, "Frank O'Hara's Open Closet," *PMLA* 117 (2002), pp. 414–27.

Hope, Clover, "Lil Wayne, Last Time I Checked," *XXL* 99 (January 2008), pp. 74–82.

Howe, Irving, "The Plath Celebration: A Partial Dissent," in *Modern Critical Views: Sylvia Plath*, ed. Harold Bloom (New York: Chelsea House, 1989).

Hume, Kathryn, "Voice in Kathy Acker's Fiction," *Contemporary Literature* 42:3 (Summer 2001), pp. 485–513.

Hungerford, Amy, *The Holocaust of Texts: Genocide, Literature, and Personification* (Chicago: University of Chicago Press, 2003).

Jackson, Victoria, *Dickinson's Misery* (Princeton: Princeton University Press, 2005).

Jacobs, Jane, *The Death and Life of Great American Cities* (1961; New York: Vintage, 1993).

Jameson, Frederic, *Postmodernism, or, the Cultural Logic of Late Capitalism* (Durham: Duke University Press, 1991).

—, *The Seeds of Time* (New York: Columbia University Press, 1994).

Jay-Z, "Money Ain't a Thing," *Vol. 2: Hard Knock Life* (Roc-A-Fella 558902, 1998).

—, "Come and Get Me," *Vol. 3: The Life and Times of Sean Carter* (Roc-A-Fella 558906, 2000).

—, "Heart of the City," *The Blueprint* (Roc-A-Fella 586396, 2001).

—, "The Takeover," *The Blueprint* (Roc-A-Fella 586396, 2001).

Johnson, John, *Carnival of Repetition: Gaddis's "The Recognitions" and Postmodern Theory* (Philadelphia: University of Pennsylvania Press, 1990).

Jones, Mike, feat. Slim Thug, "Still Tippin'," *Who Is Mike Jones?* (Warner Brothers 7YMV1K, 2005).

Juvenile, "In My Life," *Juve the Great* (Cash Money 12FXCW, 2003).

Kahneman, Daniel, and Amos Tversky, "The Framing of Decisions and the Psychology of Choice," *Science* 211:4481 (January 30 1981), pp. 453–58.

Kaufman, Robert, "Red Kant," *Critical Inquiry* 26:4 (Summer 2000), pp. 682–724.

—, "Adorno's Social Lyric and Literary Criticism Today," in *The Cambridge Companion to Adorno*, ed. Tom Huhn (Cambridge: Cambridge University Press, 2004).

Kelley, Robin, "Kickin' Reality, Kickin' Ballistics: Gangsta Rap and Postindustrial Los Angeles," in *Droppin' Science*, ed. William Eric Perkins (Philadelphia: Temple University Press, 1996).

Kirzner, Issac, "The Subjectivism of Austrian Economics," in *New Perspectives on Austrian Economics*, ed. Gerrit Meijer (London: Routledge, 1995).

Knight, Christopher, *Hints and Guesses: William Gaddis' Fiction of Longing* (Madison: University of Wisconsin Press, 1997).

Krims, Adam, *Rap Music and the Poetics of Identity* (Cambridge: Cambridge University Press, 2001).

Lacan, Jacques, "The Mirror Stage as Formative of the 'I' Function," in *Ecrits* (New York: W. W. Norton, 2002).

Lachmann, Ludwig, *The Market as Economic Process* (Oxford: Blackwell 1986).

Laclau, Ernesto, and Chantal Mouffe, *Hegemony and Socialist Strategy: Towards a Radical Democratic Politics* (London: Routledge, 1985).

Laing, R. D., *Interpersonal Perception: A Theory and Method of Research* (New York: Springer Publications, 1966).

—, *The Politics of Experience* (New York: Pantheon, 1967).

—, *Knots* (New York: Vintage, 1970).

Lanzoni, Susan "An Epistemology of the Clinic," *Critical Inquiry* 30:1 (Fall 2004), pp. 160–86.

Lash, Scott, "Pierre Bourdieu: Cultural Economy and Social Change," in Calhoun, Lipuma and Postone, *Bourdieu: Critical Perspectives*.

Latour, Bruno, *Reassembling the Social* (Oxford: Oxford University Press, 2005).

Leibenstein, H., "Bandwagon, Snob, and Veblen Effects in the Theory of Consumers' Demand," *Quarterly Journal of Economics* 64 (May 1950), pp. 183–207.

Leitch, Vincent, *Theory Matters* (London: Routledge, 2003).

Levine, George, "Introduction," in *Aesthetics and Ideology*, ed. George Levine (New Brunswick: Rutgers University Press, 1994).

Levi-Strauss, Claude, *The Elementary Structures of Kinship* (Boston: Beacon Press, 1969).

Leypoldt, Gunter, "Aesthetic Specialists and Public Intellectuals," *Modern Language Quarterly* 68:3 (September 2007), pp. 417–36.

Lichtenstein, Donald, Nancy Ridgway, and Richard Netemeyer, "Price Perceptions and Consumer Shopping Behavior," *Journal of Marketing Research* 30 (May 1993), pp. 234–45.

Lil' Flip, "The Way We Ball," *Undaground Legend* (Sony 6GOAo, 2002).

Lil' Rob, "Peek-A-Boo," *Can't Keep a Good Man Down* (Lideres 950226, 2001).

Lil' Wayne, "Loud Pipes," *Tha Block Is Hot* (Cash Money 153919, 1999).

—, "Hey DJ," *The Carter* (Cash Money 27JYPI, 2004).

Liu, Alan, *The Laws of Cool: Knowledge Work and the Culture of Information* (Chicago: University of Chicago Press, 2004).

Lodge, David, "Objections to William Burroughs" (1966), in Skerl and Lydenberg, *Burroughs at the Front*.

Lowney, John, "The Post-Anti-Aesthetic Poetics of Frank O'Hara," *Contemporary Literature* 31 (1991), pp. 245–64.

Luhmann, Niklas, *Love as Passion: The Codification of Intimacy* (Stanford: Stanford University Press, 1982).

Lukacs, Gyorgy, *History and Class Consciousness* (Cambridge: M.I.T. Press, 1971).

Lydenberg, Robin, "Notes from the Orifice: Language and the Body in William Burroughs," *Contemporary Literature*. 26:1 (Spring 1985), pp. 55–73.

—, *Word Cultures: Radical Theory and Practice in William S. Burroughs* (Urbana: University of Illinois Press, 1987).

McCaffery, Larry, "The Artists of Hell: Kathy Acker and Punk Aesthetics," in *Breaking the Sequence*, ed. Ellen Friedman and Miriam Fuchs (Princeton: Princeton University Press, 1994).

McClosky, Donald, *The Rhetoric of Economics* (Madison: University of Wisconsin Press, 1985).

McGee, Daniel, "Post-Marxism: The Opiate of the Intellectuals," *Modern Language Quarterly* 22 (1998), pp. 201–25.

McGurl, Mark, "The Program Era," *Critical Inquiry* 32:1 (Fall 2005), pp. 102–29.

McLuhan, Marshall, "Notes on Burroughs" (1964), in Skerl and Lydenberg, *Burroughs at the Front.*

McWhorter, John, "How Hip Hop Holds Blacks Back," *City Journal* (Summer 2003), pp. 2–9.

Marx, Karl, "Theses on Feuerbach" (1845), in *The Marx-Engels Reader*, ed. Robert C. Tucker (New York: W. W. Norton, 1978).

—, "The Communist Manifesto" (1848), in *The Marx-Engels Reader.*

—, "Preface to the First German Edition of *Capital*" (1867), in *The Marx-Engels Reader.*

—, *Capital Vol. 1* (1867; New York: Penguin, 1992).

—, "Critique of the Gotha Program" (1875), in *The Marx-Engels Reader.*

Mayakovsky, Vladimir, *For the Voice* (Cambridge: M.I.T. Press, 2000).

Mead, George Herbert, *Mind, Self, and Society* (Chicago: University of Chicago Press, 1967).

Michaels, Walter Benn, *The Gold Standard and the Logic of Naturalism* (Berkeley: University of California Press, 1987).

Miles, Barry, *William S. Burroughs: El Hombre Invisible* (New York: Virgin, 2002).

Mill, J. S., "Thoughts on Poetry and its Varieties," *Autobiography and Literary Essays, Vol. 1 of The Collected Works of John Stuart Mill* (Toronto: University of Toronto Press, 1981).

Mirowski, Phillip, *More Heat Than Light: Economics as Social Physics, Physics as Nature's Economics* (Cambridge: Cambridge University Press, 1989).

—, *Machine Dreams: Economics Becomes a Cyborg Science* (Cambridge: Cambridge University Press, 2002).

Missy Elliott, "Slide," *Under Construction* (Elektra 62813, 2002).

Mitchell, Juliet, *Psychoanalysis and Feminism* (New York: Pantheon, 1974).

Mobb Deep, "Eye for an Eye," *The Infamous* (Loud 66480, 1995).

Molesworth, Charles, *The Fierce Embrace: A Study of Contemporary American Poetry* (Columbia: University of Missouri Press, 1979).

Murphy, Timothy, *Wising Up the Marks: The Amodern William S. Burroughs* (Berkeley: University of California Press, 1997).

Nelly, "Ride With Me," *Country Grammar* (Uptown 1577413, 2000).

Nelson, Cary, "The End of the Body: Radical Space in Burroughs" (1973), in Skerl and Lydenberg, *Burroughs at the Front.*

Nelson, Deborah, *Pursuing Privacy in Cold War America* (New York: Columbia University Press, 2002).

—, "The Virtues of Heartlessness: Mary McCarthy, Hannah Arendt, and the Anesthetics of Empathy," *American Literary History* 18:1 (2006), pp. 86–101.

Notorious B.I.G., "I Love the Dough," *Life After Death* (Bad Boy 73011, 1997).

Nozick, Robert, *Anarchy, State, and Utopia* (New York: Basic Books, 1974).

Nussbaum, Martha, "Invisibility and Recognition: Sophocles Philoctetes and Ellison's Invisible Man," *Philosophy and Literature* 23:2 (1999), pp. 257–83.

O'Hara, Frank, *Art Chronicles 1954–1966* (New York: George Braziller, 1975).

—, *The Collected Poems of Frank O'Hara*, ed. Donald Allen (Berkeley: University of California Press, 1995).

Oliver, Kelly, *Witnessing: Beyond Recognition* (Minneapolis: University of Minnesota Press, 2001).

Owens, Craig, *Beyond Recognition: Representation, Power, and Culture* (Berkeley: University of California Press, 1994).

Parsons, Stephen D., *Money, Time, and Rationality in Max Weber: Austrian Connections* (London: Routledge, 2003).

Perloff, Marjorie, "A Ritual for Being Born Twice: Sylvia Plath's *The Bell Jar*," *Contemporary Literature* 13:4 (Autumn 1972), pp. 507–22.

—, *The Poetics of Indeterminacy* (Princeton: Princeton University Press, 1981).

—, *Frank O'Hara, Poet Among Painters* (Chicago: University of Chicago Press, 1997).

Pitkin, Hannah, *The Attack of the Blob: Hannah Arendt's Concept of the Social* (Chicago: University of Chicago Press, 2000).

Plath, Sylvia, *The Bell Jar* (1963; London: Harper & Row, 1971).

—, *The Collected Poems* (New York: Harper Perennial, 1992).

Poirier, Richard, *A World Elsewhere: The Place of Style in American Literature* (1966; Madison: University of Wisconsin Press, 1985).

Polanyi, Karl, *The Great Transformation* (1944; Boston: Beacon Press, 2001).

Polanyi, Michael, *The Tacit Dimension* (New York: Doubleday, 1966).

Price, Richard, *Clockers* (New York: Picador, 1992).

Prodigy, "Y.B.E.," *HNIC* (Relativity 1873, 2000).

Project Pat, "Rubberband Me," *Walkin' Bank Roll* (Koch VBIE5G, 2007).

Puff Daddy feat. Mase, "Been Around the World," *No Way Out* (Bad Boy 39QD, 1997).

Rabin, Matthew, "Daniel Kahneman and Amos Tversky," in *American Economists of the Late Twentieth Century*, ed. Warren Samuels (Cheltenham: Edward Elgar, 1996).

Raekwon, "Ice Water," *Only Built For Cuban Linx* (Loud 66663, 1995).

Redding, Arthur, "Bruises, Roses: Masochism and the Writing of Kathy Acker," *Contemporary Literature* 35: 2 (1994), pp. 281–304.

Reisman, David, *The Lonely Crowd: A Study of the Changing American Character* (1950; New Haven: Yale University Press, 1967).

—, *Conservative Capitalism: The Social Economy* (Basingstoke: Palgrave Macmillan, 1999).

Ro, Ronin, *Gangsta: Merchandizing the Rhymes of Violence* (New York: St. Martin's Press, 1996).

Rose, Jacqueline, *The Haunting of Sylvia Plath* (Cambridge: Harvard University Press, 1992).

Rose, Tricia, "A Style Nobody Can Deal With," in *Microphone Fiends*, ed. Andrew Ross and Tricia Rose (London: Routledge, 1994).

Ross, Andrew, "The Death of Lady Day," *Poetics Journal* 8 (1989), pp. 68–77.

—, "Introduction," in *Microphone Fiends*, ed. Andrew Ross and Tricia Rose (London: Routledge, 1994).

Rothbard, Murray N., *The Logic of Action I: Method, Money, and the Austrian School* (Cheltenham: Edward Elgar, 1997).

Rubin, Gayle, "The Traffic in Women: Notes on the Political Economy of Sex," in *Toward an Anthropology of Women*, ed Rayna Reiter (New York: Monthly Review Press, 1975).

SAMOIS, *Coming to Power* (Boston: Alyson Books, 1987).

Sanneh, Kelefa, "Gettin Paid," *The New Yorker* (August 20, 2001), pp. 68–82.

Sartre, Jean-Paul, *Being and Nothingness* (1943; New York: Washington Square Press, 1993).

Scarface feat. W.C., "I Ain't the One," *The Fix* (Def Jam 986909, 2002).

Schumpeter, Joseph, *Capitalism, Socialism, and Democracy* (1942; New York: Harper, 1976).

Sciolino, Martina, "Kathy Acker and the Postmodern Subject of Feminism," *College English* 52 (1995), pp. 437–45.

Shalin, Dimitri, "George Herbert Mead," in *The Blackwell Companion to Major Social Theorists*, ed. George Ritzer (Oxford: Blackwell, 2000).

Shapiro, Michael, *Reading "Adam Smith": Desire, History, and Value* (Newberry Park: Rowland and Littlefield, 1993).

Simmel, George, *The Philosophy of Money* (London: Routledge, 2004).

Skerl, Jennie, and Robin Lydenberg (eds.), *William S. Burroughs at the Front* (Carbondale: Southern Illinois University Press, 1991).

Smith, Adam, *The Wealth of Nations* (1776; Indianapolis: Hackett, 1993).

Smith, Barbara Herrnstein, *Contingencies of Value: Alternative Perspectives for Critical Theory* (Cambridge: Harvard University Press, 1988).

Smith, Hazel, *Hyperscapes in the Poetry of Frank O'Hara: Difference, Homosexuality, Topography* (Liverpool: Liverpool University Press, 2000).

Snoop Dogg, "Tha Shiznit," *Doggystyle* (Death Row 50605, 1993).

Sowell, Thomas, *Knowledge and Decisions* (New York: Basic Books, 1978).

Spivak, Gayatri Chakravorty, "Translation as Culture," *Parallax* 6:1 (2000), pp. 13–34.

Stewart, Susan, *Poetry and the Fate of the Senses* (Chicago: University of Chicago Press, 2002).

T.I., "Be Easy," *Trap Muzik* (Atlantic 83650, 2003).

Tabbi, Joseph, "The Cybernetic Metaphor in William Gaddis's *J R*," *American Notes & Queries* (1989), pp. 147–51.

Taylor, Charles, "Engaged Agency and Background in Heidegger," in *The Cambridge Companion to Heidegger*, ed. Charles Guignon (Cambridge: Cambridge University Press, 1993).

—, "The Politics of Recognition," in *Multiculturalism*, ed. Amy Gutmann (Princeton: Princeton University Press, 1994).

Tratner, Michael, *Deficits and Desires: Economics and Sexuality in Twentieth Century Literature* (Stanford: Stanford University Press, 2001).

Turk, "It's In Me," *Young and Thuggin'* (Cash Money 5K9R8, 2001).

Veblen, Thorstein, *The Theory of the Leisure Class* (1899; New York: Penguin, 1994).

Vendler, Helen, *Part of Nature Part of Us: Modern American Poets* (Cambridge: Harvard University Press, 1980).

Wahl, Greg, "I Fought the Law and I Cold Won: Hip Hop in the Mainstream," *College English* 26:1 (1999), pp. 98–112.

Warner, Michael, "Zones of Privacy," in *What's Left of Theory?*, ed. John Guillory and Judith Butler (London: Routledge, 2000).

Warren, Kenneth, *So Black and Blue: Ralph Ellison and the Occasion of Criticism* (Chicago: University of Chicago Press, 2003).

Watkin, William, *In the Process of Poetry: The New York School and the Avant-Garde* (Lewisburg: Bucknell University Press, 2001).

West, Cornel, *Race Matters* (Boston: Beacon Press, 1993).

West, Kanye, "When It All Falls Down," *College Dropout* (Roc-A-Fella 20300, 2004).

Westside Connection, "Gangsta Nation," *Terrorist Threats* (Priority 24030, 2003).

Wheeler, Elizabeth, *Uncontained: Urban Fiction in Postwar America* (New Brunswick: Rutgers University Press, 2001).

Whitehead, Colson, *The Intuitionist* (New York: Anchor Books, 2000).

Woodmansee, Martha, and Mark Osteen (eds.), *The New Economic Criticism: Studies at the Intersection of Literature and Economics* (London: Routledge, 1999).

Wright, Erik Olin, *Classes* (London: Verso, 1985).

Wubben, Emiel, "Austrian Economics and Uncertainty," in *New Perspectives on Austrian Economics*, ed. Gerrit Meijer (London: Routledge, 1995).

Zelizer, Viviana, *The Social Meaning of Money* (Princeton: Princeton University Press, 1997).

Zizek, Slavoi, *The Sublime Object of Ideology* (London: Verso, 1989).

Index

50 Cent 129, 194
Acker, Kathy 3, 6, 40, 41, 52, 78, 97–98,
    103–26, 196
    and AIDS 108
    on embodiment 114–16
    Empire of the Senseless 103–105, 106, 107–109,
        110, 112–19, 123–26
    In Memoriam to Identity 109, 111, 114–15,
        118–25
    on myth 103–109, 115, 125, 188
    Pussy, King of the Pirates 104, 125
    and Rimbaud 123–25
Adorno, Theodor 10–11, 70–71, 160–63
Agamben, Giorgio 162, 195
Altieri, Charles 177
Anderson, Elijah 129, 133, 135
Anderson, Paul Thomas 5, 45
    There Will Be Blood 27, 38–42, 44, 52
anti-psychiatry 34–38, 172–74
Arendt, Hannah 5, 27, 48–52, 92, 102, 133, 147,
    151–55, 156, 162, 175, 176, 183, 195
Ariely, Dan 166
Arrow, Kenneth 178–80

B.G. 127–28, 145, 164
Badiou, Alain 171
Baker, Houston 137
Bakhtin, M. M. 170
Baraka, Amiri 5, 19, 45
"Das Kapital" 27, 42–44, 52
Bateson, Gregory 34–36, 173
Bauman, Zygmunt 178
Bersani, Leo 66, 169, 172
Big Pun 142
Big Tymers 128
Bigelow, Gordon 165
Bishop, Elizabeth 159, 171
Black Rob 127
Blasing, Mutlu 177
Bourdieu, Pierre 8–11, 14, 148, 161, 167,
    195

Brennan, Timothy 136–37, 137, 142, 191
Breslin, Paul 173
Britzolakis, Christina 31
Burroughs, William S. 6, 52, 77–102, 116, 117,
    124, 187, 190, 196
    and code 81–82, 88–89
    and culture 86–88
    and embodiment 79–80, 81–87
    Naked Lunch 80
    Nova Express 78, 102, 187, 190
    and Rimbaud 90–92
    The Soft Machine 78, 80, 82, 85, 87, 90, 99,
        100, 190
    The Third Mind 99, 182
    The Ticket that Exploded 78, 80–81, 99, 100,
        101–102
    and the virtual 79, 89–90, 97–98
Butler, Judith 31, 132, 171

Calhoun, Craig 167
Callon, Michel 48, 166, 175, 176
Cameron, Sharon 168
Campbell, Colin 131
Canovon, Margaret 50, 176
Caruth, Cathy 120–23, 190
choice 20–24, 53–76
Clipse 129
collective subjectivity 21–22, 54, 61–67, 140;
    see also invisibility
Conley, Tim 169
Cooper, John Xiros 166
Crain, Caleb 177

Davidson, Donald 176
Davis, Colin 171
Deleuze, Gilles 162, 188
de Man, Paul 120, 121, 122, 174
Dennet, Daniel 185
Desai, Meghnad 175
DMX 195
Dr. Dre 129

Dreiser, Theodore 20–22, 169
  The Financier 20, 169
Dreyfus, Hubert 14, 83–84, 85–86, 88, 167, 168, 182, 183

economics 14–19
  fictional 25–26, 47–52, 108
  Marxist 42–44, 70–71, 157–59, 174
  Monetary 187–89, 105–107
  Neoclassical 15–17, 56–57, 177–78
  see also Choice *and* Price
Eliot, T. S. 78–79, 86, 87, 88–89, 99, 181
Ellison, Ralph 136, 138–39, 194

Fam-Lay 145, 195
Fanon, Franz 138–39, 194
Farland, Maria 172
Ferguson, Frances 190
Foucault, Michel 27, 34
Frank, Robert H. 166
Fraser, Nancy 28
Fried, Michael 174, 194
Friedman, Ellen 189
Friedman, Milton 2, 69–72, 74, 92, 105, 165, 179, 183, 187–88

Gaddis, William 3, 78, 98, 169, 170
  and invisibility 45
  JR 5, 25–26, 44–45
  and recognition 19–21
Gagnier, Regenia 165, 167
Galbraith, John K. 70–71, 75
Gallagher, Catherine 165
genre 4–5, 12–15, 25, 127, 170
Gibson, William 1, 4, 41, 52, 78, 97, 116, 117, 190
Gilroy, Paul 129, 135, 137, 193
Godden, Richard 167
Goux, Jean-Joseph 107, 189
Granovetter, Mark 166
Gray, John 106, 108, 115, 175, 183
Greenberg, Clement 72–75
Grossman, Allen 183
Guatarri, Felix 34
Guillory, John 8–9, 166
G-Unit 127

Halpern, Richard 167
Hansen, Mark B. N. 117, 155, 156, 182, 196
Hardt, Michael 103, 104, 106, 107, 188
Harris, Oliver 181
Harvey, David 2, 165, 175
Hayek, F. A. 23, 92–98, 100, 101, 102, 105–106, 107–109, 112, 115, 117, 125, 170, 183–85, 186, 187–88, 189

Hayles, N. Katherine 80–82, 181, 182
Hegel, G. W. F. 28, 30, 132, 138, 154–55, 157
Heidegger, Martin 12–15, 18, 20, 25, 83, 85, 87, 88, 163, 168, 182–83, 185
Henry, Michel 151, 154–56
Herring, Terrell 66, 179
Hope, Clover 192
Horkheimer, Max 71
Howe, Irving 29, 30
Hume, Kathryn 118
Hungerford, Amy 172, 175

Intersubjectivity 2, 10, 16, 20, 23, 27–28, 31–33, 36–38, 37, 40–42, 45, 47, 48, 50–51, 99–100, 100, 102, 134–35, 136–37, 138, 140, 171–73, 173, 176, 186; *see also* Recognition
invisibility 33, 45, 127–46, 197; *see also* collective subjectivity *and* Recognition
  and blackness 136–40, 193–94

Ja Rule 194
Jackson, Victoria 174
Jacobs, Jane 1, 4, 5, 59–62, 69, 75, 78, 117, 178
Jameson, Frederic 5, 6, 17, 22, 25, 37, 101, 109, 162, 167, 196
Jay-Z 129, 135, 142–44
Johnson, John 22, 170
juvenile 144–45, 145, 195

Kahneman, Daniel 62, 166, 184
Kaufman, Robert 10–12, 14, 166, 167
Kelley, Robin 137, 191, 193
Kirzner, Issac 170
Knight, Christopher 170
Krims, Adam 129, 143

Lacan, Jacques 27, 29–30, 37, 132, 171
Lachmann, Ludwig 170
Laclau, Ernesto 188
Laing, R. D. 19, 35–37, 43, 44, 99, 172–74
Lanzoni, Susan 172
Lash, Scott 167
Latour, Bruno 176
Leibenstein, H. 169
Leitch, Vincent 166
Levine, George 167
Levi-Strauss, Claude 110–11
Leypoldt, Gunter 168
Lichtenstein, Donald 169
Lil' Flip 144, 145, 195
Lil' Kim 191
Lil' Wayne 192
literature
  as example 13–14, 168

literature (*cont.*)
  and fascination 7
  and ideology 147–59
  and society 12–18
  sociology of 12
  and the virtual 79, 89, 98, 102, 140–46, 197
Liu, Alan 9, 10, 166
Lodge, David 102, 181, 187
Lowney, John 177
Luhmann, Niklas 173
Lukacs, Gyorgy 169
Lydenberg, Robin 181, 186

McCaffery, Larry 109
McClosky, Donald 178
McGee, Daniel 188
McGurl, Mark 10
McLuhan, Marshall 80, 89
McWhorter, John 137
Marx, Karl 42–44, 46, 49, 97, 148–58, 160
  The Communist Manifesto 44
  "Critique of the Gotha Program" 149–57
  "Theses on Feuerbach" 154–55
Mayakovsky, Vladimir 76, 180
Mead, George Herbert 131, 132
Michaels, Walter Benn 174
Miles, Barry 181
Mill, J. S. 174
Mirowski, Phillip 92, 178
Missy Elliott 128
Mitchell, Juliet 174
Mobb Deep 127
Molesworth, Charles 53, 176
Mouffe, Chantal 188
Murphy, Timothy 186

Negri, Antonio 103, 104, 106, 107, 188
Nelly 128
Nelson, Deborah 176
Notorious B.I.G. 127, 141
Nozick, Robert 2, 165
Nussbaum, Martha 27, 133, 193

O'Hara, Frank 1, 4, 5, 41, 53–76
  on abstraction 54
  "The Death of Lady Day" 57, 177
  on interest 72–73, 74–75
  "Military Cemetery" 67–68
  "Ode to Joy" 64–66, 76, 179
  "On Seeing Rivers' *Washington Crossing the*
    Delaware at the MOMA" 68–69
  "Personal Poem" 53, 54–59, 178
  "Personism" 54, 55, 58, 72, 76
  "A True Account of Talking to the Sun on
    Fire Island" 76

Oliver, Kelly 172, 194
Owens, Craig 30, 37

Parsons, Stephen D. 186
Perloff, Marjorie 53, 58, 173, 179, 181
Pitkin, Hannah 50, 176
Plath, Sylvia 5, 19, 28–38, 43, 45, 173
  The Bell Jar 27–29, 28, 33–34
  "Daddy" 32–33
  "Death and Co." 33
  "Edge" 32
  And hostility to recognition 28–34
  and insanity 27, 28–31, 33–34, 37, 42
  and invisibility 32–33, 45
  "Lady Lazarus" 32–33
  "The Other" 30
Poirier, Richard 168, 169, 194
Polanyi, Karl 5, 15, 27, 45–50, 51, 52, 75, 92, 102,
    162, 175, 183
Polanyi, Michael 183
price 3–4, 25–26, 46, 92–97, 166, 181–85
Price, Richard 139
Prodigy 129
Project Pat 129
Puff Daddy 134

Raekwon 128
Rakim 142
Recognition 16–18, 19–21, 25, 27–29, 30–38, 45,
    49–52, 99–102, 131–34, 147–57;
    see also anti-psychiatry *and* invisibility
Redding, Arthur 113, 117, 190
Riesman, David 5, 74–75, 177, 185
Rimbaud, Arthur 78, 90, 97, 124–25
Ro Ronin 192
Rose, Jacqueline 31
Rose, Tricia 129, 135
Ross, Andrew 177, 179
Rothbard, Murray N. 184–85
Rubin, Gayle 110, 111

SAMOIS 110, 113–14, 189
Sanneh, Kelefa 129, 142–44, 191
Sartre, Jean-Paul 173
Scarface 142
Schumpeter, Joseph 20
Schwartz, Anna 187
Sciolino, Martina 118
Shackle, G. L. S. 184
Shalin, Dimitri 170
Shapiro, Michael 107–108, 189
Simmel, George 22, 97, 169
Smith, Adam 96, 100, 105, 107
Smith, Barbara Herrnstein 72–74, 165
Smith, Hazel 177, 179

Smith, Will 194
Snoop Dogg 129
Sowell, Thomas 170
Spivak, Gayatri Chakravorty 27, 31, 51, 171
Stewart, Susan 29, 51, 133

T.I. 134, 140
Tabbi, Joseph 170
Taylor, Charles 27, 28, 51, 83, 86, 133
Tratner, Michael 165
trauma 33, 119–24
Turk 195
Tversky, Amos 61–62, 166, 184

Veblen, Thorstein 16–17, 129–31, 169, 195
Vendler, Helen 53, 176

Wahl, Greg 192
Warner, Michael 60, 178–79
Warren, Kenneth 193
Warren, Vincent 179
Watkin, William 179
West, Cornel 192
West, Kanye 195
Westside Connection 141
Wheeler, Elizabeth 186
Whitehead, Colson 193, 194
Woodmansee, Martha 165, 167
Wright, Erik Olin 188
Wubben, Emiel 184

Zelizer, Viviana 135
Zizek, Slavoi 31, 171